# BACKSTAGE AT THE OPERA

EDWARD JOHNSON AND LUCREZIA BORI

# BACKSTAGE
# AT THE OPERA

By

## ROSE HEYLBUT

AND

## AIMÉ GERBER

*Paymaster of*
*The Metropolitan Opera Association*

*ILLUSTRATED*

❧

THOMAS Y. CROWELL COMPANY
PUBLISHERS  :  :  NEW YORK

To
"THE HOUSE"

# FOREWORD

THE three sections of this book include one (the last) which explains some of the details of actual operatic routine, and two which are devoted to reminiscences. The material in those two sections is presented solely as a series of personal impressions. There has been no attempt at either criticism or banner-carrying. Aimé Gerber, Paymaster of the Metropolitan Opera Association, and affiliated with that organization for thirty-nine years, is responsible for the facts of the opera's life from 1898 to 1931. Rose Heylbut is responsible for the arrangement and writing. The material dealing with events since 1931 derives from the impressions and observations of both.

It is impossible, within the limits of one volume, to touch upon *all* the interesting names and events bound up with New York's opera since 1898. Other individuals associated with the Metropolitan on terms of equal intimacy and over an equal period of time might select quite different highlights. For one reason or another, however, the facts here presented live most vividly in the minds of those responsible for this book; their selection has been based upon general, "human," interest rather than upon formally critical evaluations or the emergence of "tendencies"; and they are offered entirely as personal recollections and observations, colored only by the nature of associations that have been happy.

Rose Heylbut,
Aimé Gerber.

*New York,*
*June, 1937.*

# CONTENTS

## Part I

### Mostly Managerial

## Part II

### Opera Glamour

## Part III

### The "Factory"

*Part One*

MOSTLY MANAGERIAL

# Chapter I

## MAURICE GRAU

### 1.

IT ALL depends upon the point of view. To one not over-afflicted with realism, it is still the same Metropolitan Opera. The main auditorium, fronting Broadway, stands forthright and yellow and square, just as it did more than fifty years ago. The thickness of its walls, the height of its archways and ceilings, the great sweep of its staircases, and the clustered crystal of its lights, all tell of time that has been—which is something of an achievement in this day of passing landmarks. The "front," though, is perhaps the only factor in the opera's life which has remained unchanged. The two wings on the side streets were added later. The neighborhood has become another world.

In the beginning, the stately Metropolitan stood in a comparatively quiet section of town. During the daytime hours, the streets had that unthronged look of the financial district on a holiday. There was no rush of crowds, and traffic consisted mostly of hansom cabs and bicycles. The Normandie Hotel was one block down, and many of the operatic folk made their headquarters there (although one French tenor of the old days, who earned nine hundred dollars a performance, complained that all hotels in New York were far too dear, and occupied a furnished room that cost five dollars a week). Lilli Lehmann selected the old Normandie, partly

3

because of its dignified accommodations, and partly because she could get to work for an odd hour of practise or rehearsal, at any moment that suited her, and regardless of weather or cabs. Rumors still live of the great Lehmann's appearing suddenly and unheralded in the midst of an ensemble rehearsal, taking charge of things in her own imperious way, singing everybody's parts in quick succession, and bringing order out of chaos for a number of choristers and secondary singers.

Around the corner was the Broadway Theater, where, some time later, a dashing young musical comedy star was to make a vast success in *The Waltz Dream*. The name of that star is Edward Johnson. On Seventh Avenue, there were low, ramshackle shops, occupied chiefly by clothing-dealers and petty tradesmen; and in Thirty-ninth Street stood a row of flats of none too savory a character, and delicately styled "Soubrette Row." Still further west, brooded the ominous shadow of Hell's Kitchen. That influence was quite counteracted, however, by the Church of St. Chrysostom, part of the parish of old Trinity, which stood on the corner of Seventh Avenue. There were frequent humorous interludes between its Rector (or Vicar, as he was called), Father Carl Mollar, and the Opera House people. Father Mollar once complained that the Opera House disgraced the neighborhood; it looked like a brewery. When the cross atop St. Chrysostom's was blown down in a storm, and allowed to remain down for some weeks, the Opera House people hastened to observe to Father Mollar that his church disgraced the neighborhood by the dilapidated condition of its steeple.

The Opera House was definitely "uptown." To-day, it is the farthest "downtown" of New York's legitimate

theaters. It stands in the heart of the wholesale clothing district, and all day long its sidewalks are crowded
with factory workers, errand-boys with open carts of
dresses, and a battery of boot-blacks with the emblem
"Peace!" marked boldly upon their blacking-boxes.

Inside, too, there are graphic markings of the finger
of progress—new seats; new facilities; new stage lights,
regulated by remote control from a point at the center
of the stage, beside the prompter's box; and a telephone
equipment of ten trunk lines and thirty-five exten-
sions, reaching from the sub-cellar to the roof-stage.
In the old days, there were just two telephones; one
in the private office of Maurice Grau, and the other
in the open hall on the street floor. There, the engineer
in the basement, the business manager at the end of the
corridor, or the house superintendent on the fifth floor,
were summoned by a breathless office-boy, to transact
their business at the old wall-bracket, in full earshot of
all and any who chanced to pass by. Also, there were
no elevators. Nobody expected them. Having two
telephones in the same house was progress enough.

The inside life of the House has undergone interesting changes, too. But for all its alterations of policy,
personnel, and equipment, it is still the same Metropolitan. No other house will ever be quite like it; for
its winding corridors enclose something more than an
auditorium and rehearsal rooms for stars and starlets.
They shelter the shades of the departed great who have
made musical history.

### 2.

The Paymaster's office is on the fifth floor, in lofty
quarters that used to be the residence of the house super-

intendent. There is a long table-desk where the dozen
different pay-rolls are signed, a shelf of books, and a
collection of photographs which have nothing to do with
the opera. Mostly, they are of dogs and catches of
fish. Aimé Gerber came to the House nearly forty
years ago.

There was excitement when young Gerber was graduated from public school. A merchant-prince named
Orr, a former pupil of the school, came back to visit.
He appeared in the room of the highest class, wrote the
words "Help Wanted" on the blackboard, and offered
a prize for the best letter applying for a position. The
nature of the prize was not disclosed. At best, it might
be a medal or a gold watch; at very least, a lucrative
opening in the magnate's own offices. The entire class
competed, and the ten best letters were sent on to Mr.
Orr. It took weeks for the decision to be made known,
during which speculation grew ever more vocal and ever
more heated as to the prize. Gerber clung to the gold
watch theory. In time, the news came. The winner
was Aimé Gerber. His letter had best pleased Mr. Orr,
as to style, content, and penmanship. The prize was
Samuel Smiles' volume on thrift, believed to do incal-
culable good to the unformed character of youth.

Shortly after this blow fell, a friend came running to
Gerber's home on West Thirty-eighth Street, with word
that they were looking for a new office-boy over at "the
House." (The young herald was Jules Judels, who
to-day is rehearsal director of the Metropolitan, numbering among his duties the scheduling of all out-going
tour trains seven minutes ahead of time, so that stellar
latecomers may not be left behind.) Arraying himself
in his Sunday best (he still wore knickerbockers), Ger-

ber presented himself at once. He was interviewed by
Mr. Ernest Goerlitz, Secretary of Maurice Grau's com-
pany. The interview went satisfactorily enough, but
Mr. Goerlitz did not commit himself as to the position.

"Go outside to the mail-desk," he said at last, "and
write me a letter of application. Then we'll see . . ."

Evidently, young Gerber had made profitable use of
his readings on thrift. He wrote precisely the same
letter which had moved Mr. Orr. In less than five
minutes it was done. The next morning, the position
was his. Goerlitz expressed confidence in a young man
of fourteen who could conceive so model a letter in so
brief a time. So Aimé Gerber became office-boy to the
Metropolitan Opera in general and to Maurice Grau
in particular. He sat at a desk in the hall, responded to
summons in four languages, and watched the making
of musical history.

## 3.

Since the present record is to be one of personal recollections, the earliest history of the Metropolitan has
no place in it. Even the briefest survey of those first
fifteen years, however, shows that, prior to Maurice
Grau's taking over the reins of operatic management,
in November of 1898, the Metropolitan had built its
traditions solidly. The first performances (1883) were
given in competition with the company of Col. Henry
Mapleson, then active in the Academy of Music. The
Metropolitan casts, assembled by Henry E. Abbey,
included Marcella Sembrich, Christine Nilsson, Italo
Campanini, Scalchi, LaBlache, Fursch-Madi, Novara,
and Del Puente. Ultimately, two opera troupes were

found to be one too many, however, and it was the Metropolitan which survived.

Abbey's first season suffered financial defeat, and the following year saw the advent of a German opera company, under the direction of Dr. Leopold Damrosch and, after his death in February of 1885, under that of Edmond C. Stanton, said to be "the most gentlemanly" director of opera New York had yet seen. The German company endured seven years. They produced a varied repertory (*Les Hugenots, La Juive, Aida, The Queen of Sheba, Lohengrin, Rienzi, Masaniello, Prophète, Tannhaeuser, Tristan und Isolde, Don Giovanni, Masked Ball, L'Africaine, William Tell, The Flying Dutchman, Norma, The Trumpeter of Saeckingen,* and the *Ring* tetralogy, all given in German and under their German titles, will serve as a sample); and demonstrated to New York the eminent art of Materna, Schroeder-Hanfstaengl, Schott, Staudigl, Lilli Lehmann, Marianne Brandt, Anton Seidl and his wife, Mme. Seidl-Kraus, Emil Fischer, Robinson, Alvary, Herbert-Foerster (the wife of Victor Herbert, who then served as first 'cellist in the Opera orchestra), Perotti, Reichmann, and Dippel (later to become Administrative Manager of the Metropolitan company). After Dr. Damrosch's death, his young son Walter became one of the conductors, and his other son, Frank (later to head the Institute of Musical Art of the Juilliard Foundation), was chorus master. That the company members spared themselves no effort to make their performances a success is attested in a note printed in the program of the matinée of Saturday, February 19, 1887; in order to assure the afternoon's *Masaniello,*

Herr Schott consented to appear in the chief tenor rôle, after having sung *Rienzi* the night before.

During the season of 1890-91, Lilli Lehmann appeared in *Don Giovanni* (or *Don Juan* as it was then billed), *The Queen of Sheba, The Masked Ball, William Tell, Lohengrin, Tannhaeuser, Tristan und Isolde,* and *Norma,* all within close intervals of each other. At that time, Henry E. Abbey and Maurice Grau were presenting Mme. Sarah Bernhardt at the Garden Theater, and a young entrepreneur named Heinrich Conried was offering the public a diversion entitled *Apollo, or The Oracle of Delphi,* with a cast including Lillian Russell, Jefferson de Angelis, and Max Figman.

In the autumn of 1891, the firm of Abbey, Schoeffel, and Grau assumed the direction of the Metropolitan Opera. John B. Schoeffel remained more or less of a silent partner, Henry E. Abbey and Maurice Grau conducting the business of operatic production.

Abbey and Grau continued to present operatic seasons until 1897, with notable cosmopolitan casts including Lilli Lehmann, Eames, Scalchi, Nordica, Edouard and Jean de Reszke, Plançon, Maurel, and Melba. During the season of 1897-98, the House was leased to Maurice Grau, but contained no formal operatic tenant and only visiting "seasons" of opera and concert. In 1898, then, Grau began his independent directorship which, with its Golden Age of "all-star" casts, was to stand as the most resplendent period of opera that New York had yet seen.

**4.**

Upon the death of Henry E. Abbey, the old firm went under completely. Maurice Grau, though, desired to continue the Opera alone. He summoned his creditors and offered to pay them his personal share, or one-third of the firm's total indebtedness, in exchange for a clean bill of health. The arrangement proved satisfactory (Grau's personal standing was of the highest), and so the operatic régime of Maurice Grau came into existence.

He needed assistance, however, to make his new venture a success. The steps he took to procure it are characteristic of the man. He did not apply to official wealth or society, but went among his personal friends. Grau's company was always to be his own, in more senses than that of stock retention. He sought backing among the men who knew him and accepted no obligations other than those which appeared on the ledgers. In directing the policy and general character of his company, Grau was supreme. He stood to gain most or to lose most, and was subservient to no one. He was never to relinquish this sense of personal pride and responsibility. Night after night, Grau could be found in the Directors' Box, over the right side of the stage, observing every movement in the performance. Messages were brought to him there, and he frequently scribbled instructions on leaves torn from the program; then he would turn back to the stage. Once, through a clerical error, a bill for the orchestra was presented to Grau calling for the services of sixty-six men.

"Oh, no," Grau said. "There were but sixty-five men playing in that performance. I counted them. Kindly verify this." And a check-up showed that there had been only sixty-five men.

At another time, a secondary singer was severely cen-

sured for some slip on the stage which had thrown the
chief tenor out of his part.  Grau heard of it.

"That is not quite so," he said in his courtly way.
"The little man did nothing wrong.  The fault was entirely Signor X . . .'s.  I was there and saw it all.  I
believe an apology is in order."

The backer-friends who became directors in Grau's
company, included Henry Dazian, the costumer; Frederick Rullmann (his name still appears as publisher of
the Opera House librettos); Charles Frazier, the
banker; Edward Lauterbach, Roland F. Knoedler,
John W. Mackay Sr., and Frank W. Sanger, Grau's
first business manager.  The Tysons, who conducted
theater-ticket agencies in the Fifth Avenue Hotel and
the Gilsey House, were also of the greatest assistance
to Grau, buying outright many thousand dollars' worth
of season subscriptions, at a slight discount for handling
them.  Grau got his money and produced opera with it.
Had the tickets failed to sell well, the agents would have
been the losers.  When Grau's venture became an assured success, with subscriptions for his "all star" casts
at a premium, he continued to give the agencies the
tickets which had come to mean as much to them as that
earlier quota had meant to Grau himself.

Born in Brunn, Moravian Austria in 1849, and
brought to America as a child of five, Grau was a
suave, polyglot cosmopolitan.  He spoke German, of
course; Italian, and careful, polished English; but the
language most used at the Opera House was French.
The American, German, and Italian singers soon fell
into the habit of speaking French to Grau, and his
closest friends were Pol Plançon and Jean and Edouard
de Reszke, the chief ornaments of the French contin-

gent of singers. A stickler for courtesy, Grau never permitted any interruptions when one of his artists came to call upon him in his office. Even emergencies had to wait if Nordica or Calvé were inside, talking to him. Only Plançon carried a safe-conduct against this rule. He announced himself at the door by three terrific raps of the walking-stick he always carried. And then, regardless of the business going on inside, the door would fly open, Grau's round head would appear behind it, and the two gentlemen would embrace. To Plançon, Grau always remained "*Mon cher* Maurice."

Grau was short, with Semitic features, keen, kindly eyes, and a close-cropped black beard. He was perhaps the shrewdest man ever to manage grand opera. Showmanship lay in his blood, but his entrance into the business was entirely through the back-door. He began as libretto boy, at the old Academy of Music, where he heard the greatest singers of the day, and saw what a judicious commercialization of such art might mean to an impresario. Later, he became advance agent for his uncle Jacob, the picturesque "J. Grau" (who directed the Ristori Company), serving as publicity man, ticket-seller, ticket-taker, and appeaser of prima donnas, and emerging from his apprenticeship with a better-grounded knowledge of theatrical management than J. Grau ever had. Maurice Grau was sympathetic, never too communicative, and absolutely sincere. He made no bombastic pretensions to an artistic mission. He simply gave fine performances, with the greatest singers. When asked about his art, he would often say,

"From my standpoint, the art lies in making money. From my ledgers I know that the bigger I find the bank account, the better is my art!"

That sounds worse than it actually was. Grau had very definite standards of artistic merit, and they were high. His business, however, was to please a music-loving public. He made it a firm policy to "give the public the best, at any cost." Choice opera seats were priced at five dollars in those days (with a later increase to seven for special performances), and Grau never lost sight of the fact that "five dollars is a lot of money!" He had the shrewd notion that "the singers made the show"; that the average opera-goer paid to hear, not *Aida,* but Emma Eames; not Wagner so much as Nordica in the rôle of *Isolde.* Perhaps he was right. At all events, he made a great success. And the "all star" casts he assembled (Nordica, Schumann-Heink, and the two de Reszkes in *Lohengrin;* Eames, Nordica, Jean de Reszke, and Plançon in *Les Huguenots;* and Lilli Lehmann, Sembrich, Nordica, Edouard de Reszke, Maurel, and Salignac in *Don Giovanni*) gave no one greater pleasure than they did to Grau himself.

Grau secured the Metropolitan lease some time before he became sole producer of opera there. In the program of January 17, 1898 (when a five-week season of operatic performances was being given by the company of Walter Damrosch and Charles Ellis), there appeared the preliminary notice that raised the curtain on Grau's future plans.

## PRELIMINARY ANNOUNCEMENT

### THE MAURICE GRAU OPERA COMPANY

*Lessees of The*

### METROPOLITAN OPERA HOUSE

will open its first season of grand opera on or about

## DECEMBER 12, 1898

and will endeavor to present to the musical public of New York City, the finest and most complete Grand Opera organization that has ever appeared in America. Mr. Maurice Grau, the Managing Director, has already consummated arrangements with

*Mesdames*

| | |
|---|---|
| Calvé . . . . . . . . . . | Soprano |
| Eames . . . . . . . . . . | " |
| Schumann-Heink . . . . . . | Contralto |

*Messrs*

| | |
|---|---|
| Jean de Reszke . . . . . . . | Tenor |
| Van Dyck . . . . . . . . . | " |
| Salignac . . . . . . . . . | " |
| Campanari . . . . . . . . | Baritone |
| Bispham . . . . . . . . . | " |
| Albers . . . . . . . . . . | " |
| Edward de Reszke . . . . . . | Bass |
| Plançon . . . . . . . . . | " |

*Conductors*

Herr Anton Seidl and Signor Mancinelli

and negotiations are now pending with a number of the leading European artists whose names will be announced later. Mr. Dangerfield, scenic artist of The Covent Garden Theatre, London, has been specially engaged. Particular attention will be given to the scenic productions. It is the intention of the management to present during the season several new operas in addition to the standard repertoire.

On November 29, 1898, Maurice Grau began his career as independent operatic impresario at the Metropolitan with a performance of *Tannhaeuser* which included Nordica as *Venus,* Eames as *Elisabeth,* Van Dyck (début) as *Tannhaeuser,* Plançon as *The Landgraf,* and Albers as *Wolfram,* Mancinelli conducting.

Grau took infinite pride in his casts, quite apart from their sheer business value to him. They were, in a sense, his form of personal expression; represented the best of his personal efforts. He kept a sharp ear open for recommendations, but never depended upon agents to select his singers for him. The summer months found him traveling up and down Europe, combing the rosters of large and small opera houses, for voices that might please him. These reconnoitering trips were always made incognito. No one ever knew when Grau was there. He would drop into a seat in the balcony, or at the back of a dark box, and leave again if he heard nothing that sounded promising. But when there was a voice he wanted, he would send his card to the singer that night still, invite him to luncheon the next day, and produce, along with the fruit and the port, a contract for the Metropolitan Opera.

Grau studied the reviews of his artists as carefully as ever a general studied campaign plans. The gentlemen of the press treated him with greatest courtesy. They respected him. Despite his close personal friendships with Henry E. Krehbiel, James G. Huneker, and W. J. Henderson (whose sensitive writings until recently constituted the chief adornment of *The New York Sun*), Grau never suggested criticisms-by-favor. His successor, Heinrich Conried, had to learn by hard experience what Grau had by instinct: that it is ex-

tremely poor policy for a Managing Director to enter
the Press Room between the acts in order to lecture the
critics on what they ought to write and what they should
have left unwritten last time.  Still, it once happened
that a Grau tenor received a criticism which was anything but "all star."  Grau summoned the hapless artist
to his office the very next morning:

"Good morning, Monsieur D. . . You have seen the
notices of last night's performance?  They were not very
good, were they?  Well, I will not insult your artistic
integrity by suggesting that you gave me less than your
best.  So we must seek another way out.  Here is an
envelope.  In it, you will find your steamship tickets
home, and a check for seventy-two hundred dollars.
That represents the amount of our entire contract—nine
performances at eight hundred dollars each.  You will
find it correct, I believe.  And now you may consider
yourself quite free to make whatever further professional commitments you desire.  Good morning, Monsieur D. . . and good luck attend you!"

The public, of course, never heard of this flying trip
in mid-season.  Monsieur D. . . was simply reported as
"indisposed" and a popular tenor took his place for the
remainder of his well paid but unsung performances.
The public had to have the best at any cost.

Grau's shrewdness lay in knowing where to spend and
where not to.  Jean de Reszke once observed,

"Grau will give you a good cigar—but not the match
with which to light it!"

The first contract that brought Schumann-Heink to
New York was not remarkable for its high fees.  To
make the terms more acceptable, however, Grau appointed the contralto's husband, Paul Schumann, to one

of the stage managers' posts, and insured both their lives, for the family's sake. These extra attractions came considerably cheaper than a star salary cachet. On the other hand, when Schumann-Heink asserted herself as an artist of first magnitude—and it didn't take long for her to do this—Grau was the first to offer her very different terms. He granted increases in salary without question if he felt they were deserved; but he refused to inflate the general expenses of the organization by so much as the cost of an extra pair of tickets.

House employes were given one pair of seats each season. If a second request was made, Grau would look at the petitioner in surprise, lift his eyebrows, and remark thoughtfully,

"A pair of tickets? *Another* pair? It seems to me that I did present you with a pair five weeks ago."

The annual cutting-down of the payroll became effective with the last note of the season's last Sunday night concert. On Sunday evening, there was a full staff of administrative and stage personnel. On Monday morning, the managerial staff consisted of Goerlitz, Frank Garlichs (who is to-day the company's Treasurer), and Gerber; while the house was taken over by one janitor, one stage-doorman, one scrub-woman, one porter, and the engineer who sent up the hot water. And so it remained until rehearsals were begun the next fall. Yet, despite his economies, Grau's sense of courtesy impelled him to provide hansom cabs at the company's expense when the artists' ships arrived and left, or when the singers came and went on tours. Thousands of dollars meant nothing to him where the glamour of the opera was at stake, but the flintiest down-East Yankee couldn't outhaggle him in small matters.

Once the Opera House scrub-women wanted their
wages increased from seven-and-a-half to eight dollars
a week. Grau lost sleep over it. Up and down his office
he paced, looking towards ruin.

"Eight dollars? But why . . . WHY? How can I
fling money about like that?" (Grau's great expression
of objection was "WHY . . . ?" When things dis-
pleased him too much, he put the problem up to Fate.)

The women got their increase in the end, but it cost
Grau more than a half-dollar's worth of nervous energy.
And he was by no account a mean man. He would
give to any street-beggar who approached him. He
endowed many a hospital bed both here and abroad.
And his office-boy was required to separate all cancelled postage-stamps from their envelopes and bind
them into packets of a thousand each, to be sent to
France to serve some purpose connected with hospital
charities. Grau never failed to look through the
waste-paper basket at the end of the day, to make
sure that no stamp had been allowed to escape detach-
ment. But the notion of spending *opera* money in any
way that failed to redound to the public value of the
"show" seemed to him an unforgivable waste. Privately, Grau was a large-scale trader in Wall Street.

Grau's personal income from salary and stock divi-
dends was further increased by a clause inserted into all
artists' contracts requiring them to give their services to
one performance a season that was known as the Manager's Benefit. All proceeds from this gala performance belonged to Grau, and each and every star took
part, great names assuming small rôles just to be on the
program, and excitement (and receipts) running high.
The Manager's Benefits continued through Conried's

régime (the most brilliant of them all, perhaps, was a certain performance of *Fledermaus,* with the entire company of notables enjoying themselves with private larks and "real champagne" in the ball-room scene, and Conried himself quitting the Manager's box to don a costume and mix with the chorus) ; but were stopped with the advent of Mr. Gatti-Casazza.   Mr. Gatti revived "benefits" during the last few years of his directorship, but only on condition that the Emergency Fund should be the beneficiary.   These performances became the "Surprise Parties."

Grau reorganized his company on sound business lines.   He held a consultation with his friend Henry Dazian, whose business was then on Union Square, and persuaded him to allow his own chief accountant, Ernest Goerlitz, to come up to Thirty-ninth Street. Goerlitz, a master of detail and precision, completely reorganized the books and originated certain competent systems of accounts which are still in use.   Later, Goerlitz was transferred to the managerial staff, rising to the post of Assistant General Manager, which he occupied through Conried's directorship.   He drilled his staff, kept accurate account of receipts and expenditures, and put the new organization on a sound working basis.   If Grau assembled "all star" casts, Goerlitz saw to it that the business paid.   The Grau régime was hailed as the first managerial enterprise to make a profit out of grand opera—after all bills were settled.

### 5.

The theory that "the singers made the show" opened epic opportunities for the flourishing of artistic whimsy.

Those, indeed, were the days of spectacular "temperament." In all reasonable requests, Grau was pleased to accommodate his stars, and he humored them in many ways that were not strictly reasonable, but which worked no harm. But when matters became climactic, Grau knew how to assert himself. He was the sole arbiter of company disputes, and his methods were a triumph of the sheer power of personality.

Imagine a beautiful prima donna, beautifully gowned, full of beautiful wiles, and giving off the perfume of sheer glamour, pouting, pleading, threatening *not to sing* unless she were immediately given her own way about . . . well, practically anything at all. Grau would listen sympathetically. First he would explain matters in a business-like way. If that failed (and this was not an impossible occurrence), he would put his head to one side, purse his lips persuasively, and confide to the lady how greatly he relied on just *her* helpful coöperation to make things come right. If that failed, too, Grau would straighten up again, alter his tone, and, in few but telling words, issue Orders. And the orders stood. The artists respected Grau even when they emerged worsted from the lists of battle.

Emma Calvé, however, did cause him some anxious moments. This greatest of all *Carmens* was a magnificent artist and a charming woman, but once she became aroused, the sparks flew. Calvé developed the disquieting habit of leaving her dressing-room just before she was called to the stage, in order to look through the peep-hole in the door that, in those days, separated the wings from the body of the house, and see how large an attendance was already present. New York opera audiences are not too punctual in arriving. It often happens that a house which is recorded as a complete sell-out at the box-office, does not settle down in its seats until the start of the second act. Indeed, a society matron once wrote a perfectly serious letter to the management, begging them to transfer the *Celeste Aida* from the beginning of the First Act to the middle of the Second, so that she would not *always* have to miss it!

This was all explained to Calvé, of course, but either she could not or would not understand it. If the House was not *full* when she was ready to appear, she felt slighted. Doubtless, something had been left undone in advising the public that she, Calvé, would appear at eight-fifteen sharp. Up to Grau's office she would storm, then, in full costume and make-up, to give vent to her opinions with a vehemence that would have left anyone but Calvé voiceless for the remainder of the evening.

"I am not appreciated here. I refuse to sing to-night!"

Grau would try to soothe her, but mostly it was a waste of time. In the end, he would order her back to her room, and send his office-boy to the various doors with strict instructions that no member of the evening's cast be allowed to pass through in street dress! After that, there were more scenes which delayed the start of the opera. Then, when it was past curtain-time, and the House began to present a more occupied appearance, which it would have done anyway, Calvé would steal out of her room to have another look through the peep-hole.

"Ah, you see!" she would say in triumph. "You *can* do something!"

Then, of course, she would be perfectly willing to go on.

Calvé's moods were no mere stage properties. At one

Sunday evening concert, in later years, she had an altercation with the conductor, Felix Mottl, about a last-minute transposition of a song. The song was to be an encore. The conductor refused to transpose it without due preparation for the orchestra, and Calvé refused to sing it untransposed. In the end, Mottl left the stage —the printed program was done—and the men followed him. Nothing daunted, Calvé came to the front of the stage, and announced,

*"Chansons de France!"*

Then, without accompaniment of any sort, she sang the simple folk songs of France and of the Basque country that she loved so well.

## 6.

There was once a young man frequenting the stage-door, who used to remark that he had been wise in his "choice" of a very rich father. Maurice Grau was wise in his "choice" of the time in which he directed grand opera. During that Golden Age of song there *just happened to be* a plethora of magnificent voices. It would be interesting to know why one generation produced a vocal galaxy like Lehmann, Sembrich, Eames, Nordica, Melba, Schumann-Heink, Calvé, Fremstad, the two de Reszkes, Salignac, Saléza, Plançon, Bonci, Scotti, and Caruso; while the succeeding one could boast but few to match prowess with the least of these. Surely, it must be the result of something more than mere accident?

Besides finding this unequalled wealth of artistic material at his disposal, Grau gave opera at a time when production costs were about at their lowest, and this quite apart from any voluntary economies of his own. To-day, opera's chief and steadiest expenses are the salaries of the chorus, the orchestra, and the various stage departments (electricians, carpenters, scenic workers, etc.). Grau worked with a chorus of sixty-five voices instead of the hundred and six of the boom days, and they took what they could get. Fifteen dollars a week and no "overtime" was an average chorus salary. The stage crews were also smaller in number, and the hands drew about thirty-seven-and-a-half dollars a week. The orchestra numbered sixty-five men instead of eighty-five. On a regular payroll, such differences make themselves felt.

Further, Grau had no storehouses to pay for. Fire laws in those days permitted the scenery to be stored pretty much anywhere under or back of the stage. And the general working equipment was fairly rudimentary, in an age of no elevators and two telephones. The star dressing rooms had no running water and only the most primitive sanitary equipment. Little was spent on uniforms for the front-of-the-House staff. Also, there was no restriction against crowding in the standees. To-day, the fire laws permit the Opera House four hundred standees downstairs and one hundred fifty upstairs. In Grau's day, all applicants could be packed in. And they were! A thousand standees was nothing unusual for special gala performances, and a thousand standees meant more than a thousand dollars at the box-office.

And the stage itself! Grau did vastly more than merely to assemble a number of splendid voices which chanced to exist at that time and would doubtless have been heard without him. He mounted truly magnificent performances with a working equipment which, in the light of to-day's mechanical advancement, must have been primitive (although it didn't seem so then!). All scenery was set and shifted by hand. The "flies" were innocent of any button-pressing. Pulleys and counter-weights were manipulated by man power. There were no electric or hydraulic systems. The sets for Wagner were freely and openly used for Verdi and Meyerbeer, and the costumes and properties which the House supplied (the principals generally furnished their own) were not refreshed too frequently. Only moderate sums were expended on stage decoration and upkeep (although new sets began to appear towards the end of Grau's directorship), and there was little worry about novelties in the repertory. And despite all this, Grau's productions were splendid. He clung to the policy of giving the best works of the standard repertory, sung in their original languages, by a company of first-rank "stars"; and the public flocked to his doors. Were audiences less exacting in those days as to scenic values? Or did a sheerly musical awareness permit them to overlook all other considerations in the presence of that magnificent singing?

People troubled not at all to examine casts before paying down their money for tickets. If Nordica wasn't billed, Eames was; if the cast did not include Saléza or Maurel, there would be Jean de Reszke or Plançon. Last-minute replacements in the cast caused little worry; any substitute from the company's roster was sure to be quite as stellar as the singer originally announced.

Grau was an indefatigable worker. For a brief time he joined forces with Colonel Higgins and produced opera at Covent Garden in London, simultaneously with his Metropolitan season. That is to say, the executive work of the two enterprises was simultaneous, although the public seasons followed each other by some weeks. At this time, Grau attended to his correspondence between two and three in the morning, so that he might be uninterrupted at his writing, and ready for regular business demands the next day. His great passion was poker. On Saturdays, he would allow himself a few hours' recreation. After the matinée curtain had gone up and the "show" was well under way, he would walk through the House, twirling his cane and whistling some incoherent jumble of notes which no one ever recognized as a tune, on his way to the Phœnix Club, at the old Knickerbocker Theater, there to regale himself with a few hours of happy freedom, intensive poker, and the company of his cronies, Dazian, Roesner, Rullmann, and Sanger. The reports of the matinée's intake would have to be brought to him there, and he was always on hand again for the evening performance. Still, he had had his bit of relaxation, and it buoyed him. Grau's opera was entirely a matter of personal enterprise. He knew what he was about and depended on himself. He never wearied of hearing people compliment him on the success of his methods.

"And the best of it is," he would confide, *"I can't even read music!"*

# CHAPTER II

## HEINRICH CONRIED

### 1.

MAURICE GRAU resigned in the spring of 1903 because of failing health. His successor came to the House in the unique position of a Director of grand opera who had had virtually no experience with either musical directorship or operatic management. Heinrich Conried was distinctly a theatrical man, and as such, he ranked at the very top of his profession: a sort of German Belasco, who was known beyond the confines of the world of German plays for his thoroughness and his sensitive artistry. Unlike Belasco, however, Conried had also distinguished himself as an eminent actor. Conried came from the Irving Place Theater which he continued, for a time, to direct along with his operatic activities, and where his troupe of regular and "guest" artists included Sonnenthal, von Possart, Barnay, Mitterwurzer, Kainz, Bonn, Helene Odilion, Agnes Sorma, Marie Geistinger, Max Haensler, and Gustav von Seyffertitz. It was by no means an unusual thing to see Broadway celebrities of the stamp of Edwin Booth, Lawrence Barrett, or E. H. Sothern down at the old, un-fashionable Irving Place, observing the Germans in Shakespeare or Goethe or Ibsen. Although Conried was to institute the most thorough scenic improvements the Metropolitan knew, people who remember his Irving Place productions insist that the stage facilities there, while faithful, were of the most meager. This was doubtless due to financial emergencies, and not to lack of artistic zeal on Conried's part.

Heinrich Conried began his professional life as an apprentice-weaver in his native Bielitz, in Austrian Silesia. When he mounted Hauptmann's *The Weavers* at the Irving Place Theater, he gave an astonishingly authentic presentation of conditions among those workers. One means by which he achieved fidelity to detail was to send back to his old home for certain looms and pieces of furniture that had lived in his memory since childhood. An unquenchable love of the theater sent him on to Vienna, and his nineteenth year saw him installed as member of the famous Burg Theater troupe, the goal of every actor in Germany and Austria. At twenty, he was distinguishing himself as actor in and manager of a company in Bremen which had fallen on hard times and which his astute policies of direction finally rescued. His work there earned him a call to New York. He became assistant to Mathilde Cottrelly, then manager of the old Thalia Theater on the Bowery (in her latter years, Mme. Cottrelly appeared on Broadway, in a play depicting the life of the House of Rothschild), and finally he took over the management of the Irving Place Theater independently. Conried effected a conquest of the universities, taking his troupe to perform the German classics at Harvard and Yale. When Grau resigned from the Metropolitan, Conried became his successor, through the formation of the new Conried Metropolitan Opera Company.

Where Grau's financial backing had come from his personal friends, Conried enlisted the aid of the city's wealth and society. Among his original supporters were Henry Morgenthau, Jacob H. Schiff, and James Hazen Hyde; and the Directors in his company further included Eliot Gregory, Alfred G. Vanderbilt, H. P. Whitney, J. Henry Smith (known as "Silent" Smith), Clarence H. Mackay, George J. Gould, Robert Goelet, and Otto H. Kahn. Mr. Kahn's début at the opera was not directly sought, although he, of all the directors, was to be so long and so zealously concerned with the welfare of the Metropolitan that it was suggested that the "O.H." in his name actually stood for "Opera House." Mr. Schiff had been invited to the Board, but, declining on the grounds of pressure of business, suggested that a younger member of his firm of Kuhn, Loeb and Company, be accepted in his place. Mr. Kahn was that younger member. With Conried, official society became allied with the opera's activities. His enemies— and he did not lack them—hinted that Conried deliberately sacrificed a measure of his artistic independence to the obligations he assumed to "society." There was an arrangement for a time, for instance, that the socially preferred Monday night performances should number the fewest possible presentations of Wagnerian opera. Unquestionably, however, the opera gained in a particular kind of glamour that had never entered the calculations of Maurice Grau.

Conried was given a tenure of office of five years' duration. His salary was fixed at $20,000. a year, to be augmented by an annual Benefit, one-half of the net profits, and a stock dividend of six-percent. The artists whom he took over from the Grau roster included Gadski, Sembrich, Calvé, Ternina, Homer, Burgstaller, Dippel, Campanari, Scotti, Van Rooy, Journet, and Plançon; and the conductors Hertz and

Hinrichs. Olive Fremstad and Felix Mottl (conductor) who made their first appearances here under Conried, had originally been contracted for by Grau. Another Grau-made contract involved the artistic services of a young Italian tenor named Enrico Caruso. His coming here was the result of chance.

Grau had contracted for Caruso to come to the Metropolitan, having heard him abroad on the recommendation of Henry Dazian. The contract became void, however, upon Grau's retirement, and needed legal renewal. Caruso's terms were forty performances at five thousand francs each. Conried found the contract along with a mass of other material on Grau's desk, and paid little attention to it. Because of his inexperience in matters musical, he had never heard of Caruso, and believed that such an outlay could be better used for a "bigger name." Conried's choice inclined to Alessandro Bonci. Caruso's agent, advised of the change of management, cabled inquiries as to whether the Grau contract was to be renewed. Conried replied that he would not guarantee the forty performances, and offered a smaller number. To this Caruso did not agree, and the matter hung in abeyance. Then Conried began in good earnest to cast about for a fine Italian tenor. He spoke to many people, from foreign music connoisseurs to Italian boot-blacks, asking who "the best" Italian tenor might be, and invariably the answer was,

"Why, don't you know? Caruso, of course!"

In Europe that summer he heard, for the first time, one of Caruso's records. Then Conried remembered about the contract on his desk. There was a further exchange of cables, a trifle warmer this time, and arrangements were concluded. Conried agreed to guarantee more performances than the original ten he had offered; Caruso agreed to accept something fewer than Grau's forty, and the tenor came here for a "beginning" of twenty-five. His arrival was celebrated by a little gathering at Conried's home, where further business details were settled in the presence of Ernest Goerlitz and Mrs. Conried. Later, Caruso reported about it gravely.

"I have see the party and I have kiss the hand of the Director's lady wife."

Caruso's "début" in New York took place some weeks before he arrived here. Conried invited the critics to his office and promised them a surprise. In a corner stood one of the old phonographs of the International Talking Machine Company. Gerber, as impresario of winding-crank and discs, ran through a dozen or more records of the tenor's earliest making, all operatic arias with piano accompaniment.

Still, though Conried was to bring to the Metropolitan artists of the stamp of Farrar, Morena, Chaliapin, and Gustav Mahler, his newcomers that first season numbered a smaller proportion of "stars" than Grau's rosters had shown; his specialty lay along other lines.

## 2.

In the early spring of 1903, the new Manager came to inspect the working conditions of his House. Goerlitz introduced him to the House staff in formal fashion, and Gerber was appointed as Committee of One to show him about, from the engine-room to the roof, and note down his instructions for possible alterations. The notes soon assumed epic proportions. Conried's genuinely

artistic perceptions were affronted by practically everything he saw. The offices! The furnishings! The
equipment! None of these was suitable to a temple of
art. Conried wished his House to be just that, and he
wished every least member of his staff to appreciate the
fact, not merely through words but by personal feeling.

Accordingly, the first change he ordered was a scrap-
ping of the entire office equipment. The old-style high
book-keepers' desks, before which one sat on a tall stool,
were banished as "inartistic." Conried's assistants were
to have fine, roll-top desks. And when they finally
arrived, the gentlemen at the ledgers felt their chests
dilating with all the pride of operatic tenors. Which
was precisely what Conried wanted. Next, Gerber was
sent to select massive, splendid furniture for the smoking-room on the Thirty-ninth Street side of the Grand
Tier floor. It was chosen in strictly gentlemanly style,
simple and without "fuss." Ladies did not smoke in
those days, at least not in public. Much of that furniture still stands in the smoking-room that adjoins the
box of the Opera Club.

Then came the fitting-up of Conried's own office. At
that time, the General Manager occupied an office on
the second floor, in which there was a spiral staircase
that communicated directly with the office of the Business Manager, downstairs. To-day, the General Manager uses the office on the first floor that the Business
Manager used to have. In the old days, Grau would
often lean over the winding balustrade, shout for "Goerlitz!" and settle the most important details of casting or
salary, from floor to floor, in a Wagnerian *fortissimo*.
Not so Conried. Conried ordered the door to this staircase sound-proofed, and all transoms darkened. He

required absolute privacy and quiet at his work—with no possible chance for leakage through either sight or sound. He scrapped Grau's big, worn old table-desk, where memoranda had so long lain, in neat little piles, all over a four-foot-square surface. Conried ordered for himself a magnificent mahogany desk, soft rugs, and fine furniture.

When he came to the ante-room outside the manager's office, he looked pleased.

"This is the very place for my lessons," he observed. "I still give dramatic lessons, you know."

And the bare little ante-room became transformed into an artistic study, with portières, curtains, couches, and easy-chairs. In the corner stood a wash-stand, and Conried considered it with care.

"It will be necessary for me to keep it, to wash my hands. But how it looks! *Furchtbar!*"

And the carpenters were summoned to build a frame around the wash-stand, camouflaging it into a desk. One rolled back the top, and there were the soap and water. It still stands there, a monument to the union of necessity with art. Conried actually did give lessons in that room, in acting and elocution.

Conried's extensive changes were not the result of mere vanity. Though he was by no means lacking in that quality, he was prompted first and foremost by a very real desire to bring the equipment of the House into line with his own standards of fitness. After tackling the administrative quarters, he set to work on the stage and the auditorium. Conried's reconstruction of the Metropolitan stage was so complete that it represents the last general overhauling to take place there, up to the present time.

At an expenditure of some $150,000, Conried trans-
formed Grau's old-fashioned stage into a marvel of
modern ingenuity.  He brought over Carl Lauten-
schlaeger, from the Prinz Regenten Theater in Munich,
as technical director.  The notable improvements included a new system of electrically controlled counter-
weights for the "drops," or flying scenery which had
theretofore been manipulated by hand; a new stage
floor; a new proscenium arch; the removal of the doors
on either side of the proscenium arch (where the peep-
holes had been and through which the singers had come
for curtain-calls); more traps, and a mechanical system
for raising and lowering them.  The stage crews were
given yearly contracts.  Further, he ordered new stage
sets, properties, and costumes, at great cost, from the
ranking firms of scenic artists in Vienna, Munich, and
Paris.  The scenery was painted abroad, and mounted
upon the battens here.

Out front, in the body of the auditorium, Conried
continued his project of offering opera patrons a house
that should be a fit setting for the finest in art.  He installed new seats, contracted for complete new decorations in the still-prevailing color-scheme of deep red and
gold, and arranged for a splendid foyer on the Grand
Tier floor.  A haunting memory persists that, back in
the very old days, even before Grau's time, this foyer
had been used for occasional and very special performances of vaudeville!  A small stage stood in the place of
the present refreshment bar, and the performances were
conducted by Otto Weil, later to become associated with
Conried, both at the Irving Place Theater and at the
Opera.  Weil was in charge of advertising and travel.

As a final bit of elegance, Conried ordered all House

employes who were seen by the patrons, to appear in evening clothes. It was with mixed emotions that the doormen, the ticket-sellers, the ticket-takers, and the ushers first donned their new "tails," along with silver badges to distinguish them from the opera's patrons. Not until there had been some embarrassing encounters with ready-made bow ties, rebellious "dickey" shirt-fronts, and over-long "tails" on over-small program-boys did the atmosphere begin to calm down to normal.

An emphasis on Conried's truly gigantic efforts in the cause of the *appearance* of opera offers the best clue to the change in managerial policy. Grau had given magnificent singing performances and let it go at that. Conried regarded the singing as but one of a number of factors all necessary to the final sum-total of Art. It now remained for him to complete his work with per-formances of musical eminence.

### 3.

Conried had gotten his training and lived most of his life in the "heroic" school of German acting, and its hall-mark never left him. He was not completely free from either egotism or pompousness. Where Grau had gone quietly to the Directors' Box to observe, Conried showed himself about the House, immaculate in his dress clothes, white gloves, and opera hat, very much the Impresario, and enjoying the full flavor of it. Also, he showed himself in the Press Room, an alcoved room behind the Second Tier boxes reserved for the critics, and delivered himself there of addresses on what should and should not be written about his perform-ances. This, naturally, did not tend to add warmth to

the tone of the next morning's reviews. Conried's relations with the press were not over cordial. However,
he knew perfectly well how to deal with the "artistic
temperament," got along very well with the singers,
and, as time went by, came to be genuinely better and
better liked. But in the very beginning, those who had
served under Grau could not help but be alive to all
that was different in Conried.    397196

During the early period of his directorship, and until
the deterioration of neighborhood drove him out, Conried and his family occupied a private house in West
Thirty-ninth Street, and he would arrive at the House
promptly at nine every day. He was proud of the fact
that he required no more than six hours' sleep. One
morning, an artist scheduled to sing that night, telephoned in shortly after nine to say that he was ill and
could not possibly appear. An immediate cast replacement was necessary, and Conried pressed the buttons
that summoned his various heads of departments. Not
one came. It developed, then, that none of the gentlemen had yet come in. Conried was irate. He telephoned
their homes, requesting them to put in an immediate
appearance. Everyone expected an ominous explosion.
But nothing happened. A few days later, then, hand-
somely printed signs were hung up in every office, publishing the intelligence that Department Heads were
required to be at their desks by nine. Grau would never
have thought of printing signs. There'd have been a
quick reproval, and then clear weather.

Both gentlemen were thorough, but their brands of
thoroughness proceeded from vastly different parent
stems. Grau did things himself—all sorts of things, from
entertaining the artists, to giving out complimentary

tickets or helping the office-boy bear down on the handle of the huge iron press that was then used to make copies of letters. Conried dwelt on the upper levels. He familiarized himself with the least detail of what was needed, and then surrounded himself with the best possible aid, both human and mechanical, to carry the program through. For generalship of this kind, he had real genius. It was Ernest Goerlitz who came to take over many of the duties of sheerly business routine that Grau had attended to himself.

At one time, too, Conried tried out a then-novel device for announcing visitors, that should spare him the noise of the telephone bell. The attendant in the stage-door lobby wrote the caller's name on a piece of paper in the machine and pressed a button which transferred the written name upstairs to Conried's desk. Then, by a buzzer that sounded downstairs only, Conried would signify his wishes in a system of signals—one buzz meant "Show him up" and two, "Show him out." Not a spoken word would be heard.

It may be that even for himself Conried "set the stage" a bit; for, when the mood was upon him, his slightly arrogant exterior could melt away as though it had never been, and there would emerge a very human man, of generous and kindly impulses. Conried was a gallant host, and for open-handed generosity, he rivaled Caruso himself. He made gifts of expensive jewelry to his assistants, at holiday time and often enough for no reason at all—perhaps in his heart he felt kindly towards them and experienced a shyness about expressing it in a less formal way. He was constantly offering people the finest Havana cigars, yet the cigars he smoked himself were fearful. He had them especially made in Austria, and when he offered a friend a cigar somewhere in transit, where the ever-ready box of "presentation" Havanas could not very well be produced, the friend felt an anticipatory wave of illness stealing over him. Conried was famous for those long, thick cigars of his, that tasted like a mixture of straw and cabbage, seasoned in tar.

Conried remained at his desk in New York during the spring of 1906 when the company made a tour that began with an anticipated visit to California, and ended with the San Francisco earthquake. Two performances had already been given, and thousands of dollars had been collected in subscriptions, when suddenly fire broke out. Goerlitz, who managed the troupe on that tour, decided that it would be impossible to present Wednesday's matinée performance of *The Marriage of Figaro,* but announced that the evening's *Lohengrin* would doubtless stand secure. By six o'clock, the Grand Opera House was down. Flames tore across the sky; the streets opened beneath one's feet; people rushed together in anguished groups, and cries of distress sounded louder, even, than the crashing of masonry and buildings. Of the entire Opera equipment—settings and properties had been taken for a complete repertory— only a scant dozen trunks were left. The men of the orchestra lost their instruments and Marcella Sembrich replaced them out of the proceeds of a special Benefit Concert, although her own resources had been depleted by losses. Olive Fremstad tended the wounded in the wreck that had been the St. Dunstan Hotel. Caruso was seen kneeling in the open street, devout in prayer. Only Frederick Rullmann, who accompanied the tour, brought pleasant recollections out of the horror that was

San Francisco. Retiring after an extremely hilarious
post-performance party, he went to bed in the Palace
Hotel, slept soundly through the entire disaster, and
came down to the lobby late the next afternoon, much
startled by the appearance of the place, and demanding
on all sides to know why the chandelier was on the floor.

The first direct news was sent through to the House
by Nahan Franko, the orchestra's concert master, in a
wire asking Conried to notify the families of the opera
personnel that, so far, all were safe. Conried was at his
desk when the word came. There was bedlam in the
House, and people rushed about talking of ruin.

"Ruin be damned!" cried Conried. "The company is
in danger!"

Immediately, he organized emergency means for getting every bit of news available. Gerber was placed at
the switchboard, where he remained unrelieved for fifty-
six hours, and all calls not directly concerned with
Western Union, Long Distance, and the various railroad lines, were cut off. Presently, the little stage-door
lobby began to fill with the families of the touring singers—wives, mothers, sisters, children, beloved ones, all
crying and wailing and asking for word and wondering
what could be done. Some stayed there in the lobby
all night, resting on the little leather settees. Conried
came out to them and stayed with them, promising that
all in his power should be done for the sufferers, and
relaying all news as it came through. By seven in the
morning Conried was at the House, bringing milk and
rolls for breakfast. He shared his own with Gerber at
the switchboard, and lent a hand at the plugs while
Gerber ate. At a time of emergency, Conried showed

with best wishes of
April 30,
1902

MAURICE GRAU

Aimé Dupont

HEINRICH CONRIED

himself as generous and human, and not a trace of the heroic acting remained.

In San Francisco, all further performances were, of course, wiped out, and the people of that city had paid vast sums for tickets. Regardless of a possible Act of God salvation, the Metropolitan Opera undertook what will probably stand as the most gigantic refund in the annals of the theater. Goerlitz had instructions from Conried to make good the lost subscription money, dollar for dollar. The question was, though, how to prove possession of the tickets, for the contents of practically every home had been destroyed either by fire or quake. Goerlitz had no money with him, but promised to return to San Francisco, after a hurried conference in New York, to refund all tickets which could be produced, or the possession of which could be legally established on evidence or oath.

When he got back to San Francisco, he was mobbed by people demanding their money back. Some could show charred scraps of tickets the remainder of which had been burned away. Some brought half-destroyed wallets with nothing but a little mound of ashes inside. Some had nothing whatever to show, but took their oath that they had bought subscriptions for such or such locations. There was that in the manner of these people who had been through such harrowing experiences, which precluded doubt. Goerlitz listened to every one, examined his evidence, heard his story—and gave the money back. When the final accounts of that disastrous tour were balanced, it was found that the money paid out in refunds exceeded the original intake by a less than negligible amount. It remained one of Conried's most cherished memories that the people of San

Francisco had not taken advantage of him under circumstances that would have made it easy to do so. On returning to New York, the company gave a great Benefit for the earthquake sufferers.

## 4.

Many notable happenings stand out as highlights of the Conried régime. The coming of Caruso, strangely enough, is not one of them. Conried opened his season on November 23, 1903, with the new Italian tenor in *Rigoletto*. Caruso was extremely nervous. Backstage, he paced up and down, gesticulated, gargled out his throat, and raised appealing glances toward Heaven. The House staff, accustomed as they were to the calm, poised reserve of Jean de Reszke, regarded this newcomer as decidedly "different." Caruso gave a fine vocal performance, but achieved no outstanding triumph. During the early part of that first season, he continued to rank as just another promising voice. It was not difficult for the House people to get complimentary tickets for Caruso performances.

But suddenly, towards the end of the year, he asserted himself. His nervousness wore off, he grew more used to the climate, and his voice rang out richer and fuller. The "differentness" of him began to translate itself into the spontaneous expression of one of the heartiest, most lovable personalities the world ever knew. At one of Caruso's final performances that season, the House went suddenly and completely mad, applauding, shrieking, stamping, and even venturing a charge through the orchestra pit and across the footlights to reach him in person. One Amazonian young woman further horrified the much-bewildered recipient of this ovation by tearing a button from his coat and then promptly bursting into tears. Caruso had caught fire. After that, the House looked back to the complimentary tickets with wistful longing, while Mr. Conried looked forward to a five-year contract with new enthusiasm.

The event which most stimulated Conried and which was perhaps the greatest achievement of his career, was the first American stage presentation of *Parsifal*—the first to be given anywhere outside Bayreuth. He made a calm announcement that he intended mounting this work, and immediately found himself the storm-center of sensational controversy. All that autumn, there were letters of objection, committees of protest, and headlines that left nothing unsaid about the legal and religious "scandal" that was about to be visited upon the American public.

Opposition to *Parsifal* was based on two counts. The legal side involved the claims of the Wagner family that they held the exclusive rights to the production, and that *Parsifal* could not be performed outside Bayreuth without their consent, which they refused to give. The moral, or religious, side centered in the belief that, because of the symbolic value of the opera, it amounted to sacrilege to present it on a public stage and in the manner of ordinary theatrical entertainment. There were those who feared that the Deity Himself was to be portrayed in "play-acting." Conried found a veritable hornets' nest about his ears.

On the "moral" side, he issued a long statement, that a performance of *Parsifal* involved no desecration whatever; that Wagner himself had intended it to be publicly presented; that no religious personages or ceremonies were brought upon the stage; and that the ultimate meaning of the work dealt, not with spiritual mysticism, but with the loftiest conception of humanity.

On the legal side, however, more was required than a managerial statement. The Wagner family, represented by Mr. Gilbert Ray Hawes, summoned Conried to court, for violation of copyright. At the trial, Conried pointed out that the careful preliminary investigations he had made showed conclusively that the copyright did not extend to America; *Parsifal* was entirely unprotected in this country. He demonstrated, further, that the work had already been performed here, as a concert without scenery or costumes, at the Academy of Music in Brooklyn on March 31, 1890 (with Lilli Lehmann singing *Kundry's* music, the cast further including her husband, Paul Kalisch, Theodor Reichmann, and Emil Fischer, Seidl conducting); and that a precedent of a sort had thereby been established. Mr. Conried was represented by Judge A. J. Dittenhoefer. The case lasted less than a week, and was decided by Judge Lacombe in Conried's favor. So the *Parsifal* plans went forward.

As a matter of fact, they had never gone backward. During all of the criticism and even throughout the trial, Conried maintained a calm confidence. He believed in the justice of his claims; and he believed in *Parsifal*. His attitude went far towards buoying up the confidence of the House.

In those days of stress, he came closer to the people who worked with him. When the court action began, he sent for Gerber and pointed a meaningful finger at him.

"Aimé, bet all you've got on *Parsifal*. If you lose, I'll pay!"

At this time, too, Conried confided that the extensive alterations he had made in the stage had been calculated especially for the best possible presentation of *Parsifal,* which had been in his mind all along. It would no longer be necessary for Americans to travel to Bayreuth, he said, in order to see the work in its finest form.

The first presentation was announced for December 24, 1903, with a cast that consisted of Ternina, Burgstaller, Homer, Blass, Journet, and Van Rooy, Hertz conducting. This, despite the ukase from Bayreuth that no one participating in the American performance of *Parsifal* would be welcomed there again. For weeks in advance, public interest ran to fever pitch. The criticisms had not abated; ministers denounced Conried's "sacrilege" from their pulpits regardless of his printed statements; and through no efforts of his own, the Director found himself deluged with the most resonant sort of publicity. On the other hand, music lovers applauded his plan, and the demand for tickets exhausted the supply almost as soon as they were placed on sale. The mail-orders from out of town were enormous, increasing finally to the point where the regular box-office staff could no longer handle them. Gerber was put into a special room, into which were poured bags upon bags of mail, all containing drafts or bank-notes in payment of the desired locations. His sole duty was to take the money from one envelope and put it into another, together with a printed slip that regretted the management's inability to furnish any more tickets. He sat there more than a week. As the room was on the street floor and accessible from the lobby, Conried locked

Gerber in there, and carried the key about with him. From time to time, he would rattle at the lock, open the door, and enter with some friend to whom he showed, with keenest pride, just how much money he was obliged to return.

Another object of Conried's pride was the extra-long pay-rolls which *Parsifal* occasioned. The friends who were treated to the sight of the mail-order room were also invited to marvel at the long sheets of additional wages, which Conried would order to be brought and spread out on the floor of his office.

Judge Dittenhoefer, who had defended Conried's case, was among those who could not secure seats for the performance. Believing, no doubt, that the Manager of the House could work any miracle, he merely mentioned to Conried that he would like to hear *Parsifal*.

"Just send me a pair of seats, will you?"

Conried tried his best to do so. He gave Gerber two hundred-dollar bills from his pocket, with instructions to go out among the speculators and spend the entire amount for any seats he could get. Hours later, Gerber returned without the tickets. Not one was available in all New York, even for Conried.

The performance began at five in the afternoon and lasted until midnight, with a pause for supper between acts. There was a special police guard about the House. As an added touch, Conried sent a squadron of trumpeters, in full costume, to the main doors, to sound a fanfare as five o'clock drew near. The audience was requested to be in their seats before the conductor took his place, as no one would be allowed to enter after the music began. The doors of the auditorium were to be closed, and all late-comers obliged to stand in the outer lobby.

When the First Act was done and the doors were
opened, a rush was expected. Then it was found that
there was not one person standing in the lobby. For
that performance, at least, there were absolutely no
late-comers!

Whatever the private attitude of the spectators, the
atmosphere pervading that performance is unforgettable. The Opera House lost its air of a theater and
took on the reverent tone of a place of ceremonial service. The settings and effects were more than splendid
and the cast surpassed itself. Mme. Ternina especially
made a notable impression as *Kundry*. The eye-trouble
from which she suffered showed itself at close range in
an expression of extreme nearsightedness, and she was
past her first prime. But she made a magnificent figure
on the stage, and the tones of that remarkable voice of
hers rang forth in splendor. One of the call-boys
voiced his admiration in terms of dubious complimentary
value but with great heartiness:

"Some may be younger and some may be handsomer,
but you never catch *her* slipping!"

The one strange note in that evening, perhaps, was
the supper hour. A supper had been arranged in the
upper foyer, to be served at tables; but many people
brought their own food, and ate sandwiches in all parts
of the House, some dragging camp-stools along with
them, thus picnicking their way through *Parsifal*.

Conried was quick to realize that these *Parsifal* performances meant more than mere operatic entertainment, and with the understatement that often showed
itself as part of his nature, he announced that there
would be but a limited number of presentations of
the work that season. (There were eleven in all.) He

could have given it every night, and probably kept the House open all summer with it, besides. He intended, of course, to hold it in reserve as a permanent and very special feature of his repertory. But a circumstance arose which skimmed the cream, so to speak, from his plans.

The legal proceedings, during which Conried had taken such pains to demonstrate that *Parsifal* was unprotected in this country, were not wasted upon other impresarios. The most enterprising of these, Col. Henry W. Savage, saw which way the wind of public interest was blowing, and quickly organized an English version of *Parsifal,* which he gave at the Madison Square Theater and later on tour. The English performance was nothing like as magnificent as Conried's production; still, it served to acquaint with the wonders of *Parsifal* those who could not go to the Metropolitan. The English production undoubtedly harmed Conried's business interests. Presently, the novelty of the opera wore off, and there was a time when tickets for it could not only be gotten, but could be gotten free. During that first season, however, the opera's dividend to its stockholders was paid chiefly by *Parsifal.*

Not all of Conried's novelties were destined for such a glorious reception. During the season of 1906-07, he announced his intention of mounting Richard Strauss' *Salome.* Because of the unsavory theme of the work, there were once more rumblings of disapproval; but objections of that kind had worked no harm to *Parsifal,* and Conried paid them no heed. Again he took infinite pains with cast and settings, for he believed that *Salome* offered something new and distinctive as a work of art. The opera was announced, its nature was known, and rehearsals went forward without official remonstrance of any kind. During that winter, Conried had been exposed to much nervous tension of an unpleasant character, and though no one realized it at the time, he became stricken with the first symptoms of an illness from which he was never to recover. Many of the *Salome* rehearsals were hastily transferred from the stage to Conried's bedside, so that he might be advised of and responsible for every bit of the production's progress.

In due time, the dress rehearsal took place, in the presence of directors of and stockholders in the organization, together with members of the press and personal friends of sound taste, whose opinion might be taken as a gauge of the chances for *Salome's* public success. There were differences of opinion, of course—there were those who criticised the dancing of the *première danseuse* who "doubled" for the prima donna in the scene of the Seven Veils; there were those who dwelt upon the striking realism of Mme. Fremstad's performance with the severed head of John—but such comment went no further than an expression of opinion, and all went well. The performance was given as Conried's Benefit, on January 22, 1907, the cast including, besides Fremstad, Burrian, Van Rooy, Journet, and Dippel, Hertz conducting.

Because it was the Director's Benefit, arrangements were made for the appearance of more of the singing personnel than the small cast which the opera demanded; and because *Salome* is a brief work, requiring less than an hour and a half to perform, it was decided that a Gala Concert of ten numbers should precede the novelty on the evening's bill. The actual performance of *Salome* did not begin until a little before ten o'clock. The performance was brilliant and aroused great controversy. The theme and the music were heavily scored, but the artistic value of Conried's presentation earned praise. Then, a few days later, the bombshell burst.

The directors of the Real Estate Company, which granted Conried the lease on the House, requested that *Salome* be withdrawn from the repertory, as "objectionable." Conried was furious. It was the only time, perhaps, that he was seen to lose control of himself. His position was that all objections to the work should have been entered when it was first announced and before he had gone to an expenditure of over $20,000. in mounting it. He replied to his censors and asked to have their request set aside. Several of the directors in the opera company took up the cudgels in Conried's behalf, but a second resolution was passed, officially ending, for a time at least, the Metropolitan career of *Salome*. It was rumored that the objections were first put forward by several ladies of the Diamond Horseshoe, who brought pressure to bear on the Directorate in general and on the Morgan interests in particular.

When the decision was made public, the I-told-you-so's began. It was stated in the press that the first note of public horror had been sounded when several groups were seen to leave the Opera House before the performance was over. Conried was more angered by such items than by the official ban itself.

"That is a ridiculous thing to say," he cried; "of course some few left before it was over. It was a very late performance. Don't some of them do just that during every opera we give? I don't mind being censured for honest mistakes, but I hate unfairness!"

Conried never lost faith in the artistic possibilties of

*Salome,* and predicted that the day would come when the same House would suddenly re-discover it. During the season of 1933-34 *Salome* was again presented at the Metropolitan, as a novelty revival. While the opera was hardly hailed as an overwhelming work of art, it was no longer found "objectionable" and finished out the season as an honorable member of the repertory.

The opera chorus, which up to this time had been quite unorganized, took steps during Conried's régime to band together under union protection. The pros and cons of bickering over conditions and terms headed up, at last, into a formal strike of the chorus which lasted three days. The "show must go on," of course, and all sorts of frantic means were tried to make the absence of the chorus as little noticeable as possible. At one point, the enesemble parts were taken over by a small organ and a couple of violins. Students in the Opera School, which Conried had founded, were hastily summoned to fill in the gap, together with the half-dozen chorus members who remained loyal to the company. And the "stars" themselves rose to the emergency. During the nights of the strike, there were no rest periods in the dressing-rooms. As soon as the principals in the cast left the stage, they hastened to the wings where they took up the part of the choral ensemble. During one memorable performance of *Tristan und Isolde,* this off-stage chorus comprised the voices of Nordica, Knote, Bégué, Blass, Dufriche, Goritz—and Caruso. Caruso had come into the House that night (as he often did, to hear those works in which he did not take part), and the excitement of the strike and the off-chance that "something might happen" soon drew him from his seat to the wings. When he found his distinguished colleagues singing the chorus' music, he cast aside his hat and coat and joined them. He was quite familiar with the music. Although Caruso never sang in German opera because of language difficulties, he admired it intensely, and was entirely at home with all of the great tenor arias, which he sang on "Ah." More than once, while visiting in one of the administrative offices for a comfortable chat, did Caruso raise that unmatched voice of his to sing the *Preislied* from *Die Meistersinger*. He sang it magnificently, too. When these impromptu performances of foreign music were over, then, Caruso would applaud himself, make all sorts of grimaces, and rattle off a string of disconnected German words, including items from the bill-of-fare and ending up with *"sehr schoen."* After the strike was settled, with a bit of victory and a bit of compromise on both sides, Conried had little gold medals struck, commemorating the valuable assistance of his "all star" chorus. Caruso wore his on his watch-chain for a time, and took keen pleasure in displaying it and telling of the time when he had been a "chorus man."

Conried's sheerly artistic zeal led, in one instance at least, to rough weather. Although Grau had built his greatest success upon his casts, Conried determined that the "star system" must go. From the viewpoint of abstract artistic theory he was correct. People *ought,* no doubt, to listen to music for the sole sake of the music itself; listeners *ought* not to be deflected from their appreciation of melodic line and harmonic splendor by the face or personality of a dynamic "star." But in dealing with audiences, "oughts" do not count nearly so much as facts. And the fact is that, regardless of right or wrong, people *do* come to hear the "stars." Grau had this axiom of showmanship perfectly well in hand without theories.

Conried did not. It must be remembered that Conried had already done fine work with his Irving Place company, where all the members were equally competent and no "stars" stood out. Perhaps he believed he could accomplish the same results at the Opera House.

At all events, where Grau had presented "all star" casts, Conried offered Operas. There is a tremendous difference. Conried himself was ultimately to appreciate it. Through the lapsing of some of the old Grau contracts and through replacements of his own, Conried presently found himself with a roster that included many "stars" and still more very competent singers, but which lacked the old-time splendor which Grau had taught Metropolitan audiences to expect. During the second and third years of Conried's régime, the profits began to fall off.

One astute gentleman lost no time in turning Conried's decision against the "star system" to excellent account for himself. His name was Oscar Hammerstein, and he was conducting a rival enterprise less than half a mile away, at the Manhattan Opera House, on West Thirty-fourth Street. Hammerstein was a formidable showman. He gave the public what it wanted, which included several things which Conried was not giving it. With casts headed by Bonci, Renaud (whose Grau-made contract with the Metropolitan, Conried had failed to renew), Sammarco, Mary Garden, Lina Cavalieri, Tetrazzini, Dalmores, Campanini, Bressler-Gianoli, Melba, and Calvé, he presented a popular repertory which laid stress on the newer French works, and "sensations" (*Salome* among them), as well as on the familiar musical fare. Altogether, he gave fine "shows." Whether or not Hammerstein's purely artistic methods were equal to Conried's, there was a time when the comparative box-office figures told a startling story. Some years later, when Conried was gone, the Metropolitan entered into an arrangement with Hammerstein which bound him not to give competitive opera in New York. But long before that happened, Conried's face began to wear an anxious look.

Where Conried depended chiefly on the drawing powers of Caruso (in one season, Caruso appeared in more than fifty performances), Hammerstein added to his "stars" and promised the return of the De Reszkes; and while the promise was never fulfilled, Conried was nonetheless aroused to a sense of danger. When the seasons were over, Conried left speedily for Europe and began what amounted to a raid on the foreign opera houses. "Stars" were what he wanted now, and "stars" were signed up anywhere and everywhere. The Director came back with an amount of contracts which were not entirely liquidated until years after his death. But the "stars" shone once more at the Metropolitan.

### 5.

Conried's illness had been making rapid progress. His movements had become painful and halting. For a while, he came down to the House on crutches. Later, a special elevator was said to have been built into his home, and he appeared at his office in the care of a trained nurse. The opera's destinies lay in the hands of a tired man, and the time came when he slipped almost unconsciously into the habit of prefacing his plans with "*If* I come back next season," instead of "*when* I do." Conried's activity of mind and zeal of spirit were never to flag, despite the handicap under which he worked. When he was no longer able to come to the House at all, he directed much of his work from his bed. At this time, Ernest Goerlitz proved his worth, both to the organization and to Conried. The actual work of directing the Metropolitan fell on his shoulders. All House problems, the castings of the operas, and the arrangement of the repertory were in his care. Yet, after his duties were done, he would go up to Conried's home and give him a detailed report of the day's business, discussing plans with him and taking his instructions for the next steps.

Harassed by ill health and over-work, Conried was forced to resign from the Directorship of the Metropolitan during the winter of 1908. A Conried Testimonial gala was given at the Opera House in March. He left for Europe that spring, never to return. He died in Meran, April 27, 1909. His body was brought home for burial, and a memorial service for him took place at the Opera House on May 13. More than four thousand cards of admission were issued, and crowds lined the streets waiting for the cortège to pass. The body lay in state on the stage of the Metropolitan, flanked on either side by the seven-branched candlesticks of Hebrew ritual. The Opera House orchestra played Beethoven's Funeral March from the *Eroica* Symphony, and Mmes. Rappold and Homer and Messrs Martin and Blass sang Handel's *Largo*. The atmosphere of reverence reminded one strangely of that which had pervaded the House during that first, unforgettable performance of *Parsifal*. That, perhaps, was the tribute which Heinrich Conried would have valued most.

There was speculation, of course, as to who would become Conried's successor in the post of General Manager of the Metropolitan Opera. Suggestions were put forward which included the names of everyone who had ever been even remotely connected with any form of musical directorship. More than that, since Conried himself had come from the world of the theater, some quarters insisted that Dillingham, Frohman, or even the Schuberts should take over the House. Hardly a week went by that the newspapers did not hail some new candidate. At this time, it was said that Ernest Goerlitz entertained hopes of being appointed to succeed his former Chief. However, time passed, new names kept cropping up, and nothing happened. And then, suddenly, there was news.

An appointment had been made. A name that New York hardly knew. The name of Gatti-Casazza. In the very beginning, there were those who asked if the name were that of a city or an opera house. Then it developed that the name belonged not only to a Director of Opera, but to the Director of the Teatro alla Scala, in Milan. La Scala was the one house before which even the Metropolitan accepted second place.

The pictures of the new Director showed a dignified gentleman with a close-cropped beard and handsome patrician features. The House staff began to wonder what he would "be like." He was an Italian; he spoke little English; he had no personal acquaintance with the tastes or habits of New York; there was an air of calm mastery in his face; and he had guided the destinies of the finest opera house in the world. A man like that could be either entirely stimulating or entirely crushing.

At last came the day, in the spring of 1908, when the

Jishkin

To Mrs Aime Gerber very Cordially
n.y. 19. 9. 3? Ll. XXX Cassed

LONG LIVE
OUR BELOVED GATTI

FAREWELL PARTY FOR GIULIO GATTI-CASAZZA

new Director was to arrive.  A cab drew up before the
Thirty-ninth Street entrance, and someone got out.
A tall, dignified man, with a close-cropped beard
and patrician features.  He approached the door with
measured step, the thumb of one hand caught under his
coat lapel.  That was the first glimpse the House had
of Giulio Gatti-Casazza.  In the spring of 1935, Mr.
Gatti left the House.  With measured step, and the
thumb of one hand caught under his coat lapel, he
entered the taxi-cab that was to bear him away.  Never
once in the intervening years was his demeanor to vary
from the patrician poise, the aloof yet kindly sincerity
that marked him as a young man.  The wonderings of
the House were set at rest.  The newest office-boy
breathed a sigh of relief.

"That man," he observed, "has *class!*"

CHAPTER III

## GIULIO GATTI-CASAZZA

### 1.

AGAIN, the advent of a new General Manager brought an entirely new atmosphere into the House. Mr. Gatti was no "showman." He was a scholarly gentleman who happened to be an expert impresario into the bargain; but the other came first. Gatti never had to assert his authority; it resided in his very person. Where Conried had insisted upon quiet and privacy, and the sort of aloofness that became the opera's Director, Gatti had but to show himself and other people accorded those things to him. The noisiest press-agent ever to disturb the House lobbies, who wore down celebrated nerves by slapping celebrated shoulders and shouting celebrated first-names over the heads of a crowd that stood three-deep, stood silently aside to make way when Gatti passed by. Simply, there was that in his person.

Gatti was born in Udine, Italy, in 1869. He studied at the Universities of Ferrara and Bologna and at the Reale Scuolo Superiore in Genoa, specializing in mathematics and engineering. Later, he attended the Accademia Navale, and received the diploma of a naval engineer when twenty-two years old. His studies in music and the humanities were conducted privately, under the supervision of his family. His father had been one of Garibaldi's famous "Thousand," and later

became a Senator of the Kingdom of Italy. Gatti's
interest in matters of musical organization were a direct
inheritance; his father had long served as head of the
board of directors of the Teatro Communale of Ferrara.

When the elder Gatti was called as Deputy in the
Italian Parliament in 1893, he relinquished his activities
in the Ferrara directorate, and his son became his successor. The younger Gatti was then but twenty-four,
and immediately asserted himself as a sound custodian
of operatic matters.

During this time, the financial affairs of the great
Scala were undergoing difficulties. In 1897 no state
subsidy was granted the theater and it remained closed
during the carnival season. In 1898, La Scala was
reorganized, and its headship was offered to young
Gatti. He hesitated to accept the post because of his
youth, together with the fact that there were men in
Italy who had had greater theatrical experience than a
brief five years in Ferrara. The Milan authorities
urged his acceptance, however, and his father finally
advised him to go.

In the summer of 1898, the new Director of La Scala
was presented by Boito to Verdi. Verdi took the young
man aside.

"I have a piece of sound advice to give you. Remember that this theater is intended to be full, not
empty. Never forget that."

Gatti never did forget it. He often referred to that
bit of advice from the greatest composer of Italian
opera. Whatever means he was destined to use—and
often he had to forge them for himself—his policy was
to keep the theater full. He did it by a system that
sounds simple enough: that of offering the finest pro-

ductions possible, mounted in the finest way possible, and sung by the finest casts possible. The surplus he brought into the Metropolitan treasury was perhaps the main factor in enabling the House to survive the years of economic depression.

After his meeting with Verdi, Gatti went to confer with a highly promising young conductor, who had been appointed Musical Director at La Scala. His name was Arturo Toscanini. The conference inaugurated a close artistic association that lasted some sixteen years, and crowned the musical traditions both of Milan and New York. There was brief interruption when Toscanini left La Scala abruptly (and temporarily) for South America. It was reporied that he had been offended by repeated requests for encores.

Gatti began his directorship of La Scala in December of 1898 (less than a month after Maurice Grau opened his first independent season at the Metropolitan), with a performance of *Die Meistersinger*, in Italian, and with Antonio Scotti in the rôle of *Hans Sachs*. Gatti's vision definitely strengthened the position of Wagnerian opera on the Italian stage. It was Gatti, too, who tried the experiment of bringing a Russian singer into La Scala. There had been some doubt as to how the experiment would succeed, but Gatti stood his ground. When the singer came, the doubts vanished; his name was Chaliapin.

## 2.

Dissatisfaction with certain of Conried's methods led the directorate of the Metropolitan to the conclusion that the new Chief must be an executive who was thoroughly familiar with all branches of operatic

management, and who could put the Metropolitan on
the same basis of permanence and artistic soundness
that was enjoyed by "the greatest opera house in the
world." Thus Gatti was called to New York.

The Conried Metropolitan Opera Company was dis-
solved and the Metropolitan Opera Company came into
existence. Among the new provisions it was decided
that the General Manager was to have no further
financial interest in the concern. He was to be engaged
at a salary, to share in none of the profits, and to require
no Benefit. Further, since Mr. Gatti was unfamiliar
with his new sphere and since he represented traditions
which, in their turn, were foreign to New York,
the directorate tried the well-meant but unfortunate
experiment of dual management. Gatti, as General
Manager, was put in charge of the artistic welfare of
the organization. Andreas Dippel, of the German contingent of singers, was named Administrative Manager.
His duties were to employ his tact in assisting Gatti
with such matters of detail as might be unfamiliar to
him, and to keep an eye open for the welfare of the
German repertory. Despite Gatti's notable furthering
of German opera at La Scala, the feeling persisted,
in some quarters, that "an Italian" might possibly
become obsessed with the notion of cutting from the
repertory everything but Verdi, Rossini, and Puccini.

It was hardly likely that such a joint arrangement
could endure and it did not endure. Any administrative
friction which might have arisen and then died down
again, was brought to a head by the action of five members of the company. It having been learned that the
contracts of Gatti and Toscanini were to be extended,
a letter was sent to the Board of Directors requesting

equal security and equal freedom for Dippel. The letter was signed by Mmes. Sembrich, Eames, and Farrar, and Messrs Caruso and Scotti. The reply from the directorate made it plain that the Metropolitan Opera was to have but one head, that Gatti was to be that head, and that Dippel was to be subordinate to him. Thus the air was cleared. In 1910, Gatti entered upon his individual directorship, which was to endure twenty-five years.

On assuming his new duties, Gatti found a well equipped house and a gratifying degree of public opera-interest. In most other respects, he had to pull himself and his organization out of a morass of difficulties. His first movements were encumbered by the yoke of dual management. His policies could not be framed without some regard for the competition of Mr. Hammerstein. And within the company itself, he found little discipline. The artists had been granted a fairly free hand in arranging repertory and casting to suit their personal tastes.

While it took some two seasons and a bit of directoral pressure to clear away the first problem, Gatti set about solving the other two at once. In his policies, he showed himself a seasoned and experienced impresario. Gatti often said that, in his opinion, the finest voice in the world was worthless unless it projected, along with its tones, the human power of communication. Singing wasn't enough. Gatti demanded the utmost of his artists, and got it. His tastes were extremely broad. There was never the first trace of that "Italianization" of the repertory which some over-anxious spirits had thought it necessary to guard against. German, French, Italian, Russian, Spanish, Bohemian, and American works were mounted by him, and the German operas fared distinctly better under Gatti than they had under Conried.

It has been said that Gatti was prejudiced against American singers and American works. That was not the case. Gatti gave a willing ear to any artist who, by virtue of vocal ability and stage experience, seemed to merit membership in a company of expert operatic performers. When an American showed these qualities, he was included; when he did not, it was a lack of rounded experience rather than his Americanism which excluded him. Even before the music-world became nationality-conscious, Gatti's American roster included Geraldine Farrar, Riccardo Martin, Allan Hinckley, Putnam Griswold, Clarence Whitehill, Josephine Jacoby, Herbert Witherspoon, Herbert Waterous, Jeanne Gordon, Kathleen Howard, Rita Fornia, Henrietta Wakefield, Marion Telva, Thomas Chalmers, Mario Chamlee, Ruth Miller, Reinald Werrenrath, Florence Wickham, Basil Ruysdale, William Hinshaw, Louise Homer, Anna Case, Arthur Middleton, Mabel Garrison, Mary Lewis, Grace Moore, Marion Talley, Queena Mario, Gladys Swarthout, Helen Jepson, Lawrence Tibbett, Richard Bonelli, and Richard Crooks. Together with these came numerous lesser singers, some of whom have gone on to bigger things, and some of whom have been heard from no more, regardless of Mr. Gatti.

As regards American operas, Gatti mounted Converse's *The Pipe of Desire*, Cadman's *Shanewis*, Damrosch's *Cyrano*, De Koven's *Canterbury Pilgrims*, Parker's *Mona*, Gilbert's ballet, *Dance in the Place Congo*, Breil's *The Legend*, Hugo's *The Temple Dancer*, Herbert's *Madeleine*, Carpenter's ballet, *Sky-*

*scrapers,* Taylor's *The King's Henchman* and *Peter Ibbetson,* Hadley's *Cleopatra's Night,* Hanson's *Merry Mount,* Gruenberg's *Emperor Jones,* and Seymour's *In the Pascha's Garden.* Considering the total American operatic output, such a proportion is not inconsiderable. At all events, it serves to clear away any question of "prejudice." When an American public demanded American operas, they were presented. The ultimate duration of the works depended upon their own merits and not upon the presence or absence of good-will on the part of an impresario. In any case, Gatti had given the works a chance, under the best possible auspices, and in a house that was dedicated to operatic entertainment and not to laboratory experiments.

Gatti gave great attention to scenic decorations (many of the sets were built by Josef Urban, who worked with astonishing realism and detail. Mere painting on canvas was not enough. An Urban church was a real church, and one that could have done duty in many a small town, while an Urban ship stood ready to launch); rounded out the standard repertory with many interesting novelties; and secured the finest casts available. Gatti often said that the odd circumstance of an apparently general vocal deterioration could not help but be felt, and that it grew harder and harder to find complete casts of the old-time "all star" splendor. But through a judicious combination of casts, he managed to offer the public the values it demanded.

After the first two seasons of Gatti's directorship, the company's business reports showed a healthier complexion, which continued until the recent years of depression. Gatti's most notable achievements were a general raising of standard in the opera's productions, and the placing of the organization on a permanent basis. The season-to-season existence was at an end. It now became possible to work and plan in advance. Gatti definitely took the opera out of the ranks of exhibitionistic entertainment and fortified it with a background of dignity and good taste.

After two years of Gatti's leadership, the danger of Hammerstein's competition seemed less acute. Comparative attendance in the two houses pointed to the victory of the Metropolitan. Hammerstein was reaching the end of his resources. At last the arrangements were concluded which bound Hammerstein to give no more opera in New York, and though there was an attempt made to evade this bond, it was stopped by court order.

In his attitude towards his artists, Gatti enforced the discipline that was part of his nature. It soon became understood that his word was law. To say that this *became understood* is no understatement. There was that in his personality that made any more active self-assertion quite unnecessary. For Gatti, there were no "stars." There was only a company of singers. No artist was indispensable to that company; the company, rather, was indispensable to the artists. Such an attitude cleared the air. The "temperaments" quieted down; the "scenes" were known no more; and the singers were satisfied to sing, leaving matters of administrative policy in the hands of the General Manager.

Gatti often employed humorous means of convincing his artists that their own way wasn't always the best way. No one enjoyed those jokes of his better than he did. At one time, Olive Fremstad complained that she was being assigned too many "heavy" dramatic parts.  Gatti listened to her sympathetically, and then said that he believed that type of rôle best suited to her talents.  Still, Fremstad objected.  She wanted something "lighter."  Gatti shrugged, at last.

"Well, if you are sure you want to try something of that type, you must certainly be allowed to do so."

When the next season's rôles were assigned, Mme. Fremstad found herself allied with the extremely "light" and also somewhat vapid part of *Giulietta*, the Courtesan, in Offenbach's *Tales of Hoffmann*.  The part was "light" in more senses than one, and Fremstad found her valuable histrionic gifts required for no more strenuous service than decorative reclinings upon a couch.  She went to Gatti to suggest that this was not quite the sort of rôle she had had in mind!  But Gatti headed off any further objections with,

"Ah, now you are happy.  You wanted a light part and you have one!"

Mme. Fremstad appeared, at last, as *Giulietta* and found (not without critical aid) that the part did not suit her at all.  After that, she was quite satisfied to stay with the more dramatic rôles, for which Gatti had wished to reserve her in the first place.

Another time, and in dealing with the same artist, Gatti further showed his mellow diplomacy.  A performance of *Tales of Hoffmann* was to be given this night and, at the last moment, the new *Giulietta* was caught in a mishap.  The elevator in her hotel jammed between floors and couldn't be budged.  Time passed, it grew nearer and nearer curtain-time, and while the elevator-passengers still hung suspended in mid-air, word was gotten to the House that, in all likelihood,

*Giulietta* would not descend in time to appear. It was too late to change the bill, and the only other *Giulietta* available was Fremstad, who by this time had gotten to abhor the "light" part. Gatti went to the telephone himself.

"Ah, Madame Fremstad! And how are you this evening?"

"I am very well, thank you."

"I know you often retire early. Perhaps you are already resting?"

"Yes, I am."

"Ah, that is too bad! For in that case, I should never have the courage to ask a favor of you. A favor which would incommode you a very great deal."

"Well, why not ask it, at any rate?"

"Never! I would not dare. I know that you are . . . well, temperamental. Sometimes . . . well, perhaps a bit difficult to deal with. For that reason I would not . . ."

"What? I, temperamental? I, difficult? Nonsense! Surely, you know me better than that. Ask what you like."

"And you will promise not to be angry with me?"

"I promise. If only as a test of character!"

Whereupon Gatti unburdened himself of the story of the entrapped *Giulietta*.

"And what I wished to ask of you," he concluded, "was to assume that rôle to-night. But, of course, if you are comfortably resting, I cannot ask it."

"You don't need to," laughed Fremstad. "I'll be down in ten minutes."

And she came and sang the detested rôle, and refused to accept the evening's salary, saying that her "character" was worth more than a check and that Mr. Gatti was kindly to remember that she was not at all "difficult"!

Never, during that telephone call, had there been a breath of hurry, a suggestion of excitement. Had the result been different, Gatti would simply have made other plans. But his manner would not have changed. Whatever his problems or worries or fears, no one ever saw him other than the suave, poised, assuring Chief.

### 3.

From the time of his coming to the day of his going, Mr. Gatti remained a profound mystery to the public. Cartoonists pictured him as a majestic sphinx. He gave no interviews. He was little in evidence. No one was familiar with his tastes or his habits. He went but rarely into society. He had little to say. Yet Gatti was sincerely beloved by his associates, to whom he revealed himself as cordial, frank, and absolutely just. One of the most gifted of theatrical entrepreneurs, he hated anything that savored of "showmanship." At the Gala Farewell performance tendered him just before his departure, he sat well towards the back of Box Forty-eight, deeply moved by the ovation given him, yet loath to have either his person or his emotions set off by spotlight. In response to the cheering, he waved his hand, still from the rear of the box. Giuseppe De Luca pushed him to the front, and Gatti trembled. His reserve proceeded not at all from purposeful austerity. First, it was his nature; and in addition, he believed that, personally, he had nothing with which to interest the public. He came before them as a director of opera,

and as such, the only thing that could speak adequately
for him was his work.

It is a pity that this public did not know the real
nature of the man. It would have found him a kindly
person, of great enthusiasm and an astonishingly wide
range of interests. He could talk with authority on
every conceivable subject, from music and opera personalities to politics, agriculture, engineering, and
science.

His cloak of reserve could be deceptive. During
the earlier years especially, House people had a dread
of being "called on the carpet" before him. Experience
soon showed, though, that Gatti was regularly on the
side of the under-dog. He never discharged anybody
if there were a possible loophole by which to retain him;
and such culprits as came before him knew in advance
that they would be justly dealt with.

When occasion warranted it, though, Gatti could
thunder his displeasure in no uncertain terms. He was
constantly in the dark auditorium at rehearsals, walking
up and down the aisles, standing at the side, sitting
towards the rear, everywhere at once and attending
every move on the stage. He never saw—and never
remembered!—such slips that arose from nervousness
or an over-striving to get things right. But the least
evidence of negligence called forth immediate comment
in tones that rang through the darkened house. Once
a carelessness in following the stage directions raised
an outburst. Later, Gatti assured the offender that the
censure implied no personal ill-will: he had been aroused
by "an injustice to the performance."

It was said that Gatti never learned to speak English.
That was not quite the case. He spoke the language,

and understood it even better, which sometimes led to amusing situations, when people who took the "no English" reports too seriously expressed themselves over-freely in his hearing. But he never mastered the spoken tongue perfectly as to pronunciation, and felt reticent about doing an unfinished job with it. Thus, he clung officially to Italian and French, but was in no wise handicapped in speaking to the House personnel, some of whom knew English only.

He never grew entirely accustomed to the severe New York winters. With the steam-heat turned on, he would sit at his desk with his hat on, his muffler about his throat, and his overcoat buttoned.

Though he was seldom seen at performances, Gatti was present at all operas and watched them in their entirety. He had two favorite vantage-points: one was an old wooden chair in the left wings, and the other, a single seat that stands quite alone in the curve of the rear of the Orchestra Circle. Before the house lights were due to go up, he would escape—chiefly to the dressing-room of the tenor or the baritone, for a friendly between-acts chat.

Gatti liked riding in taxi-cabs. He never kept a car of his own, preferring to go to the curb, hail the driver who habitually waited for him, and drive off with him. Some of his gravest problems were settled in that cab, circling Central Park. Yet when the company gave performances in Brooklyn, Gatti would often save time by riding over in the subway.

Although Gatti's nature was hardly the one to invite practical joking, he had humor enough to take it in good part when he found himself involved in it. A performance of *Tristan* was in progress one cold, snowy

night and the staff of attendants in the Thirty-ninth
Street stage-door lobby was waiting, with somnolent
patience, for the long last act to end.  One of the
younger department members passed through and,
noting the sleepy silence that had settled over the mail-
desk and the switch-board, cast about for a novel and
sprightly means of "waking 'em up."  A glance at the
snowy street outside suggested what this means should
be.  Slipping out, the young gentleman returned with
a handful of soft, wet snow, aimed it at the wooden
partition alongside the mail-desk, and let fly.  At precisely that moment, Mr. Gatti walked out from his
office and received the full benefit of the snowball on
his beard.  The aim could not have been more perfect.
After which, the sleepy quiet of a moment before
seemed like a celebration in comparison with the awful
silence that brooded over the little lobby.  But Mr. Gatti
merely raised his eyebrows, and made his way on into
the auditorium, without waiting for a word of explanation.  Nor was the incident ever referred to by him.

Some time later, another member of the staff acquired
a gadget which struck terror into as many of the House
people as got caught by it.  The thing was a book;
looked like a book, was bound like a book, and covered
like a book.  The chief point of difference was that it had
a spring and a cap inside, instead of characters and
incidents, and went off with an ear-splitting report when
opened.  The "joke" was scarcely the sort that might
be thought to delight purveyors of *Tristan und Isolde;*
still, it provided its measure of amusement, in the days
of its freshness, and was carried about to pretty well
all the desks in the House—exclusive of Mr. Gatti's.
In time, Gatti saw it lying on the desk of its owner.

"Ah, a new volume?" he observed, picked it up, and proceeded to open it.

Cannon-fire resulted, and Mr. Gatti let fall the toy and left the room in haste. Never did he refer to this incident, either.

During the war, when Gatti was straining every effort to keep politics out of the House, a furious dispute arose one night in the Press Room. All shades of opinion were represented, and voices were rising, when suddenly a hush fell over the room. There, in the doorway, stood Gatti, who normally never entered the Press Room at all. The men apologized for their disturbance, the nature of which was contrary to House policy, but Gatti waved apologies aside. That night, he came out of his shell. He sat down with the men and threshed things out with them, pointing his talk with such a scholarly and unimpassioned survey of European history, finance, and economics, that the original dispute was forgotten. The fundamental humanness of the man showed itself the day that he insisted on lending his own violet-ray lamp to a House employe, for his sick child.

4.

The highlights of Mr. Gatti's régime! How to choose them? Extending from 1908 to 1935, they include most of the happenings in the course of living, remembered Metropolitan Opera. There are comings and goings, premières and parties, anniversary celebrations and deaths, the meteoric appearance of new "stars" and the passing into history of people who still seem young. There is the war, the banning of German opera, Wagner in English; there are boom years with such resplendent "openings" that the frequence of smoking camera flashes caused one well-intentioned bystander to turn in a fire alarm; there is a depression, the first broadcasting of opera from the Metropolitan stage, and the unbelievable occurrence of a public appeal for opera funds. It is not musical or critical values that set some of these events apart.

With the opening of the season of 1908-09, it became known that Marcella Sembrich would retire from the operatic stage. Her going was in no wise related to the circumstance of the letter referring to Mr. Dippel. Mme. Sembrich had been allied with the Metropolitan for twenty-five years, and felt that she wished to leave at the zenith of her powers, "before there should be an afterglow of pity." The news came as a shock, for Sembrich was sincerely beloved. Always reserved, never "a good mixer," she won hearts through her kindness and sincerity. Those qualities shone forth from her and no one could help but feel them.

Neither her voice nor her appearance bore testimony to more than a quarter-century of professional activity. In more than one instance, the House has had to witness the gradual waning of some favorite singer's powers, a slow fading that matches step with sagging muscles and graying hair. And it is always a sorry thing to see. But for Sembrich there was no sunset. Her voice remained fresh and pliable, and her assumption of the "young" rôles carried convincing illusion. She was never beautiful, yet her flawless taste in costuming, her fine care for the detail of her appearance, and the sheer zeal of purpose that animated her, caused her not to represent, but to *become* the part she sang. And

a Houseful of spectators watched her become the part
and believed it.  Sembrich's art was always and utterly
dependable.  News of personal sorrow that reached her
before a performance did not cast its shadow upon her
work during that performance.  For exquisite musician-
ship and gallantry-of person, Marcella Sembrich has
never been replaced.

On February 6, 1909, her departure was formally
recognized in a great special performance made up of
single acts of three of her best beloved operas (Act One,
*Don Pasquale*; Act Two, *The Barber of Seville*; Act
One, *Traviata*), with the entire company taking part
where possible, and merely sitting about the stage as
"supers" where the rôles did not go around.  Geraldine
Farrar appeared in a minor part.  Of the entire band
who sang and danced their way through the scenes that
night, only Angelo Bada is still with the company.  The
evening's program was printed on white silk, and the
crowd that thronged the House was the greatest to have
been admitted since the stringency of the fire laws.

At the close of the musical program, the festivities
began, in that curious tension that invariably follows the
attempt to make a celebration of an occasion which in
its nature is more moving than gay.  A throne had been
set on the stage, the entire company was grouped about
it, and Mr. Gatti, arm in arm with Mme. Sembrich,
made a tour of the stage, towards the place of honor.
That was the first time ever (and one of the few times
ever) that Gatti appeared on the Opera House stage.
His nervousness was apparent.

On behalf of the company, Dippel presented Mme.
Sembrich with a great silver punch bowl, together with
a set of resolutions appointing her an Honorary Mem-

ber. A pearl necklace and a watch and chain set in diamonds had been purchased entirely by public subscription, as a tribute from Sembrich's unknown admirers "out front," and these were presented by Seth Low, a former Mayor of New York City. But the gift that touched Sembrich most was a loving-cup offered by the men of the orchestra, who had not forgotten her generous assistance to them at the time of the San Francisco earthquake. Then Sembrich, in turn, presented some mementos, including in her gift list four members of the orchestra who had played there since her own coming in 1883. And the applause rose louder and the cheering grew, and under it all lay the knowledge that this night marked the passing from the operatic world of one of its truly great figures.

It was one of Sembrich's chief charms that she never forgot old friends or old happenings. During his first years with the House, Gerber (still in knickerbockers) was summoned to her apartment in the Savoy Hotel, to transact an errand involving press clippings; and besides cutting the clippings, he also cut his hand. Sembrich fainted at the sight of the blood. When she came to, she apologized for her "lack of consideration," and ministered to the young sufferer, who was far more awed by the attention accorded him than by his mishap. Throughout the years of their acquaintanceship, Sembrich never failed to enquire, first solicitously and later laughingly, for his "poor wound."

Less than a fortnight after the Sembrich farewell, Emma Eames announced her intention of quitting the organization, too; but confined her formal leave-taking to a speech to the audience during one of the entr'actes of a performance of *Tosca*. It was said that Eames was not entirely in sympathy with the "Italian" régime.

Despite his personal reticence, Gatti was the first of the General Managers to put gala entertaining on a company basis. What entertaining Grau and Conried had done, was done privately. Gatti very definitely heightened opera interest and general good feeling by using special musical events as the background for great gala parties, all given in the House and including the entire House membership. It was "the sphinx," oddly enough, who promoted the most informal jollity the House had yet known.

Gatti's long directorship saw many new works, many premières with their attendant excitement, many notable casts, and many interesting visitors. But two events combining all those elements stand out—possibly because of the splendid entertainments which followed them! These performances took place within three weeks of each other. The world première of Puccini's *Girl of the Golden West* was given on December 10, 1910, to be followed on December 28 by the world première of Humperdinck's *Koenigskinder*. The Metropolitan was by no means accustomed to world premières, and the normal excitement of being the first house to witness the works was heightened by the presence of the two composers. Both Humperdinck and Puccini had visited the Metropolitan before, to attend performances of *Haensel und Gretel,* and *Manon Lescaut* and *Madama Butterfly,* respectively; but their second appearances in the House seem the more vivid.

While *Koenigskinder* was possibly the more musically successful (at least, it endured longer), *The Girl* caused the greater sensation. All in one, here was a

new work, a first performance, an American theme and
setting, a splendid cast, and a definite note of "human
interest." The play from which the opera's libretto
was adapted, had enjoyed a run on Broadway. Blanche
Bates was its star, and its author and producer was
David Belasco.

Belasco was now invited to assume full charge of the
stage for the opera's presentation. At first glance, this
wizard of the theater seemed singularly unimpressive.
A short man, with silver hair, mild brown eyes, an
habitually low voice, and a most untheatrically quiet
manner. He wore his familiar dress of a priest of the
Roman Catholic Church, and everyone (particularly the
religious Italians) derived a special sensation from seeing "a Father" take hold of the stage. And he did take
hold of it!

Belasco was in the House early and late. Watching
him rehearse, one was again struck by the mysterious
workings of the sheer power of personality. He never
raised his voice. He was never "spectacular." He
simply impressed people with what he wanted—and got
it. Belasco and Gatti had many qualities in common
and their association was a happy one. Belasco often
said that the biggest dramatic job of his career lay in
making that polyglot company of principals and
choristers, all firmly rooted in the operatic school of wide
gestures, look and act like the uncommunicative type of
cowboy Westerner. Without Belasco, the visual part
of the presentation might easily have approached the
burlesque. In rehearsing the chorus and the "supers,"
his method of quenching gestures was simply to order
all hands in trouser-pockets unless actually needed for
lifting a glass or drawing a gun. With the principals,

though, the process was more involved. The cast
included the Italians, Caruso and Amato, the Czech
Emmy Destinn, the African Dinh Gilly, and the Russian Didur. All had to be re-born as folk of the Bret
Harte school. For half an hour at a time, Belasco would
sit quietly in a corner with one or the other, patiently
coaching a single motion, a single expression of face.
Suddenly, then, he would call for silence, go to the
center of the stage, and act out a full scene, assuming
every part. The "stars" were deeply interested—partly
in their rôles and partly in observing the wizardry of
Belasco.

It took much convincing to persuade Destinn to part
with her silk stockings and don cotton ones. Caruso was
happy as a schoolboy in the novelty of it all, and took
great pains learning to handle himself "like a cowboy."
The lesson was never forgotten, and odd moments of
exuberant spirits often called back those gestures of gun
play. But it was Gilly who most won Belasco's heart.
Gilly was powerfully built, with a nose that looked as if
it might once have been broken, and naturally "bandy"
legs. He alone had the appearance of a cowboy without special coaching!

The musical direction was in the hands of Toscanini,
and Puccini was present, at rehearsals and at the première. Puccini made a tremendous impression, with his
handsome face and his suave, kindly manner. And
since interest has already centered in the shape or covering of people's legs, it must be stated that the House
fell into a rapture of admiration for Puccini's trousers.
Wide at the hips, tapering tight at the ankles, and held
by a strap under the feet, they looked like nothing so

much as the costume of *Rodolfo* in the Maestro's own
*La Bohême.*

*Koenigskinder* saw one of the most moving of all
operatic characterizations in Geraldine Farrar's appealing delineation of *The Goose Girl*.  The picture she
made as she walked through the old arched gateway,
surrounded by a flock of live geese (which never quacked
once!), is indelible in the memories of those who were
fortunate enough to see it.  Alfred Hertz conducted the
performance, which was under the general supervision
of Engelbert Humperdinck, a small, old-world gentleman whose face looked as if it might have come out of
one of those fairy-tales he loved to set to music.

After each of these performances, Mr. Gatti entertained for the guests of honor.  The parties were given
in the foyer of the House, and the invitation list included
the Directors, the entire company, the press, and certain distinguished guests.  Formality soon departed, the
champagne was plentiful, and the sheer good feeling
that was stimulated between the House and the outer
world did much towards heightening the strictly musical
success of Gatti's opera.

Another memorable party was the one which Clarence H. Mackay gave to celebrate the first New York
performance of Victor Herbert's *Natoma*, in February
of 1911, when the foyer was decorated with smilax and
orchids, and canary birds sang.  Though the performance and the party both took place in the House,
*Natoma* is not strictly Metropolitan history.  Dippel,
then active in the Chicago-Philadelphia opera organization, brought his company to New York for a series of
guest performances, and *Natoma* was given by him.

5.

Mr. Gatti was presently to find himself beset with graver responsibilities than those involving operas and "stars." His directorship might be said to fall into three sections. Prior to 1917 there were simply the problems of management, which are by no means so simple, but which were made to seem so in the light of later events. From 1917 to 1929 came the years of war emergencies and a post-war rehabilitation that rose to a boom; while from 1929 to his resignation in 1935 there came the problems of depression which threatened the life of the organization itself.

The season of 1913-14 was a singularly brilliant one. Gatti had undertaken the tremendous task of mounting five complete novelties in addition to the regular repertory (they included *Der Rosenkavalier* and *L'Amore dei Tre Re* with Lucrezia Bori's unforgettable delineation of *Fiora*), and his plans for raising musical interest still further were well under way, when war was declared.

The position of a director of polyglot opera in a neutral land was by no means an easy one. There was fear that the war might cause a falling-off in subscriptions (it did harm the financial security of opera organizations in other cities), but even more than that, there was fear for the unity of the company. Most of the principal singers gave their allegiance to their own countries, which they were quite free to do while the United States remained neutral; but such allegiances caused an inescapable tension between individuals whose business it was to work together harmoniously, in foreign parts, for the common purpose of art. Besides the threat to the company's spiritual harmony, there was the very real problem of assembling all performers in New York in time for the opening of the new season. Most of the artists and many of the choristers and orchestral players had gone abroad for vacations or additional guest seasons; and to assure his own season, Gatti had to set his hand to tasks that stretched from diplomatic intervention to the hurried cabling of funds. Albert Reiss, committed to a concentration camp in France, secured his release only through the offices of the French Ambassador. Rothier went to war. Gilly, a war prisoner in Austria, could not be released. Gatti's leadership through those hard years stands as a greater achievement than any presentation of opera.

He was never heard to "take sides" himself and requested his artists to refrain from all discussions. Whatever people were feeling, the surface of harmony was maintained, and the House's policy of strict neutrality was attested by the revival of Weber's *Euryanthe* (December 19, 1914), with a cast that included Frieda Hempel, Johannes Sembach, Hermann Weill, and Margarete Ober (all Germans), under the baton of Toscanini. During the following seasons, Gatti continued his splendidly imperturbable policy of presenting the operas of all lands as universal works of art and leaving politics outside the door. The German repertory was in no wise slighted, and when Alfred Hertz resigned (1915), Artur Bodanzky was brought over to take his place. (An Austrian by birth, Bodanzky was then Musical Director of the Royal Theater of Baden, in Mannheim, and his coming required permission from the French and English governments.) Until America entered the war, there was no appreciable change of policy on Gatti's part, and no demand for one on the part of the public.

A shock to public sensibilities, however, came from reports in the press that, at a New Year's Eve party given at the home of Johanna Gadski (1915), Otto Goritz, another member of the German contingent, had sung a gay song that alluded sarcastically to the fate of Americans aboard the ill-starred *Lusitania*. For some time before this, Mme. Gadski's presence in the company had aroused public resentment. Her husband, Captain Hans Tauscher, had been an agent of the Mauser and Krupp munitions concerns, and had served his country during the early war years in some extra-military capacity. Later, he was arrested by officials of the United States Secret Service on charges involving the destruction of the Welland Canal. Mme. Gadski was felt to be rather more than a mere purveyor of foreign art, and protests were heard. Before that season was over, Mr. Gatti announced that Gadski would not rejoin the company the following year. Otherwise he continued steering the course of his activities serenely through all these disturbances.

And then American neutrality was over. During a performance of *Canterbury Pilgrims,* word was brought into the House that President Wilson had asked Congress to declare a state of war between the United States and Germany. Excitement mounted at once to fever pitch. Mr. Bodanzky, at the conductor's desk, rose gallantly to the occasion and led the orchestra through an impromptu performance of *The Star Spangled Banner*. (Though an "enemy" by birth, Bodanzky had already declared his intention of becoming an American citizen, and there was never the slightest doubt of his loyalty.) James W. Gerard, the Ambassador to Germany, was present in the House and rose in a box, to call for cheers for the President. On the stage, the German Mme. Ober broke down at the news and had to be assisted to the wings.

When the United States severed its relations with Germany, Captain Tauscher came rushing into the theater at the end of the performance, his face blanched and a terrified look in his eyes.

"I never thought it would come to this," he cried, "I never thought they would actually do it!"

That season's final performances of German opera were allowed to continue undisturbed, and the Good Friday presentation of *Parsifal* was received with reverent respect, although that day marked America's entrance into the war. But the new season pointed to new needs for policies concerning the language and nationals of an enemy land. In November of 1917, Gatti let it be known that there would be no German performances and that the repertory would include "nothing that could cause the least offense to the most patriotic Americans." The contracts of the German singers were cancelled. Artistically, Gatti was one of the staunchest supporters of German opera; and from a business point of view, the Wagnerian repertory could not afford to be overlooked. He took the position he did to avoid embarrassment to his American public.

6.

With their characteristic adaptability, American audiences used the Armistice as a safety valve for blowing off the last of their animosities, and soon settled down again to a willingness to accept German art. Wagnerian operas were back in the repertory by the winter of 1920, although they were then sung in English; and November of 1921 saw them restored to full polyglot equality, in their own tongue.

Caruso opened the season of 1920-21 with his magnificent characterization of *Eleazer* in *La Juive*. It was the last time he was to inaugurate the new operatic year. To see him that night, no one would have imagined that the cloak of the reaper was spreading out to enfold him. *Eleazer* was undoubtedly Caruso's finest rôle. Although he had been the outstanding public favorite for nearly two decades, hypercritical opinion contended that, despite the opulence of his voice, he was not a "thorough artist." With *Eleazer* (which he coached under the direction of a veteran Jewish actor from one of the lower East-side theaters), Caruso emerged as a complete and mature artist, and one of the finest the world ever saw. There was infinitely more than a great voice to make *Eleazer* an unforgettable stage portrait.

Early in December, Caruso strained his side while singing a performance of *Pagliacci*. The opera was delayed some half-hour while he gave care to himself, but he insisted on "going on with the show." He was in great pain, though, and the pain remained. He complained during the next day or so, of feeling "a hurt." Three days later, while making up for a performance of *L'Elisir d' Amore,* in the Academy of Music in Brooklyn, he was stricken with a severe attack of coughing. Presently his handkerchief came away from his mouth red with blood. The dressing-room presented a frightful aspect. Everything Caruso touched was instantly blood-soaked. Messrs Ziegler, Swin, and Gerber, who were with him, became gravely alarmed, and begged Caruso not to attempt to sing that night. But again he insisted on appearing. It was nearing curtain time, the house out front was filling with people who had come especially to hear Caruso, and "the show must go on." During the First Act, a relay system was arranged with members of the chorus, whereby a supply of clean handkerchiefs was constantly passed to Caruso, without knowledge of the audience. They, too, came away blood-stained. By the end of the act, Caruso was in no condition to continue, and despite his protests, an announcement was made from the stage. The audience was told that Caruso had been taken ill, but that he was willing to go on if the people wished it.

"No, no!" shouted the house. "Let him stop!"

Ticket refunds were promised, the audience filed out, and Caruso was taken home, gravely ill. His chest and upper body were tightly strapped with adhesive tape, to guard against further hemorrhages, and he was ordered to stay quiet. Within a fortnight, however, he was back at work, still strapped, still suffering great pain, but insisting on resuming his performances. The *Eleazer* he gave on Christmas Eve was the last performance he was ever to give. Caruso's career stopped with his attainment of artistic perfection. The strain of singing had brought on a relapse, and there followed weeks of critical illness, through which he was carried only by his heroic determination. Friends who visited his bedside found him reading his prayer-book. A picture of his mother stood on the table beside him.

As spring approached, there rose the hope that Caruso would one day be Caruso again. But when he

came over to the House on a visit (which turned out to
be his final one), the hopes sank.  In the familiar clothing of the vital, vigorous Caruso, with his broad
shoulders and developed, arched chest, there came a
bent, shrunken figure.  His garments hung upon him
and his face was drawn.  The one fear in everybody's
mind was that he would see some reflection of the piti-
ful change, in the eyes of those who greeted him.
Caruso drew out his cigarette case to offer its contents
to his friends, dropped it and though the dozen men
sprang to pick it up for him, he insisted on retrieving
it himself. On his way out, then, he came upon one of
the scrubwomen.

"Mr. Caruso!"

He stopped and shook hands with her.

"I'm awfully glad to see you back . . . but, my, how
thin you got!  I hardly knew you again."

Caruso turned to the group about him, who had been
mendaciously assuring him how well he looked.

"There is one person here, at least, who tells me the
truth."

He left for Italy that spring, never to return.  There
are those who still feel that a quiet rest in the Adiron-
dacks, without the commotion of travel, might have prolonged his life.  But he would journey to Italy, where
he further exhausted himself by a taxing foot-pilgrim-
age to a favorite shrine.  Less fervent souls make the
trip on mule back.  He died in his beloved Naples, in
August.

The following season marked another departure, but
of a less tragic kind.  Geraldine Farrar had announced
her intention of retiring from the operatic stage at the
age of forty, and she kept her word in the face of spec-

tacular public protest. This was entirely characteristic of the forceful "Gerry." The undisputed queen of the operatic world remained "Gerry" to the entire House staff. To make her departure final, she gave away every bit of costuming she owned . . . gowns, shoes, properties, stage-jewelry; she summoned the members of the chorus and ballet to her dressing-room in little squadrons, and handed the beautiful things about. To the House staff, she presented gold watch-chains, and charms engraved with her autograph. Her farewell performance of *Zaza* was a "100% American" demonstration. From the look of the House that day, one might have thought a political rally was in progress. Flags fluttered, horns tooted, bouquets flew towards the stage, Gerry-flappers shouted, and Gerry-flappers wept. Miss Farrar was carried from the theater and borne in triumph to her waiting automobile.

Within the House, Miss Farrar was regarded as what the stage carpenter called "one of the boys." Everyone felt sure of her friendship and everyone loved her. For some obscure journalistic reason, the much-publicized doings of this much-admired "star" were habitually set forth in terms of her "temperament," her "differentness," and her favorite breakfast foods. Few accounts ever mentioned the fact that this "glamorous personality" was also one of the hardest and most faithful workers the company ever knew. Farrar devoted endless time and energy to the study of her rôles; she had definite reasons for every look or gesture. Yet she was always receptive to expert advice . . . more so than many a novice. The headlined aspects of "temperament" were entirely foreign to the Farrar whom the House knew.

The year of Farrar's departure saw the arrival of Maria Jeritza. Although her début (in *Die Tote Stadt*) marked her at once as an interesting artist, it was her *Tosca* which established her in public regard. Operatic audiences were accustomed to hear the *Vissi d'Arte* music sung as a formal aria, with the singer occupying a good position near the footlights, and addressing herself to the House in the development of a "big moment." When the cue came at Jeritza's first performance of the part, a shiver of consternation ran through the House. Suddenly the singer dropped to the floor; it looked exactly as though she had become stricken by illness. Lying flat on the stage, then, she presented the music not as an aria but as a cry of anguish. One marvelled that she could produce her tones in a posture so disadvantageous to singing. But she did, and the House went mad. Here was something entirely new! One of the city's severest critics—an acidulous gentleman who expressed headlined scorn for every manifestation of "commercial opera"—was seen to rise to his feet and cheer. Jeritza had asserted herself, not only as an artist but as a "hit."

Early in 1925, there occurred a demonstration that left no doubt as to the direct means of ascertaining "what the public wants." The performance was a revival of *Falstaff* and the ovation that rose in the House had nothing to do with any of the principals in the cast. It concerned itself, rather, with a tall, slim young Californian, who had been heard in the company during some seasons, and always in secondary parts. His name is Lawrence Tibbett. Actually, his name is Tibbetts, but the final *S* was omitted in the program through a print-

A SCENE FROM "MANON," TAKEN DURING A PERFORMANCE. LUCREZIA
BORI AND RICHARD CROOKS

A SCENE FROM "MANON," TAKEN DURING A PERFORMANCE. LEFT
FOREGROUND, LUCREZIA BORI AND RICHARD CROOKS

er's error, and the nature of what befell him has caused him to continue without it.

*Falstaff* was revived especially for the veteran Antonio Scotti, and Tibbett, who then ranked as just another baritone, was assigned the secondary rôle of *Ford*. After a duet between Scotti and Tibbett, there came a sudden and astonishing thunder of applause. The usual bowed acknowledgments were made, but the matter did not end there. The clapping grew louder, shouts and cheers rang out, and it became evident that something out of the ordinary was developing. Embarrassingly enough, Scotti interpreted the outburst as directed to himself, and stepped before the curtain alone. Then someone shouted "Tibbett!" and the House took it up. Tibbett had already gone to his dressing-room to prepare for the next act. The conductor hastily sent one of the 'cellists upstairs to summon him. On the way, the man encountered Gatti in the wings, explained his unusual errand, and asked if he were willing to have Tibbett called. Gatti said, *"Si, Si,"* in his imperturbable way, and the bewildered young man was pushed to the footlights alone. There was no doubt then for whom the applause was meant. Lawrence Tibbett had come into his own. After the performance he stopped in at a telegraph office to send the good news to his mother. Then he rode home in the subway. By morning, he discovered that he had wasted the cost of his telegram. Every newspaper in the country carried enthusiastic accounts of the young American's triumph.

Another of Mr. Gatti's American discoveries who "stopped the show" is Richard Crooks. Crooks has always had very definite ideas of what he wants. As a child, he wanted music, and sang soprano solos in the

church choir of his native Trenton, New Jersey. He
tells one that it is often embarrassing to him, to-day, in
his thirty-fifth year, to receive the greetings of people
who remember his work "a quarter of a century ago."
When he lacked the money for the vocal lessons he
wanted, he set about earning it by painting gas tanks,
and loading blocks of ice on to the delivery wagons that
began their route at seven in the morning. Long before
he had asserted himself, he refused an engagement in
comic opera at a thousand dollars a week because he did
not want comic opera. He refused a music patron's
offer of the funds for foreign study because he did not
want to live on money he had not earned himself. He
refused five consecutive contracts with the Metropolitan
because he did not want to appear in a House of great
traditions before he felt himself ready for it. When he
did appear there at last, his début performance of
*Manon,* in 1933, was delayed for fifty minutes by the
demonstrations of the audience. On both sides of the
curtain, "Dick" Crooks is one of the best beloved members of the opera's forces.

## 7.

Then came the years of high living, free spending,
and quick replenishment from the whirling dance of
figures on ticker-tape. One result to the House, of
course, was an immense box-office intake. Shop clerks
and office boys, who had never before seen the inside of
an opera house, were purchasing orchestra chairs at
eight dollars apiece. But the boom years also ushered
in what threatened to become one of the most vexing
problems since the war. That was the matter of oper-

atic salaries.  All demands were high in those days, and
those for artistic honorariums proved no exception.
Even a sold-out House for every performance would
hardly have yielded enough to meet them, and suddenly
the surplus which had been accumulating under Gatti's
able management, began to mean something more urgent than a mere statement on the ledgers.

This condition grew aggravated when a financier
named Samuel Insull emerged as operatic impresario
in Chicago.  Insull had vast sums at his command, and
he wanted to make the Chicago operatic organization
the most splendid in the country.  Here was competition
which was rather different from Mr. Hammerstein's,
and which might have proven even more troublesome.
Hammerstein had tried to lure away Metropolitan audiences.  Chicago tried to lure away Metropolitan casts.
As soon as an artist made good in New York, he was
likely to be offered double the salary from the apparently limitless coffers of the windy city.  Many of the
artists came to Mr. Gatti with troubled faces.

"I have enjoyed my work here with you, and I'd love
to stay on with you.  But . . . *this* is what I'm being
offered in Chicago!"

Thus, there came into existence the hitherto-unknown
necessity for contract bidding.  To keep the Metropolitan roster at the level which the public expected,
Chicago's offers had to be met.  And all the while, the
surplus was shrinking.

Mr. Gatti always seemed favored by Fate.  Whenever things got too black for human handling, something unexpected happened, quite from the outside, to
alter conditions beyond the wildest imaginings.  When
the salary question got to the straining point, the de-

pression struck. It seems hard to believe that the depression should have worked good to anyone, but in one sense, it helped the Metropolitan. What it did in Chicago is financial history. Mr. Insull departed, his opera was disbanded, and the fabulous salaries were as done as though they had never been. Some of the artists for whose services bidding had been necessary, were happy to come back at their former terms. More than that, when the pressure of conditions seemed to threaten the Metropolitan too, there developed a loyalty among company members that outweighed any question of fees. Celebrities, secondary singers, choristers, House employes, all pledged their support to Gatti, regardless of terms, some of them offering to accept less than was promised them. Gatti himself led the way towards a general voluntary salary cut by proposing to work without any pay at all, should it prove necessary for him to do so. Beniamino Gigli refused to reduce his demands, on the grounds that such a step would injure his artistic status. He has not sung with the company since.

Those were the dark days when the "Save the Opera" drive was begun, largely through the splendid efforts of Lucrezia Bori. Bori installed a clerical staff in her own apartment, and threw herself completely into the task of retaining old subscribers and finding new ones. Many a subscriber who "cancelled with regret" was invited to tea with Miss Bori. And when the tea was over, the cancellation was cancelled! The drive was met with an overwhelmingly generous public response. Contributions and "radio subscriptions" poured into the House from people in all parts of the country, many of whom had never seen the Metropolitan. Farmers, with no cash to spare, sent eggs and produce, with instructions that the goods be sold and the proceeds devoted to the Fund. Children enclosed dimes and nickels in laboriously written notes that told of candy that had been given up so that the contribution could be made. Any doubt as to the hold which Metropolitan Opera has come to take upon American life was dispelled by the attitude of the public during those days of depression.

Fate had still another trick in store, and played it at another of those moments that were of greatest advantage to Gatti. During the last year of his directorship, the opera needed a new stimulus of human interest. The worst of the depression emergency had passed, but *something* was needed to keep general opera-interest at a high level, and nothing spectacular seemed in sight. No unusual novelties were ready; no breath-taking conductor was coming over; no glamorously heralded "stars" seemed to shine. There was, however, among the regularly announced newcomers, a stranger from Norway. She had never sung in America; it is by no means certain that she would have been engaged, had Frida Leider renewed her contract with the company; no one knew much about her; she was unfamiliar to Covent Garden, Milan, Vienna, Paris, and Rome; she was past thirty, and not at all the cotton-batting-wrapped type of prima donna. She was announced as just another soprano. And then came the day of her début and people discovered that the unknown newcomer was Kirsten Flagstad. The stimulus of new interest had come.

To-day, Flagstad stands as the greatest individual attraction the House has ever had. In former days, when money was plentiful, the regular subscriptions took up most of the seats. People *wanted* to buy tickets when some favorite "star" or some especially alluring cast combination was announced, but the regular subscribers held such a corner on them that single-performance tickets were hard to obtain. Hardly any subscribers withdrew, and those who died generally bequeathed their Metropolitan seats to their favorite sons. When Flagstad arrived, the depression had caused something of a falling-off in the regular subscriptions, with the result that there were more seats for sale at the box-office. And these she sells out, to the last inch of standing room. Never before was the entire quota of "stand-up" tickets sold out for the German repertory. Flagstad's *Kundry* helped to put *Parsifal* back into the "popular" list. Gatti often said that the one emotion attendant upon his departure from the House not tinged with regret, was the thought that he was "bequeathing" Kirsten Flagstad to the coming régime.

### 8.

Gatti had worked valiantly through a succession of grave difficulties. In the winter of 1934 he announced his intention of retiring from the Metropolitan. There was a final Gala Performance, of course, in which the entire company took part, and the proceeds of which were devoted, at Gatti's request, to the Opera Fund. Gatti had been urged to show himself on the stage for the last time, but he refused. There was great surprise then, when suddenly he did appear, walking on with his slow step and familiar gestures. Only after the first excitement had subsided did "Mr. Gatti" remove his beard and his make-up to reveal tall Emanuel List disguised as a striking likeness of the departing Chief.

Then the orchestra rose to its feet, the audience stood at attention, and a spotlight was thrown upon Box Forty-eight, where the "real" Mr. Gatti was seated. He responded with a salute and had to be pushed to the front of the box to be seen.

On the day of his departure, Rosa Ponselle gave a final party for him on the Lido Deck of the *S. S. Rex*. The invitations had been sent by telegram. Many of the artists were present, together with the chorus, orchestra, ballet, and House staff. Gatti sat in an armchair, receiving his co-workers of so many years, and disguising the emotion he felt by laughing at the impromptu parade that was organized. Someone took up a large banner that wished *"Long Life To Our Beloved Gatti!"* and the march was on. Round and round the deck they went, laughing, cheering, some cutting capers, some biting back tears. One of the Italians began the final farewells by kissing Gatti on both cheeks, and everyone followed suit, to the trepidation of some of the younger American gentlemen of the company. And then the going-ashore whistle blew, and the House people had their final glimpse of Giulio Gatti-Casazza, leaning over the rail and waving his hat. Beside him stood Giulio Setti, the chorus master. Setti had come to the Metropolitan with Gatti, and preferred quitting it with him, too.

CHAPTER IV

## EDWARD JOHNSON

### 1.

GATTI was gone. Through arrangements concluded with the Juilliard Foundation and which bore materially upon the financial well-being of the Metropolitan, the new General Manager came in the person of Herbert Witherspoon, who had formerly been one of the leading bassos of the company. Years had passed since Witherspoon's activity in the House, and while his artistry was remembered, there were comparatively few among the company's changing personnel, who really knew him well. Witherspoon returned as something of a stranger.

Again the company was reorganized, and the new plans included arrangements for a supplementary spring season of lighter opera. In administrative charge of this spring season came Edward Johnson, who was no stranger. Johnson had been a member of the company for some time. Artistically, he stood unmatched for his sensitive interpretation of lyric tenor rôles (notably, *Romeo* and *Pelléas*) ; and personally, he ranked in the Farrar class for being "one of the boys." Johnson always managed to know how many children the various House people had, and never forgot to inquire for "the family." Everyone felt the stimulus of personal kindliness that radiates from him. When it became known that he was to be one of the "bosses," there arose a new spirit of animation. Here was the best news since Gatti's resignation!

For some weeks, Mr. Witherspoon busied himself with plans for the new season. He was a tireless worker, and spent up to twelve hours a day at his desk. On the morning of his departure for Europe, on a reconnoitering tour for new vocal material, he stopped in at the office of the Assistant General Manager, where the two were joined by the Box-Office Treasurer, who came to make a final report on subscriptions. Mrs. Witherspoon was waiting in her husband's private office. At the end of the conference, they were to leave the House preparatory to boarding the ship. The three gentlemen talked, and presently the meeting was over. Witherspoon rose, walked to the swinging door that leads into the offices of the General Manager, and suddenly dropped to the floor. A moment before, he had been talking and there was no indication that he felt unwell. He died, of a heart attack, before the sailing of the ship. His death was doubtless hastened by the strenuous routine he had imposed upon himself.

### 2.

On the day that Edward Johnson was appointed Witherspoon's successor as General Manager of the Metropolitan Opera Association, a property man met him crossing the stage and stopped him.

"I've just heard the news, Mr. Johnson, and I want to offer my congratulations."

"What do you mean by talking to me like that?" demanded Johnson with a frown.

The man drew back in alarm.

"After all the years we've worked together here, swapping stories and calling each other names, you come at me now with 'Mr. Johnson'? I'm Eddie to you —just as I was when I was simply one of the tenors. And thank you very much for the congratulations, but don't forget that it'll be you and the rest of the crowd who are going to make my job a success!"

That is the best explanation of the man—and the best explanation of the fact that everybody is eager to please him.

Like Grau, Johnson is always out front during the performances, alert to every moment in the opera's progress, and to the reactions to it, as well. At the end of each act, he hurries backstage and visits with the workers on the sets and the "stars" in their dressing-rooms, encouraging them, telling them pleasant things about their work, and leaving behind him the desire to do even better. At the close of his first season as General Manager, Johnson did an unprecedented thing. He gave a dinner for the heads of the House departments, and the press. When the time for the "speeches" came, he thanked the critics for the splendid co-operation they had given him. Those among them who remembered Conried's tirades in the Press Room, drank lengthily of the ice water. Next, he asked each of the department heads to rise, while he told of special things they had done to help him in his task. Never before had these workers realized what really splendid fellows they were! The much embarrassed Master Mechanic sat down and wiped his face.

"That," he observed to his neighbor, "is what I call a boss!"

Johnson's transfer to administrative duties was a

singularly fortunate one. As an experienced singer, he came thoroughly familiar with the most important problems of managerial policy: the selection of the repertory, the judging of the singers, and the actual routine working of "the show." He had not been ambitious for the post of Chief. He had set his heart on developing the spring season of opera, which was to prepare a much-needed proving ground for promising young singers, and offer to the public the orchestra, scenic equipment, and general atmosphere of the Metropolitan at popular prices. He was called to assume the general headship because of his artistic integrity, his intimate knowledge of conditions, and the cordial sympathy with which he is regarded by the entire personnel.

The unexpectedness with which the rudder of operatic organization was thrust into his hands, together with a desire to carry out certain policies indicated by Mr. Witherspoon, placed a dual responsibility on Johnson. In assuming it, he was materially aided by two members of his administrative staff: the Assistant General Manager, Edward Ziegler, and the Box-Office Treasurer, Earle R. Lewis.

Mr. Ziegler embodies a singular combination of sound scholarship and vast practical experience. From 1916 on, he has been Assistant General Manager of the Metropolitan, working in close association with Mr. Gatti and sharing the problems of both artistic and administrative management with him. Before that, he served as music critic on *The New York Herald,* and as musical adviser to the Aeolian Company. A gentleman of seasoned judgment, he unites musical erudition, critical ability, and managerial experience with an unfailing tact which enables him to stand as general buffer between the

House and any possible emergency that could arise from outside. His talent for heaping duties upon himself has built up an attitude of mind among the House people whereby the solution of any difficulty is found in the phrase,

"Don't worry—go to Ziegler!"

Only those closely associated with Mr. Ziegler can appreciate the responsibilities he assumed during the critical years of depression. That the Metropolitan survived is due largely to his efforts. After the death of Mr. Witherspoon (which occasioned Mr. Ziegler more than professional regret, since the two had been close friends), there was a time when the House had no official head, when normal administrative duties were plunged into confusion, and when the full burden of keeping the wheels in orderly motion rested solely upon his shoulders.

Even at such a time, Mr. Ziegler could raise his head from an important consideration of contracts to give one, in four languages, the detailed musical background of the lady who sang the *Second Flower Maiden* in *Parsifal* in 1914, the difference in curtain times between the cut and the uncut versions of *Die Meistersinger,* the cue for the tenor aria at the end of the First Act of *The Girl of the Golden West,* the demands of the chorus' union in 1920, the name of the city Statute which refers to fire hazards, the number of times a certain child appeared as the Baby in *Madama Butterfly,* the condition of the locks on the closets in the first tenor's dressing-room, the words of any of the German *Lieder,* and the sequence of themes in the Brahms First Symphony. His presence in the House is a bulwark of surety. Personally, he is a charming *raconteur* and a notable wit.

Earle R. Lewis is the son of one of the world's foremost handwriting experts. He sleeps six hours a day, eats less than one, and devotes the remainder to his work. He generally arrives in the House before nine, has his barber meet him in his office, and gets through much of his mail while under lather, to have more time for conferences when the day's duties begin. Lewis came to the House over twenty-five years ago, as a very young boy, and was given the post of selling tickets for the Family Circle. This was perhaps the least attractive position the House had to offer. The Family Circle is kept apart from the rest of the auditorium. It has its separate entrance, its separate stairs, and its separate ticket-window, in the draughtiest corner of the Fortieth Street door. The patrons are generally in a hurry. Behind this cold little window, then, young Lewis took his place.

Before long, the patrons seemed to be in less of a hurry. The young man talked with them as he dealt out the tickets and made the change. He asked about their likes and dislikes in the matter of repertory and casts; why they bought seats for one performance and not for another. Presently, very interesting reports were finding their way back to the General Manager's office. Lewis had inaugurated a system of tabulating the patrons' preferences. For the first time, he introduced the element of popular psychology into a position that had theretofore concerned itself solely with tickets and cash. When Max Hirsch, the veteran Box-Office Treasurer resigned, the management decided that this alert youngster from the Family Circle window was the best qualified to take his place, and apply his novel methods to the tastes of the better-paying patrons.

Lewis has made it possible to establish a systematic check-up, not merely on the elements of operatic popularity, but on the definite reasons for such popularity; and the reasons extend from an opening up of Wagnerian cuts to a preference for rose or green in the stage sets. He has a genius for figures, adding up a column by glancing at it. His hobby is golf. Lewis and Richard Crooks once played their way across the country, motoring from one famous course to the next. They often go away on golf-week-ends together. At the end of a Friday night performance, Lewis has more than once stood in the wings, equipped with golf bags, and urging Crooks to "hurry up with the curtain calls," so that they might start out that night still. The only thing Earle Lewis does not do successfully is to manipulate a cigarette.

Lewis once carried through a novel and daring scheme for protecting the Opera's patrons from the gouging of ticket speculators. For a certain Special Performance, when prices were doubled, Lewis and his staff made a note of the purchasers' desires as to locations, took the money for the seats, wrote down each patron's name, and gave them no tickets at all! Instead, the total number of tickets were evenly distributed among the three House entrances, and the purchasers were instructed to go to one of these doors, half an hour before curtain time. On the night of the performance, then, an extra staff was placed at each entrance, and each applicant for admission was asked to identify himself. Only then were the tickets given out.

The speculators and their "diggers" soon got wind of the new arrangement, and realizing that a close check-up would take place at the doors, the majority of them felt the risk too great a one upon which to venture the expenditure of double prices.

With the invaluable assistance of Messrs Ziegler and Lewis, Mr. Johnson began his directorship at a time when the country's financial conditions were by no means settled, and when voices were heard to cry that the age of grand opera had passed. The public was thought to want something more in harmony with its own problems than vocal dialogue and costumed gestures. A prima donna (whose affiliations with the House had been terminated for some time) gave forth the view that opera, as a medium of popular entertainment, was quite dead, and that its prostrate form was rapidly being blocked from sight by the livelier manifestations of the "jazz age." The practical answer to such opinions has been—sold out houses for *Parsifal!*

THE METRO-
POLITAN AUDI-
TORIUM

*Part Two*

## OPERA GLAMOUR

# Chapter V

CONCERNING LIFE IN THE "HOUSE"

1.

THE opera carries a glamour all its own. It has nothing to do with the derivation of the word, which deals with a plurality of artistic output; and little even with the nature of the entertainment. Opera, as a matter of fact, is the most complete of all dramatic forms, blending musical values, singing, orchestral accompaniment, and often dancing, with the regular facilities of the theater. But the average conception of opera glamour does not concern itself with philological derivations or an analysis of art forms. It is best explained, perhaps, by the impulse which caused our grandfathers to call the amusement center of the smallest small town "the Opry House." Nothing even remotely approaching grand opera ever came there. The attractions were chiefly itinerant melodramas, trained-bear exhibits, or Sacred Concerts. But the name in itself meant something special. The Opera House! Immediately, one became translated into a world of wealth, distinction, elegance, smart sophistication, and "temperament"!

Raise the glamour of "the Opry House" to the Nth degree, and you arrive at the Metropolitan. New York's "Met" ranks as the only permanent operatic organization, to carry through a full season of its own, in quarters of its own, and with a roster and equipment of its own, in the entire country. Opera is given in other American cities at the present time, but usually for a briefer season, and at such times as the Metropolitan singers and conductors are free to appear. Theoretically, of course, this is all wrong. There *should be* regular, permanent local opera in all of our larger cities, partly as a means of familiarizing our public with one of the pleasantest forms of dramatic entertainment; and partly as a means of furnishing our talented young performers with that necessary routine experience which alone can help them to "rub off the corners." But practically, and until "should be" becomes converted into "is," the Metropolitan continues to occupy a unique position. If you speak of "the opera" in any of the foreign countries where companies of experienced singing-actors abound, you will be understood to mean a familiar and popular form of diversion: if you speak of "the opera" here, you mean the "Met." The "Met" is "the Opry House," in all its connotations, come true.

By no means least among the causes of the opera's glamour is the special effulgence shed upon it by society. The opera is to society what the "movies" are to the man in the street: something to be attended regularly once a week, something to be enjoyed if possible, and to be endured for conversational purposes, if enjoyment is not possible. The list of the Diamond Horseshoe boxholders reads like an Almanach de Gotha of New York aristocracy, and the opening night of each successive season is as regularly chronicled in terms of Who Was There and What Was Worn, as in terms of musical values. The lobbies are crowded with news-cameramen, and the air is rent with the glare of flashlights.

Outside, from seven-thirty o'clock on, the thrill-seekers line up on the sidewalk, to enter vicariously into the spectacle by recognizing much-photographed faces (whose owners range the social gamut from international bankers to Hollywood starlets), to make special note of fashion items, and to ask each other, as the steady stream of vehicles discharge their glittering cargoes,

"D' you happen to know who *that* is?"

To-day, the question is often justified, despite the services of the ubiquitous camera-men. Many of the socialites arrive in taxi-cabs or hired equipages, the ladies keep their jewels well covered by scarfs, and most of the jewels that do flash forth are reported to be valueless paste copies of the original parures, securely reposing in safe deposit vaults. In the old days, it was different. Then, the sight-seers were rewarded with a spectacle of their own. The "Four Hundred" drove up to the carriage entrances in their private turn-outs, and the coaches, the coachmen, the footmen, the liveries, and the very horses were recognizable on sight. From the color of the carriage's wheels, one might know whether the Astors or the Vanderbilts were arriving, and the accuracy of the identification was further established when the footman sprang down, flung open the door, and assisted to alight a dignified lady who wore a tiara, a stomacher, a dog-collar, or a sunburst which was quite as familiar as the vehicular turn-out had been. And the jewels were not paste imitations. Often, a murmur of sheer admiration went up from the crowd, and society would bow its acknowledgements. There were no organized "rackets" to cause haste and the concealment of display. Also, there was less nonchalance and more elegance. Society's arrival at the Opera was a "show" in itself.

Monday is the "fashionable" night at the opera, out-ranking all other subscription performances in social and sartorial splendor. It has been suggested that society favors Monday nights simply because most other pleasure-seekers save up their energies for the end of the working week. Actually, there is a more valid reason for the choice, which roots into what might be called a "social tradition." In the very old days, there were three extremely fashionable dancing classes, which met on Monday nights. Society distributed its prefer-ences among them all, and took pains to appear in the most gala attire that even society could muster. The classes met late in the evening, however, and it seemed a waste of splendor not to be seen *somewhere* before the dancing began. Thus, the opera became a con-venient place for putting in time, and Monday nights acquired a luster all their own.

Thrill-seekers of a different stamp are those who line up outside the stage-door. "Johnnies" is scarcely the name for them to-day, for they number as many young women as men. During a recent season which the Rus-sian Ballet presented at the Opera House, a group of enthusiastic girls took their stand outside the stage-door. Expectantly, they watched the stream of dancers, orchestral players, and stage-hands hurrying from the House at the end of their day's work. But no celebrity showed himself. Presently, one of the porters came out, a tall, well-knit fellow, whose lithe figure was set off by a fitted coat. The young ladies grew visibly excited.

"Oo, look! There he is—that's Messine, the top dancer! Now we needn't wait any more."

Happily, they followed him to Seventh Avenue, and only a merciful surge of traffic spared them the sight of "Messine's" descent into the subway.

Social history has been written inside the Opera House. In the days of Ward McAllister, when social passports were issued in terms of *Who* rather than *How Much*, the beautiful wife of a certain railroad baron had tried, unsuccessfully, through a number of seasons, to insert a wedge into society. The names of the "Four Hundred" were conspicuously absent from her dinners, and the most superlative lists of charitable Patronesses excluded her name. One night, at the Opera, this lady arranged to sit a few boxes away from Mrs. Caroline Schermerhorn Astor, the undisputed leader of society, whose word was law as to who might and who might not be formally recognized. During the first intermission, Mrs. Astor turned from her companions, and began to survey the adjacent boxes. At once, the eager lady arose and bowed to her deferentially. After a second's consideration, then, Mrs. Astor rose in her box and returned the salute. Publicly. From that moment on, the saluted lady's entrance into society was assured. She had been publicly recognized. Before the evening was out, other society ladies had bowed to her, and a murmur arose in more than one box:

"She's in at last!"

The Metropolitan was the scene of the famous Old Guard Balls, which ranked as the most impressive social events of each season. The House had constructed a complete ball-room floor, in movable sections which were stored in the cellar, directly beneath the orchestra chairs. These flooring sections still exist, but are no longer stored under the orchestra. The fire laws ordered them off to the storehouse some fifteen years ago, whence they were brought forth again, after a long period of disuse, to serve their purpose in the Opera Balls which were given, within the past five years, as part of the "Save the Opera" campaign. The floor is laid over the stage and carried straight across toward the Broadway doors, over the tops of the orchestra chairs, thus covering a space nearly a city block in depth. The recent balls were adorned by specially built ball-boxes on the dance-floor level, but the old days knew nothing as elaborate as that. Then, the only boxes were those of the Diamond Horseshoe, one flight up, and the dance-floor was marked off by a plain brass rail, also built in sections and stored in the cellar. The highlight of those galas was the Grand March, around the entire floor; and the sumptuous toilettes of the ladies, and the uniforms of the "Old Guarders," with their great bear-skin shakos, offered a spectacle that vied in splendor with the settings of many an opera.

The sheer glamour-value of staging an event at the Metropolitan has led to the occasional inclusion of singular forms of entertainment. Once there was a Dog Show. Once there was a large and very select political dinner, for which occasion the Thirty-ninth Street carriage entrance was sealed up, and a temporary kitchen installed in that lobby. Thus, the diners enjoyed piping hot food. But for a week after, the corridors of the temple of music gave forth an altogether singular aroma, strangely reminiscent of soup and sage-dressing. And once there was a wrestling match. That was an affair.

The match was an important sporting event, and the audience included noted figures from the turf and the ring. James J. Corbett and "Bob" Fitzsimmons were there, attracting quite as much attention as the wrestlers themselves. The bout began, and then, suddenly, something happened. There was a question of some violation of rules, and the principals and their seconds grew heated. Presently, the place was in an uproar. Cheers and boos arose. People took sides. What had begun as a "private" wrestling match, took on the proportions of a "free for all" fracas. Corbett and Fitzsimmons were soon in the thick of it. Fists were flying and blood was to be seen. And then the police wagon arrived—at the Metropolitan Opera House. The now-numerous contestants were unceremoniously bundled off, and the police blotter, that night, read like a record of Olympic games. But there has never been a sporting event in the House since.

### 2.

The best glamour resides in the performances themselves. In the old days, it was a common practice among opera-smitten executives of big business, to hire themselves out as "supers," for the pleasure of going backstage, marching to music, and carrying an authentically operatic spear. Lawyers, bankers, merchants, all used what influence they could muster up, to obtain a "super's" assignment, and then hurried delightedly to the long, sparsely-equipped common dressing-room, to be arrayed in bear-skins and pelts. Once Gerber was sent to carry through some business negotiations with an executive of the Aeolian Company. The business required reflection, the official was a person of formidable manner, and the interview ended with Gerber's being asked to wait for a few days.

"I'll see you next week, and we'll talk about it then."

Early the following week, the executive presented himself at the Paymaster's office.

"You've come to settle that matter we were discussing?" asked Gerber.

"N-no, not exactly," replied the gentleman, with a very unformidable grin, "I've come to collect my pay. I walked on last night."

In those days, a "super's" remuneration was fifty cents a performance.

The one performance that lives as the most exciting of all, perhaps, was the great gala presented by Maurice Grau to celebrate the visit to New York of Prince Henry of Prussia, brother of the Emperor William II (February 25, 1902)). There have been dozens of Special Performances since then, some to honor visiting notables, some to raise funds for charitable causes, and all brought their share of glamour and excitement. But the Prince Henry performance stands out. It was no Benefit enterprise. Grau was shrewd enough to see that a vast amount could be got by giving a performance which would afford the public a chance, not so much to hear an opera, as to see a Prince. Princes enjoyed a special status in those days. Thrones stood more secure; uniforms held a Graustark splendor for a generation that had never seen them on a battle-field; and society buds were just beginning to discover the advantages of bestowing their hands and their fortunes upon titled foreigners. So the coming of a truly royal Prince was in many ways an event, and Grau took advantage of it by mounting his affair for the exclusive benefit of his own organization. Orchestra chairs for that night sold at thirty dollars each.

Certainly, Grau mounted a remarkable spectacle. The House was festooned with garlands of smilax and banked with flowers. During the afternoon, dozens upon dozens of hampers were carried into the House, and the front of the parterre boxes was completely hidden by American Beauty roses. The florists' bills mounted to over five thousand dollars. The box which the Prince was to occupy was further decorated with draperies and American and German emblems. The proscenium was brilliantly illuminated, and there was a special curtain of lights, hung some six inches apart on vertical cables, and giving the effect of a single glittering cascade. Outside, lights were strung along the façade of the building, while atop it floated a replica of the royal yacht, emblematic of the sailor Prince. The evening's program opened with the First Act of *Lohengrin,* with Gadski, Schumann-Heink, Dippel, Edouard de Reszke, and Bispham—with the result that the German singers were finished and off the stage long before their Prince arrived! Then there came the Second Act of *Carmen,* the Third Act of *Aida,* the Second Act of *Tannhaeuser,* and excerpts from *Le Cid,* all with resplendent casts, including Calvé, Scotti, Eames, Homer, Ternina, Journet, and Campanari.

A special cordon of police surrounded the House, and after this assignment had been made, a number of city officials asked for complimentary tickets. The requests were refused, and the political powers who attended that performance tasted the unaccustomed sensation of paying for their seats. The German singers, of course,

were in a state of special excitement, each of them entertaining hopes of being in the center of the spotlight at
the moment when the Prince should arrive.

The Prince and his party were assigned boxes in the
Diamond Horseshoe, but not until after some keen controversy had taken place between Grau and the owners
of the seats, who were loath to part with them for the
great night. The performance progressed, the audience
grew more and more restless. Every seat was occupied,
except the state boxes, and every head was turned away
from the stage. Viewed from the wings, it made
a strange sight. Grau, fortified with a new pair of
white kid gloves, stood waiting in the Thirty-ninth
Street lobby, growing more and more nervous as the
moments sped by. There was but perfunctory interest
on both sides of the footlights. Word was carried backstage that the Prince had not yet arrived, and the
singers drew out their high notes as long as they could,
while those in the cast who were to come later, fetched
deeper breaths and showed more enthusiasm. There
was a tense cast, a restive House with reversed heads,
and a nervous General Manager pacing the lobby. At
last the first part of the program was done. The singers
who had given their best without having been heard by
the Prince were plunged into a bog of resentful gloom,
and the gloom spread to the others, some of whom refused to go on until the Prince should actually be in the
House. While the arguments were in progress, then,
word came that Prince Henry had arrived. Then there
was peace once more, and the performance moved on.

Prince Henry and his party came in full dress uniform, exchanged affable greetings with a singularly pale
Mr. Grau, and went up to their seats. The lights went

up and there was a greater craning of necks than ever.
Then it developed that only those spectators who occupied chairs in the front part of the orchestra could see
the Prince at all.  The rear of the orchestra, under the
boxes, saw nothing; the surrounding boxes saw chiefly
the uniforms of the gentlemen in attendance; and the
top of the House saw only the swell of the rose-decked
box railings, which gave no evidence that they were
sheltering royalty.  After but a brief attendance, then,
Prince Henry and his party took their leave.  The still-
unheard singers were in a state verging on collapse, in
which they were joined by those who had already finished.  Mme. Sembrich, who had been scheduled to
appear in a scene from *Traviata,* refused to go on.  The
House craned its necks once more toward empty boxes.
The excitement was over.  But Grau was himself again.

Directly after greeting the Prince, he disappeared.
He had been asked to escort the guests to their places,
but refused.  He had been asked to make an address
from the stage, but refused that, too.  He gave orders
to Gerber to tell all who might seek him that he "just
was not about," and vanished.  Long after the Prince
had left, someone knocked on the door of Grau's private office.  There he sat, in a cloud of cigar smoke and
with his collar loosened, counting up the evening's
receipts, which were the largest the House had ever
taken in.  Only the fewest of the artists had performed
for the Prince, and only the smallest proportion of the
spectators had seen him.  But the Prince had come to
the Metropolitan!

The largest receipts since Grau relaxed over the
princely intake that night, were brought in by the program given in honor of Marshal Joffre and for the bene-

fit of French war charities.  Patrons paid for their seats in hundred dollar bills, regardless of the price of the tickets; and many who could not be accommodated in the House at all, refused to take their money back.  Another performance of sheer excitement-value was the one attended by the then Prince of Wales, on November 18, 1919.  The bill presented scenes from *Pagliacci, Oberon, Forza del Destino,* and *Samson,* and Caruso participated.  This time, the visiting royalty appeared according to schedule, was received by Mr. Otto H. Kahn, and Mr. Clarence H. Mackay in a lobby that had been spread with red velvet carpet, and showed himself in his own box and in several others which he visited, to the entire satisfaction of the audience and the cast.  But neither evening provided quite the same spine-chilling thrill of the brief visit of the Prussian nobleman.

### 3.

To the uninitiated, life in an Opera House has a tendency to offer the aspect of a sojourn atop Vesuvius. What else could result from the clashing of "temperaments," the last-minute emergencies, the tension, the mishaps, the freakishness, the general sum-total of the layman's conception of stellar activity?  Such an impression is traceable, less to the stellar activity, than to the "man-bites-dog" gauge of news values.  One opera singer who takes it into his head to enter a lion's cage (in company, perhaps, with a news photographer), can brand the entire race of singers as "queer."  The oddities make the news, and so the odd happenings have come to set the standard of Opera House life.

As a matter of fact, the oddities—real oddities, that

is to say, which crop up without benefit of news pho-
tographers—count for very little, and the "insiders"
regard them as just as queer and exceptional as the public does.   The House sees little of the garish aspects of
"temperament."  Inside the House, there is work to be
done.  And it is done.  Piano rehearsals, ensemble rehearsals, orchestral rehearsals, stage rehearsals, dress
rehearsals.   Rehearsals in cloak-rooms and dressing-
rooms, in foyers, and on the roof-stage.  Inside the
House, the performance is the one thing that counts.
Every moment of every performance looms as a life-
and-death matter to the professional standing of some
individual or group in the company.  And once that
moment comes, it stands as history.   The interested
parties cannot raise a hand and say,

"Wait a minute—I'll do that over again and make
some improvements!"

When the singers rehearse, they are on call from ten
in the morning until midnight.  Rehearsals are often in
progress while a public performance goes on in the auditorium.   Singers are always on potential call for a last-
minute cast replacement.  And they must keep fit to
meet the demands made upon them.  Too many "indis-
positions" have a tendency to wear the bloom from the
cheek of operatic glamour.  The House doesn't see
much "temperament."  There isn't time.

There have been slips in the best calculations, of
course, and real "oddities" have occurred, with consequences that range from the ludicrous to the tragic.

In the old days, there was a time when *Carmen*
seemed to call forth a "jinx."  At one of the performances, just as Saléza, the tenor, was about to make the
final death-stab at Calvé, suddenly, from nowhere at all,

a scrub-woman wandered on to the stage from the wings, her lunch-box under her arm, all ready to go home. The stage manager, entrancedly watching Calvé, had neglected to pull her back, and the woman did not realize what she was about until she was a few feet out. Then she gave a horrified cry and looked helplessly about for a place to run to, while the audience tittered, the principals glared, and the conductor added volume to the tones of the orchestra. Another time, Calvé lost an important part of her attire which, normally, should have remained invisible to all but the diva herself and possibly her maid. The loss occurred at the wildest moment of her *Seguidilla* dance, and, in the hope of drawing as little attention to it as possible, Calvé cleverly brushed the article towards the back of the stage, as part of her footwork. But there it was recognized, taken up by others in the cast, kicked about, and made much of generally, to the dismay of the prima donna and the abashed amusement of the House.

A serious accident occurred, again in *Carmen,* during the season of 1904-05. The First Act set represents a public square with a bridge over which the chorus of soldiers marches on to the stage. Suddenly, this bridge came crashing down, with a vicious cracking of timber and the cries of the men who were hurled to the stage below. No one could acount for the accident; the bridge had been as solidly set up as ever. Later, then, it developed that the tread of the chorus' marching had set up sympathetic vibrations which caused the entire structure to rumble itself to bits. But while the causes were being sought, there was panic in the House. The performance was halted at once, and the curtains hurriedly closed upon a stage that looked like a miniature battle-field.   There were serious casualties among the choristers who had been hurled from the bridge, and where the flying bits of broken wood struck, ugly red gashes showed upon the faces of the bystanders.   People were screaming from pain and from fright, and presently all of the city hospitals had ambulances drawn up before the stage door.   No one was killed, but one of the choristers, a no-longer young man named Cornaglia, was permanently crippled.   After weeks in the hospital, he came back to work, and his place was held open for him. That same matter of sympathetic vibrations once caused a minor mishap, when the tenor, Perotti, sang a long-sustained high C, and one of the electric bulbs in the top lights suddenly came splintering down at his feet.

There was a performance of *Faust,* with Eames and Saléza, when the House cat walked on in the Garden Scene, and rubbed itself comfortably against the tenor's legs, in one of the most ardent moments of the love duet. It took some time for the interest of the audience to divert itself from the cat and rivet itself once more upon the performance.   But the cream of the jest was reserved for the intermission, when one of the House staff chanced to hear a perfectly serious argument in progress among a group of patrons, as to whether or not the appearance of the cat was part of the "show," regularly inserted to provide a measure of relief against the lugubrious atmosphere of *Mephisto.*

There was the performance of *Meistersinger* in which Grete Stueckgold, the comeliest of *Evas,* sang the passage that announces the arrival of her tenor-lover, waited in vain for him to appear, and finally had to begin the love duet as a solo.   Once the mechanism of the Swan in *Lohengrin* grew balky, with the result that the tenor, at the tense moment of his departure, stood gracefully posed in his boat, and remained standing there, one foot resting on a plain, unpainted board, while the fabulous fowl skimmed lightly—and boatlessly—off-stage.

There was the Brooklyn performance of *Lohengrin,* when the truck with the orchestra's instruments broke down in the snow. An hour's delay in starting the performance was filled in by a choral vaudeville-show, the chorus singing excerpts from assorted operas, all in *Lohengrin* dress. The truck was rushed through traffic lights under police escort, at last, and the audience awaited the performance with perfect equanimity.

And there was the performance of *Siegfried,* when Curt Taucher, made up for the title rôle, stepped through an unguarded trap-door and crashed to the floor of a platform, below. The opera was already under way, it was nearly time for *Siegfried's* next cue, and there was the greatest consternation as to what should be done, both for Taucher and for the performance. Taucher was lifted from the floor somewhat dazed. His first question was, whether his sword had been broken. Assured that the sword was in excellent condition, he next asked whether he had missed his cue. Assured on this point, too, he rose to his feet, tried out his voice, and, despite all protests, insisted on going upstairs and finishing out the performance. Not until the end of the opera did he permit medical examination. Then it was found that he had broken two ribs in his fall. But the "show" went on!

The spirit of "carrying on the show," regardless of all else, is the best and oldest test of the seasoned trouper. Two years ago, Queena Mario underwent an appendi-

citis operation.  The week in which she came home from
the hospital, the company was scheduled to give a performance of *Manon,* in Brooklyn, with Bori in the title
part.  On the day of the performance, Miss Bori was
taken ill and could not possibly appear.  Only Miss
Mario could take her place at such short notice.  Hoping
against hope that the entire bill would not have to be
changed at the last minute, the management telephoned
to her apartment.

"Of course I'll do it," Miss Mario replied, "only don't
let my doctor know."

She arrived in Brooklyn, pale but determined, the
opera began, and the First Act went splendidly.  No
one out front could have guessed that the lively prima
donna was less than two weeks out of an operation.  But
just as the curtain went down and the stagehands began
clearing away the scenery, she dropped down in a dead
faint.  She was carried to her dressing-room and given
such aid as could be administered by House people.
When she opened her eyes, she thought she was still in
the hospital.  But then her presence of mind returned.
Sipping teaspoonsful of champagne, she repaired her
make-up, changed her costume, and was ready to go on
with the Second Act before call time.  And she did go
on, and the performance went forward without a hitch.

4.

The House has had its mysteries.  A great copper
bell, that weighed something over a ton, used to be
stored in the basement because it was too heavy and
cumbersome to carry in and out of the storehouses.  This
monster property was used chiefly in *Tosca,* and it was

always a problem to move it about and set it in place. At the end of a long-ago season, it was put away in its basement corner where it had spent many years; and when the properties were gone over the following autumn, preparatory to the new season's start, the bell was gone. Watchmen had been on duty all summer; no one had seen or heard the first trace of a ton weight of copper bell; the floor where it had been stored showed no signs of its having melted or rolled away; no suspicious groups had been seen about the House; and no single pair of arms could have picked the thing up and tucked it out of sight while in transit. And yet it had completely vanished, and has never been heard of since.

Exactly the same fate befell the great brass rail that used to outline the dance-floor for the opera balls, and also a concert grand piano. How were these massive objects spirited away without leaving so much as a trace of a clue? Those in the House who still remember the shock of their disappearance would give a great deal to find out.

The House has had its tragedies. During the very old days, the superintendent and his family occupied living quarters on the fifth floor, in rooms that formed an old-fashioned "flat" and which are used to-day as the offices of the auditing and accounting departments. The bath-room (long since vanished) lay at the head of the steep flight of stairs leading down to the body of the House; and the night watchman, in making his rounds, often stopped in there for a wash or a drink of water. On entering the bath-room one morning, the superintendent found the body of the watchman lying drowned in a tub full of water. It was never cleared up whether the man deliberately drowned himself, or whether, under the influence of some seizure, he had got himself into the tub and lost consciousness. But for weeks afterwards, the stair corner of the fifth floor held a feeling of "spookiness," and the more superstitious of the chorus men blessed themselves devoutly before venturing to enter their own dressing-room, directly below.

Just this dressing-room on the fourth floor was the next to come under the spell. Late one afternoon, while setting out the costumes for the evening performance, the wardrobe-man entered the chorus' dressing-room, jerked back with a violence that sent the pile of gaudy clothes sprawling to the floor, and gave forth a shriek that roused the House. Gerber rushed from his office, and reached the spot first.

"What is it? What's the matter?"

Too shocked to speak, the man simply pointed.

There, in the long, unlit room that was soon to be piled high with gay motley, hung the body of one of the chorus-men, suspended by his own belt. Gerber cut him down, and the news was carefully kept from the man's colleagues until after the performance was over.

The chauffeur of Beniamino Gigli came into the lobby of the Thirty-ninth Street entrance one morning, called for the tenor's mail, exchanged a word or two with the postmistress, and dropped dead from heart failure. Ten minutes before, he had been driving Gigli and his family through traffic. And having worked its way from the top of the House to the street door, it is to be hoped that the evil spell has departed.

The House has had—and does still have—its superstitions. The classic "jinx" of every theater, of course, is whistling. To emit a whistle in any of the dressing-rooms, corridors, or wings, is tantamount to breaking a mirror, sitting down thirteen at table, or failing to knock on wood, all at once. Grau caused much heartache by whistling his tuneless tunes as he crossed the stage, but Grau was "the chief," and such resentment as followed in the wake of the heartache restrained itself within exclusively emotional bounds. Often young singers who are still innocent of this super-tradition of the theater come into the House and give vent to their feelings by whistling; but a consideration for the opinion of the majority—often inculcated by reminders from which "a chief" is immune—soon parts them from this particular form of self-expression.

The most acute sufferer from the whistle-fever was Leo Slezak, the giant Czech tenor, whose height and breadth of shoulder seemed to indicate that the man could have no conception of the nature of fear. And yet the sound of whistling reduced him to a state of nervous trembling. Slezak took the word "whistle" extremely literally. Not only did he shy at the ordinary labial variety; a cab whistle, a policeman's whistle, a toy whistle, all sent him into a frenzy.

It didn't take long for Caruso to discover this, and immediately he set about plaguing Slezak, with whom he was on the best of terms. At this time, the Master Mechanic, who controls the stage crews, gave his signals for hoisting or letting down scenery, by clapping his hands. Caruso presented the man with a whistle, made of gold, "to make the signaling easier," he explained, "only blow it hard, *hard!*" But this form of plaguing did not bring about the demonstrations for which Caruso had hoped. Slezak was never on the stage when the crews set the scenery, and the doors between the stage and the dressing-rooms are sound-proof. So Caruso hit upon another plan.

He got himself a set of tiny toy whistles, all of different keys and different degrees of tinniness, and on the nights that Slezak sang, he would come backstage at dressing time, pace up and down outside the tenor's room, and give sudden little blasts on his instruments. After every blast, a loud groan would be heard from within the room, and then Slezak's partially made-up face would appear in the door, to be followed by a hearty expression of personal opinion. Finally, almost in tears, he asked Caruso why he bothered him so.

"For your own good," explained Caruso amiably. "You are afraid of the whistle. So I whistle, and what happens? You sing better than ever . . . *magnifico!* So then I whistle more, to teach you not to be afraid."

The lesson was never completely mastered, however, and to the end of his connection with the company, Slezak continued to dread whistles.

As to Caruso himself, it is characteristic of the man that his superstitions were expressed in terms of what he loved, rather than of what he hated, or feared. And the things that he loved! Old play-bills; amusing cartoons; any quantity of dolls, some new, but most of them indescribably dilapidated from traveling about. Any funny little gift of this kind that chanced to be sent to Caruso's dressing-room on a night when he felt himself to be singing especially well, was treasured as a bearer of good omen, and was straightway added to the collection, which had to be spread about his room in its entirety for each of his performances. None of these toys was ever too old or too used or too ragged to appear.

And the worse they looked, the better Caruso loved them.

Tetrazzini, of the flute-like coloratura voice, had a pet superstition that concerned a dagger. The dagger was a property that she first used in *Lucia di Lammermoor,* and one night it fell from her hand and stuck upright in the floor. Tetrazzini was especially pleased with her reception this night, and from that time on, she kept the dagger with her as a species of barometer-before-the-fact. As she was about to leave her dressing-room to go to the stage, she would let the dagger slip from her hand, and watch eagerly to see how it landed. Did it stick upright in the floor, she was jubilant, and went to the performance confidently. Did it fall flat, she was disconsolate, and seriously expected ruin with every breath she drew. And no matter how well she sang after a flat landing of the dagger, nothing could convince her but what she *might* have done much better, had only a kindlier fate presided over the descent of her barometer.

Nearly all of the artists cherish superstitions of some sort or another, although the fewest admit them to be that. Some refuse to wear their wedding-rings while in character, and some refuse to take them off. Many wear lucky charms carefully concealed about their persons—a cross, a bit of polished stone, a tiny ivory animal, a ring of elephant's hair, a locket containing the picture of some beloved one. Many bring special pictures to their rooms, which must be set at a certain angle on a certain spot of the make-up table. Some must have red flowers beside them, and some yellow. Some sip a given number of sips of some special kind of mineral water. One lady could not be gotten to leave her room for the stage without stopping first at the practise piano, on her way out, to play three special chords. The German contingent of singers believes it bad luck to express a wish for "good luck" to a performer on his way to the stage. The notion is that a spoken wish for good may tempt the less kindly fates into a spiteful working of just the opposite effect. Thus, the ritual is to wish the departing one *"Hals und Bein Bruch"* which is translated as a breaking of the neck and the limbs. Such a wish can have only happy results!

One sees the crosses, and the pictures, and the lockets; one smells the roses; and hears the wishes and the chords.

"Is that a superstition?" one asks.

"N-no, not exactly a superstition . . . but it makes me feel good!"

All of these oddities have brought their share of amusement or excitement into the House, but none has loomed sufficiently important to influence the even tenor of House life. That is built from a solid foundation of hard work, responsibly met and intensively carried through, and illuminated by the varied and colorful personalities of the workers.

If "temperament" is largely a hybrid creature, bred from headlines and press-agents' tales, personality is a very real thing. It is perhaps the most important part of a public singer's equipment—as important as the voice itself. It is defined, not in terms of garish clothes, freakish coiffures, or idiosyncrasies of behavior, but of that subtle power of human communication which Gatti set forth as the first requisite of public artistry. Personality is the quality which enables a singer to project himself across the footlights, to convince his hearers, to touch them. A singer either has it or lacks it. The House has seen the coming and going of superb voices which failed completely to make an impression deeper than that of momentary agreeability to the ears. And there is nothing that can be done about it. The House has seen the rise of distinctly less-than-superb voices which were fortified by that human communicativeness that always causes an immediate "click." And there is nothing that can be done about that, either. Critical deliberations cannot always establish an artist's popular success. But the audience, composed of four thousand different tastes and needs and fancies, rises as one man to hail the performer who has something warm and personal to say. And the test never fails. Those singers who combine the voice with the human "click"—and they have never been too many—stand forth as the truly great. It is the sheer personality-value of the artists which provides most of the opera's glamour.

# Chapter VI

## THE OLDER PERSONALITIES

### 1.

IN THE old days, the personalities of the artists expressed themselves in terms of what they were rather than what they did. As a matter of fact, they *did* little besides attend to their work and then retire to the privacy of their personal lives. There was an aloofness about them. They believed that their responsibility to the public ended with the closing of the final curtain, and they knew not the secrets of Hollywood publicity. Indeed, Grau encouraged the idea among his singers that their public value became enhanced by the aura of mystery and apartness with which they surrounded themselves. It is inconceivable to think of their deliberately "putting on stunts" to attract public notice. Sembrich, Nordica, Eames, Melba, Plançon, the two de Reszkes, Maurel—it is interesting to speculate upon the Olympian outbursts which would have followed the suggestion, to any of them, that they model clothes in a department store, or advertise some smart café by allowing themselves to be photographed at one of its tables! And yet the public of that other day was by no means ignorant of the existence of its "stars" despite the lack of such memory-aids, and the personalities asserted themselves regardless of "stunts."

This is not a glorification of the past merely because it is past. Forty years from now, when the opera season

opens, a new *Isolde* will be discovered, and the Young
Enthusiasts will cry,

"She is absolutely the greatest *Isolde* the world ever
saw!" To which one of the old-timers will lift a quav-
ering voice in objection.

"*She* the greatest? You should have heard the casts
they had when *I* was young! You should have heard
Flagstad."

And the Young Enthusiasts will laugh, as Young
Enthusiasts have a habit of doing. "That's pure imagination."

Those who have heard Flagstad as *Isolde* will appreciate the state of mind of the forty-year-hence old-timer
who is asked to believe that her greatness is pure
imagination. Again, it is all in the point of view.

The remembered Metropolitan activity of the magnificent Lilli Lehmann is brief, and remains full of awe
to the possessor of the recollections. Lehmann's reputation for superb artistry surrounded her with a majestic aloofness, which her personal manner was not
calculated to dispel. She had no patience with anything
short of perfection, and expressed her opinions with a
frankness that caused trepidation. A singer who, in
performance, fell short of Lehmann's standards would
find himself immediately pierced with a look of towering
scorn, in full view of the others in the cast, and even
when the lapse had caused no unpleasant consequences
to Lehmann's own work. After, then, she would regard
the offender with an air that said, "there is a right and a
wrong way to do these things and *you,* very evidently,
have taken your place on the wrong side!" Her most
exacting demands, though, were those she made upon
herself. On the day of a performance of *Isolde,* she

would rise extra early and go through the entire part in full voice, to assure herself of how her evening's singing would sound.

Whenever she sang, Lilli Lehmann's place on the set became the center of the stage. She assumed full responsibility for the opera's preparation. Conductors and stage-directors asked her advice; celebrated colleagues deferred to her wishes. All found in her an unfailing source of authority and support. She was present at all rehearsals of the works in which she appeared, whether or not she participated in the scenes being coached. From the dark of the auditorium, she observed and corrected; and her corrections invariably added to the value of the performance. In her habits, she was extremely simple, preferring a room to a suite in her hotel, and attending to much of her laundry. One cold, rainy afternoon, Lehmann and Nordica chanced to leave the House together. Nordica's carriage was waiting for her. Before Nordica could offer its shelter, Lehmann eyed the vehicle with a look of superiority, raised her skirt to reveal tall, stout boots, and remarked,

"You r-r-ride? *I valk!*" And off she set into the thick of the downpour, head high and masterfulness in her very stride.

Rose Heylbut is the last reporter to have been received by her, shortly before the great diva's death. As Frau Lehmann would not tolerate a telephone in her home, the arrangements for the interview were made in person.

Lehmann lived in the Grunewald, a park-like section of Berlin, dark with trees and densely-planted gardens, within twenty minutes of the congestion of Unter den Linden. The house stood in a terraced garden that was reached by a tall gate and a short flight of steps. A ring at the bell brought no response. A second ring and then a third. The house looked occupied; windows were open, and from the rear there came an occasional note of singing. After an interval of intermittent ringing and waiting, an upward glance toward one of the second-floor windows showed a stout serving-woman leaning comfortably on the sill and observing the bell-performances with genuine interest.

"May I come in? I've been ringing here . . ."

"The bell's broken," she replied without stirring. "Didn't you know that? Everybody knows that."

It was explained that the news had not yet penetrated beyond Berlin.

"May I speak with Frau Lehmann?"

"Of course not. Not now. She's giving a lesson."

"Her secretary, then? It's important."

At last, then, she moved. Later it came out that Emma ruled the Lehmann household. No one might enter without her approval, and world-famed musicians were sent into Frau Lilli's presence with a curt, "Now see you don't stay too long!" Emma ignored her imperious mistress' early tirades against the radio and bought herself a small set with ear-phones. When good programs were on the air—and Emma was a judge—she would clap the phones on Frau Lilli's ears, with an unperturbed,

"Don't scold; you'll like it!"

In the end, she converted Lehmann into buying a radio of her own.

So Emma left the window, but did not come to open the gate. Presently a step sounded along the garden path, and there approached an elderly woman of erect

carriage and firm walk. Her iron-gray hair was bound
into a tan silk "sport net"; she wore flat-heeled linen
shoes; a long, none-too-fresh blue overblouse; and a full,
old-fashioned skirt. Her face was unsmiling and her
rather remarkable brown eyes emanated masterfulness.
After Emma, this secretary's appearance made one feel
that Frau Lehmann surrounded herself with formidable
protectors.

"I have come to ask the privilege of an interview with
Frau *Kammersaengerin* Lehmann . . ."

"I am Lehmann," said the old woman of the out-
moded dress.

Within a few months of her eighty-first birthday, she
radiated pulsing vitality. She had lessons to give that
day, after which she went, quite alone, for a four-mile
walk in the woods. So that afternoon was occupied.
However, she suggested luncheon for the next day.
Then she demonstrated how, by reaching one's hand inside the grill of the gate, one could find the key and
admit one's self, without depending on the broken bell.
This was an expedient system; the people who were
wanted let themselves in, the others kept out.

The following morning, Frau Lehmann was waiting
in the garden. She led the way into the house through
the kitchen, where a vegetarian lunch was in preparation. Vigorously opposed to the slaughter of animals,
Frau Lilli would touch no meat. Later, she opened
the great music-room. Long windows gave upon the
garden. There were mementos—but not so many as
decorate the average "studio"—of her illustrious career:
canvases of herself in character, autographed photographs, letters, scraps of manuscript. The room lived
in an atmosphere of the days of Lehmann's prime, as

though the stride of time had been brought to a halt outside the door. The massive chairs wore antimacassars; there were glass lamps, and a round center table, spread with a cover embroidered in colored wool.

Lilli Lehmann spoke of music. She told stories of her own great day, of Wagner, of the beginnings of Bayreuth. She spoke lovingly of her pupil, Geraldine Farrar; told of having "ordered" her to come for a lesson at six o'clock in the morning, on the day after a taxing operatic performance, in order "to test the child's character," and of her own surprise on seeing Geraldine step from her carriage, pale after three hours' sleep, at seven minutes before six. She asked about New York and people whom she had known there.

Suddenly, she grew heated. As certain names entered the talk, her fine eyes flashed and she loosed the floods of abuse for which she was famous. She raged against Germany's foremost modern composer; dismissed with scorn the achievements of certain of to-day's "stars"; expressed loathing of a popular American soprano. At last she tore the pedestal from under the feet of a veteran conductor, in terms that would have done credit to a Billingsgate fishwife.

"A fool! A know-nothing! A miserable *poseur!* I despise him!"

"But I know he admires you very much. He would feel sorry to think you dislike him so."

Her eyes softened.

"You don't understand, child. *Personally* I don't dislike him. He doesn't touch me. Few people do, any more. But musically. Ah, that's a different matter! This man has treated music shabbily. He's had opportunities, and what's he done with them? Worked for himself and not for art.  He's been satisfied with success —and mediocrity—when there was real work to be done, a real goal to achieve.  Admires me, does he?  Let him keep his admiration!  Certainly, I don't want it.  He has not kept faith with the things that mean much to me.  Take F . . ., for instance."  (Mme. F . . . was a prima donna of note; between her and Frau Lilli there existed an historic personal enmity.)  "F . . . has harmed me, made me suffer.  But she is an artist, an ornament to music!  She has given herself unsparingly and with ardor, to art.  And I admire her and love her.  I wouldn't speak to her, of course.  Not if she came crawling to me on her knees.  But just the same, I love her!"

Pol Plançon had only to show himself to conjure up the very atmosphere of a French court.  The impressive grace and suavity of the man told the complete story of what he was, without his doing or saying anything further to underscore the emphasis.  Plançon's "war horse" was *The Palms,* which he sang at Sunday night concerts, and, after a time, he was not allowed to leave the platform without singing it.  The picture he made as he appeared on the stage, with his tall, lithe figure, his immaculate grooming, and his poised dignity, is unforgettable.  Plançon was always the gallant gentleman, of impeccable taste.  He was immensely fond of the good things of life, and even his little foibles added to the impression of an old-world courtier.  For one thing, he used perfumes.  At first, it was rather a shock to the younger, native-born element around the House, to perceive these delicate scents outside the door and then to discover that they emanated, not from some equally

delicate lady, but from a bearded gentleman. But—it
was Plançon. Presently the perfumes became not only
tolerable but actually expected to make the picture complete. Plançon never endorsed the brand of perfume he
used, however. His beard was the French imperial, and
it was carefully trimmed and tinted every day.

As Plançon sang basso rôles, nearly all of them old
men, his beard never marred his stage impersonations.
Indeed, it rather heightened the illusion, since his old
men never suffered that lapse of dignity that proceeds
from a sudden slipping of false whiskers.

Plançon was fond of fine food and champagne, and
the French restaurants he patronized undertook to im-
port the choicest native wines, pâtés, sausages, and poul-
try, for his exclusive use. As Plançon grew older, it
was feared that his taste for rich fare might harm his
voice. Scotti once remonstrated with him about it.

"My dear friend," said Plançon, holding his wine-
glass up to the light and studying its color with the eyes
of a connoisseur, "I shall live but once. And I can pay
no higher tribute to life than to enjoy to the full all the
fine things it has to offer."

Conried was fond of food, too, though he was less
philosophical about it. Instead of philosophy, he kept
a large box of bicarbonate of soda within reach on his
desk. Many a night would he hurry into the House,
after dinner, and hear no word of business until he had
reached for his box.

"Ah," he would say with a deep sigh, "this is my life-
saver!"

Conried was also an accomplished cook. He gave
much time to searching out new recipes in the countries
to which he traveled; explained them in detail to his

friends; demonstrated them at his parties; and enjoyed
his own concoctions with a relish that is said to be absent
from the equipment of the ordinary cook. But then
came the bicarbonate.

Nellie Melba left few impressions behind her in the
House save those of her superb artistry. A vigorous
person, she came silently, left silently, and lifted her
voice only in song. She was an excellent trouper,
though. Although her voice was a brilliant coloratura,
she wished to sing the rôle of *Elisabeth* in *Tannhaeuser,*
learned it, and determined to make a success of it. On
more than one occasion Melba set herself to mastering
the heavy Wagnerian rôles, but never with the success
that attended her other performances. Her efforts were
not impossibly stimulated by the fact that Nordica was
earning triumphs in just these parts. A coolness existed
between these two artists, and the matter of rôles had its
share in maintaining it. Her first appearance as *Elisabeth* was a distinct novelty, and a début of great importance to herself, as marking a possible entrance into
a different field of activity. Her tenor for the performance had for some days been suffering from a severe
cold, and though the cold grew worse, he insisted upon
singing the title rôle of the opera that should mark Melba's first *Elisabeth.* The worst happened; the tenor
broke down before the performance was half over, unable to squeeze out another note. The opera was halted,
and Grau made an explanatory speech from the stage.
But the audience was not to be disappointed, and
Melba, still in her *Elisabeth* costume, consented to fill
out the disrupted program by singing her familiar
coloratura arias. And though she, of all the cast, was

most disappointed in her hopes for the new part, she was less severe in her judgment of the hapless tenor than any of the other singers. Melba's favorite rôle was *Mimi* in *La Bohême,* although it gave her less opportunity of displaying her vocal fireworks than any other part she sang.

It often happens that the very time in which an artist launches his career helps to make or mar it. Had the charming Zelie de Lussan managed to project her vocal arrival a decade earlier or later than the time which Nature chose for her, she would have made a sensation. She was beautiful, magnetic, and greatly gifted. But her best rôle was *Carmen,* and she presented it to a public that knew Emma Calvé. Grau considered de Lussan the finest *Carmen*—after Calvé. But ranking second to anyone is not the best recommendation, and de Lussan had to content herself with critical encomiums and the devotion of a loyal if limited public.

Miss Norton, of Maine, whom the world knew as Lillian Nordica, brought into the theater and maintained there the strict, self-denying discipline of her "down-East Yankee" inheritance. She never spared herself and often said that, in her opinion, her success was due to no superiority of voice, but to a greater talent for sheer hard work. Nordica would master rôle after rôle, without visible prospect of appearing in any of them, in order to be ready for all emergencies of cast replacement. And she was always to be counted on. It happened more than once that Nordica was called to replace some other soprano at a time when she herself was ill and in bed. She would leave her bed, sing the rôle, and go back to her rest again, without saying a word of her own indisposition until the following day, when the thanks of the management and the praise of the critics were accomplished facts, behind her. Nordica was the only artist able to eat a hearty dinner within half an hour of a performance, and suffer no vocal ill effects.

Nordica's majestic manner cowed even Grau himself. One night, her maid had inadvertently brought the wrong costumes down to the House, and the error was not discovered until Nordica arrived and made ready to dress for the performance. The girl was at once sent hurrying back to the hotel to fetch the proper robes. This took time, in a day of horse-cabs, and Nordica paced up and down her room in a tension of anxiety, realizing perfectly well that the seven-thirty start of the opera would be considerably delayed. But she said nothing. Grau, in the House as always, saw the clock point to seven-thirty, and then watched many more moments pass, without any sign of activity on the stage. His questions met no more satisfactory explanation than that Mme. Nordica "just didn't seem to be ready." At last he stormed to the stage and found Nordica just taking her place on the First Scene set, calm, serene, and showing no traces of her half-hour of nervous waiting.

"What does this mean?" Grau began, but she stopped him.

"If I speak to you now, Mr. Grau, my voice will be impaired and your performance will suffer. Come to me at the end of the opera, and I will give you the necessary explanation."

Grau left her with his wrath still unexploded, and

Nordica sang the performance with firm voice and calm mastery. After which no explosion was necessary.

Kind and helpful as she was, Nordica always maintained an aloofness of manner, and did not welcome any attempts to break through it, no matter how innocently they were meant. At Conried's Benefit Performance of *Die Fledermaus,* the entire company came on in the Ball-Room Scene, and, partly to add to the stage festivities, and partly to work off their own high spirits, some of them cut very fancy capers. Caruso, dancing with Nordica, suddenly bent over and kissed her cheek. There was no possible harm in such an extremely be-witnessed salutation, and anyone who knew Caruso could have known that only his love of prankishness had prompted him to do it. But Nordica was seriously and sincerely disturbed by this public affront to her dignity. To Nordica, easy familiarity was not part of a "star's" equipment.

There was never the first trace of aloofness about Ernestine Schumann-Heink. She was as she was, without pretense of any sort, and needed not the mellowing influence of time to reveal her utter warmth and sincerity. She lived at the old Belvedere Hotel, on Fourth Avenue and Eighteenth Street, a first-class establishment but an unpretentious one. When her fame and her earnings increased, it was suggested to her that she move to more "elegant" quarters.

"More elegant than *this?*" she exclaimed. "You should have seen how I had it in Hamburg, that time the bailiffs took all my nice furniture away!"

Schumann-Heink disarmed criticism by speaking openly, even pridefully, of circumstances which, in an age of elegance and delicacy, were not habitually thrust into the glare of public attention—of her poor, plain-looking Jewish grandmother, whom she loved devotedly and from whom, she declared, she had inherited her music; of her hard youth; her bitter poverty. And never before, surely, had a prima donna made open announcement of the fact that she needed to work extra hard because she was "too, too homely to give any pleasure to people otherwise!" Schumann-Heink had her first official meeting with Maurice Grau in London. Nordica knew her, had every faith in her, and wanted to see her succeed; and because Schumann-Heink's wardrobe was too scant and too shabby to permit her to appear before an impresario with anything like prima donna *éclat,* the generous American loaned her a silk dress ("with a train on it," as Schumann-Heink never failed to point out), and some handsome jewelry. Later, when the two artists met again in Grau's Metropolitan company, Schumann-Heink somewhat scandalized the dignified Nordica by making frequent and public reference to the loan, thanking her, lauding her kindness, and describing her own emotions when she surveyed herself in such splendid and unaccustomed things.

Schumann-Heink could speak some English when she arrived in New York, and her complete lack of "effect-making" allowed her to plunge straight into the strange tongue and then extricate herself from its pitfalls as best she could—often to the convulsed amusement of her hearers. But Paul Schumann, her husband (whom Grau had brought over as one of the stage-managers), knew not a word of English and had to keep silent in the company of any but Germans. He often marveled at his wife's superior attainments in conversational ease.

"Ach, it iss nothing; this English, it speaks itself," she would say modestly—after having just let off some expression which electrified the group about her.

Finally, Schumann hit upon a plan of exchange language lessons with Gerber. Each spoke in the other's tongue, and carried on elaborate bi-lingual discussions. This arrangement brought Gerber into terms of intimacy in the Schumann household, where many home-cooked suppers were prepared over a gas-burner, and many glasses of beer consumed. But the results of this friendship proved embarrassing to the young man when they were carried into the House itself. Promoted by this time to long trousers and to administrative responsibilities in the auditing department, Gerber fled in blushing panic from Schumann-Heink's motherly embraces and hearty salutations of *"mein liebes Kindchen"* (my dear little child).

Gerber was on duty at the hotel when one of Schumann-Heink's children was born; wired the news to Schumann, on tour with the company (in his whimsical English, Schumann referred to it as *breaking* the news); and also announced, but a few days later, that the contralto was once more able to resume her full professional schedule.

At one of the performances of *Tannhaeuser,* the *Shepherd Boy* became indisposed at the last minute, and Schumann, the stage-manager, commandeered his distinguished wife into the small part, as substitute. When the cue came for the *Shepherd Boy* to greet the pilgrims and wave his cap, no one appeared. Presently, then, a head and no more came warily up from behind the stage rock, and a voice sang the music. That was all. After, Schumann-Heink was asked why she had made so limited an appearance.

"The *Shepherd Boy's* costume calls for tights," she explained, "and that husband of mine—do you think he would let me step out before an audience and show my legs? Not he!"

There was a definite glamour about Jean de Reszke— about merely looking at him—and yet he never did a spectacular thing. A more poised, controlled, gallant gentleman never lived. Simply, one felt the fervor he brought with him into the House, and it made its impression. De Reszke was more than a singer. He was a consummate actor, a master of make-up and stage deportment, with an almost psychic power of seeing straight to the core of any stage situation and then bringing it to the surface. Yet his methods had nothing of the "dramatic" about them. Everything was calm, orderly, controlled.

No matter how familiar he was with a part, he began putting himself in the mood for it the day before the performance. On the nights that he sang, he would arrive in the House before six o'clock, preparing himself slowly, with the minutest detail. De Reszke disliked much make-up; he held that it spoiled the illusion if the audience were the least conscious of grease-paint. He would stand for half an hour at a time beside the hanging electric light bulb in his dressing-room, holding it close against every inch of his face, to draw the blood to the surface and thus produce the effect of high natural color without having to use too much paint. Then the wig would go on, and be brushed slowly, on his head, with an eye to the position of every hair. When he was dressed, then, he would go out to the stage, where he had been rehearsing the day before, and re-familiarize himself with the set, so that the least of his gestures would seem, not like acting, but the only natural thing to do. He must have put in a good two hours of work before the first call to the stage. (The opposite to Jean de Reszke in this regard was Chaliapin. When Chaliapin sang, the management was regularly in a frenzy of tension, waiting for him to arrive. He would walk leisurely into the stage-door less than half an hour before curtain time, and it always remained a mystery how he managed to adjust his superlative make-ups in so amazingly short a time.)

De Reszke was just as meticulous in his personal habits. At the Christmas season, he and his brother Edouard would take their station in one of their dressing-rooms, and make a little banker's counter of the dressing-table. On it would be spread, in the neatest piles, bank notes of all denominations, from one hundred dollars to one dollar. One of the brothers held the carefully prepared gift list, marked with the name of every member of the House staff and the amount to be bestowed on each; the other sat before the piles of notes and another pile of envelopes. Then one of the errand-boys was sent to round up the House people. One by one they came, were received with a sincere and graceful speech, and presented with their Christmas gifts, the master of ceremonies indicating the amount in a polite undertone, and the banker folding the notes into their envelopes. It was altogether an elaborate process, which was allowed to take its full time, without a trace of hurry; and the intervening moments were more than adequately filled in by the cordial words of presentation.

Jean de Reszke had a dry, salty sense of humor. He had the born actor's gift of mimicry, and would often put it to use at unexpected moments. Coming off the stage, for instance, he would meet some friend in the corridor, and pretend that this friend was Jean de Reszke, while de Reszke himself would impersonate a whole series of admirers coming to congratulate him on his performance. First came the exuberant Frenchman, who began his felicitations with many gestures and many expressions of *"mon cher Jean, mon cher collègue."* Next came the important German, bowing stiffly from the waist and assuring *"meinem sehr geehrten Herrn* de Reszke" of the extreme state of *"Hochachtung"* he felt for him. Then came the Italian, then the Pole, each with his own mannerisms and his own congratulations, expressed accentlessly in his own tongue. And finally, then, came the American, who stood stock-still before "de Reszke," fixed him with an unmoved stare, and said,

"Gene, you done a fine job!"

De Reszke's health necessitated a temporary withdrawal from operatic activities. He went to the south of France for a year, to rest and recuperate, and re-joined the company on December 31, 1900. Everyone was overjoyed to see him again, but there was just a little fearfulness, too, in the hearts of those who loved him. Would the year of absence and illness have taken a cruel toll of him? Would it show? Would he still be the same Jean? The night of his re-début arrived (the performance was *Lohengrin,* with a cast that included Nordica, Schumann-Heink, and Edouard de Reszke); Jean made up with his habitual care, and stepped out for his cue. His brother was visibly nervous, and many of the House staff stood waiting in the wings, with bated breath, afraid of losing something that meant infinitely more than the momentary success of a tenor aria. The swan-boat brought him on, at last, he stepped "ashore," looking as splendid as ever, and then he began to sing. At the first notes of that unforgettable de Reszke voice, those in the wings actually embraced one another. The voice was there. And Jean was there. And it was the same Jean. The House gave him a tremendous ovation, and he and Nordica were obliged to march up and down the stage in a sort of triumphal procession. But those in the wings experienced something very deep and real in those moments, fearing a disenchantment that would have spoiled so much and then finding that the fears were not needed.

Chaliapin combined a magnificent basso voice with perhaps the most compelling stage personality that ever graced the Metropolitan boards. The House people used to derive a sort of entertainment from watching him at his work and then trying to discover "how he did it," but no one ever found a solution which got beyond the sheer magnetism of the man. Which is the best explanation. In his person, Chaliapin was quiet, unassuming, and sympathetic. He spoke in a soft voice, and in describing his manner, the same word, "soft," suggests itself, not as proceeding from any lack of strength, but as hinting of tremendous, almost uncanny, powers deliberately held in check. If, in speaking, Chaliapin let his eyes wander to a point on the floor or the wall, his listener would presently find his own glance irresistibly drawn to the same point. Whatever part

Chaliapin played, he was completely that part, and the stage character assumed gigantic proportions.  His effects in costuming and make-up were hailed as original, and so they were; but they went deeper than a desire to be merely "different."  A more recent member of the company aroused considerable comment by dressing a highly conventional operatic character in a highly unconventional color.  When asked why he did this, the singer thought a moment and replied,

"The best costumer in Milan said that I ought to!"

Chaliapin's approach to his visual effects was a different one.  He tried to symbolize his personal conception of the character's essential meaning.  He presented *Mefistofele* (in Boïto's opera) as nearly naked as he dared, because he felt that the forces of evil *are* stripped and stark.

Chaliapin often left the door of his dressing-room open when he made up—and he accomplished this with astonishing speed—and the younger members of the House staff would devise the most impossible errands to carry them past the door, especially when Chaliapin was preparing to play *Mefistofele*.  It was always an uncanny thing to watch.  First, Chaliapin would be sitting before the dressing-table, stripped to the waist, a perfect human specimen.  Then, a deft, quick stroke of the pencil transformed the face.  Another touch, and the expression of the eyes would be completely altered.  The ears were built up, the nose accentuated, the sparse, shorn wig went on and outlined an entirely different head.  Suddenly then, without one's realizing how or when it had happened, Chaliapin would be gone, and the Devil himself was in that room!  Accustomed as the House people were to eccentricities of make-up, a shudder ran through more than one as Chaliapin strode out to the wings. Once he had gone on, he seemed to fill that vast stage with his body. When he stretched out his arms, in those sweeping, sinuous gestures of his, his right hand seemed to touch one side of the set, and his left hand the other. He completely dominated every scene in which he appeared. For all his power over other people, though, he suffered from stage-fright. Just before his cue, he would walk up and down in the wings, the beads of perspiration showing under the paint, and no one ventured to address a word to him at such moments. Many of the younger members of the company disliked being in the cast with him, because the aspect of his nervousness loosened their grip on themselves. Once he began to play, though, and the feeling of his rôle took hold of him, the nervousness vanished, and the sheer magnetism of the man became a thing to marvel at.

Chaliapin's domination of every scene in which he appeared was never the result of "temperament" or willful assertiveness. He inspired the most unusual support in the other members of the casts with whom he worked; indeed, he soon converted the ordinary rehearsal into a sort of illustrated conference on vocal and dramatic technic. Chaliapin was completely familiar with every note and every gesture of every part, in every opera in which he appeared. At rehearsals, he would go through his own business and, at the same time, keep a penetrating eye on the rest of the scene. There was nothing of the critically "superior" about this; no one ever resented it. Simply, he built towards a sum-total of perfection, and everybody felt it, knowing that the suggestions he had to make would result to the advantage of all. The stage-director frequently stepped into

the background, leaving the building of the performance in Chaliapin's hands.

One of the most accomplished artists in the company
was rehearsing a scene opposite Chaliapin one day, and
played it splendidly. Chaliapin watched, and applauded.
But when the scene was done (the stage-director was
entirely satisfied with it), Chaliapin held up his hand
for a pause, and addressed his colleague, in French.

"It is because of the artistry of your performance that
I venture to suggest to you certain shadings which, I
believe, would make it still more effective . . ."

Whereupon Chaliapin took the tenor's place on the
set, went through his part in finished style, and actually
brought something into the scene which had not been
there before. The other singer was the first to recognize
it.

"I shall play the scene as you suggest, sir"; he said
with a courtly bow, "and it is a pleasure to learn from
you!"

Chaliapin was always generous in bestowing praise
where he felt it to be due. He particularly admired
Caruso. There was a time when Chaliapin used Caruso's
dressing-room, and one night, he took up a dark make-
up crayon and wrote a glowing tribute to Caruso's art,
upon the wall, in Russian. This was greatly prized in
the House, as a solemn and beautiful thing; there was
that about the unconventional inscription—its strange
characters, its bold handwriting, its wholesouled sincerity—which lent it special significance. When the
dressing-rooms were freshened up, each spring (there
was wall-paper in those days), the decorators had special
instructions, either to leave that part of the wall un-
touched, or to cut around the piece of writing and re-

affix it to the new paper. For years it remained there, one of the "sights" and one of the inspirations of the House. But decorative efficiency triumphed over sentiment in the end. The old wall-papers were removed, a painter's brush wiped out Chaliapin's tribute with one neat stroke, and the wall was left with a freshness and cleanliness which is never regarded without regret. It is Leonard Merrick who pointed out that mere advancement does not always make for progress.

The House's worst case of stagefright belonged to a singer who shall be unknown for the reason that he remained so to his public. He was a young American tenor, who had a splendid voice, fine presence, and had built up a notable reputation in the vocal studios. He was suggested for a Metropolitan audition at last, and made so favorable an impression that a contract was signed. He practised faithfully, mastered his rôles, and gave an excellent accounting of himself at all rehearsals. But as soon as he was billed in a cast, a sort of personality-paralysis overcame him. He grew more and more nervous, and regularly, on the day of his performances, he telephoned in to the management to say that he was in such a condition that he could not possibly appear. And he never did appear, regardless of his contract, his opportunities, and his very earnest desire to make his career amount to something.

In the early days, there was a clause in the company's lease on the Opera House which gave the owners of the building, the Metropolitan Real Estate Company, the right to choose one tenor and one baritone each season, regardless of the management's further plans for the roster. On December 27, 1899, a new *Don Giovanni* made his New York début. He was young, handsome, spirited, and came with considerable acclaim from La Scala. After his first appearance, he was chosen by the House owners as "their" baritone, and continued so until that particular clause in the lease was retired. His name was Antonio Scotti. Scotti did not interpret the rôles he played; he lived them. As *Scarpia,* he became the grim essence of gentlemanly villainy —and he began to assume *Scarpia's* stride in the corridor outside his dressing-room, while he took off his tie and unbuttoned his vest. As *Escamillo,* he made one feel, not the hail-fellow-well-met spirit of the public entertainer, but the dignity of the greatest toreador in the world. His command of gesture was superb. As the *Count de Nevers* in *Les Huguenots,* he made his entrance descending a long flight of steps, and completely acquainted his audience with the character of the part before he had uttered a note.

During the latter years of his activity, Scotti's voice showed more than traces of wear, and no one realized this better than he did himself. On the nights when he was billed, he would always ask for a pair of complimentary seats for his friends, and always in the same formula.

"I want especially good locations for to-night. I appear in the performance. You notice, I do not say *'I sing'!*"

Scotti had a gift for friendship. Each one upon whom he bestowed his regard had his special name (Gerber was "my little son"), and was always greeted by some special, private joke. Scotti and Caruso were the closest of friends, occupying suites in the same hotels so that they could be constantly together. During Caruso's last illness, Scotti came close to a nervous breakdown. He was always in attendance at the sick man's bedside, talking to him when Caruso was ready for talk, and otherwise simply sitting beside him, sharing the silence of perfect understanding.

In a day of commercialism, when every celebrated trill can fetch its price from public or sponsor, it is hard to realize that accurate recordings of Metropolitan performances were made, forty years ago, for no other return to the artists than the pleasure of being able to hear their own voices. During the first beginnings of phonographic reproduction, when such records as there were, were made on wax cylinders, which no ranking artist would have dreamed of regarding seriously, the opera's librarian, Mr. Lionel Mapleson, began investigating the new device as a private hobby. Mapleson would take his machine down to the prompter's box during a performance, insert a blank cylinder, and "take" the different arias and often entire scenes, at the moment they were being sung to the House. No one thought of objecting; no one had the faintest notion that Mapleson's hobby might contain the germ of an important commercial enterprise, involving permissions, restrictions, rights, and fees. It was considered to be simply a wonderful lark, and the next morning would see the artists who had been "taken," and many of their colleagues, hurrying at an early hour to Mapleson's office, to hear the results. There would be comments, then, on the wonders of an age that could make such things possible. That was all, and it was quite sufficient for all concerned. The voices of Ternina, the de Reszkes, Saléza, Nordica, and many others who made no (or few) public recordings, were faithfully caught by Mapleson's wax cylinders. These cylinders are still in existence, though frequent use and the wearing down of the soft wax have made them less than worthy replicas of the glories they once held.

In time, word of this novel hobby was carried outside the House, and presently, the representative of one of the talking-machine companies arrived with an out and out bribe. He offered Gerber a machine and a dozen band records (all to be new), in exchange merely for pointing out the various stars and refraining from barring the way to them. So the fourteen-year-old office-boy acquired a phonograph of his own; and the following season, contracts began to be offered for the recordings of the more distinguished artists.

### 2.

Some of the company permitted themselves more spectacular pursuits, and some were out and out pranksters. Bernard Bégué led what he called "a double life." Besides singing at the Opera, he conducted an excellent French boarding house, on West Thirty-ninth Street. The lunch hour there was one o'clock and regularly, along towards twelve, Bégué would grow noticeably restless at rehearsals. The moment he was free, then, he would rush home, don a white apron and a chef's cap, and fall to with a will, preparing the entrée. He also assisted with the serving. The meals at Bégué's were famous, and many of the opera people got into the habit of going over there for lunch. Bégué himself saw nothing incongruous in sing-

ing romantic rôles in the evening and preparing meals
by day. Both offices held dignity for him and he accorded it to them. In time, he retired to a comfortable
little home in France—on the profits from his boarding
house.

Luigi Mancinelli, conductor of the French, German,
and Italian repertories and composer of the opera *Ero
e Leandro,* which was given at the Metropolitan
(March 10, 1899), with Eames, Saléza, and Plançon in
the leading rôles, was the least pretentious of men. Entirely unassuming, he could never understand why ac-
complishment in the field of music should set about a
person the sort of special glow that is not shared by
achievement in other fields. He always insisted that a
good doctor was more important than a good soprano!
Mancinelli had no special dressing-room of his own, or
if he had, he never made use of it. He would arrive in
the House in good time, hang his hat and coat in some
unused corner of another artist's room, and wait un-
obtrusively in the wings until it was time for him to go
down into the orchestra pit. The moment the opera
was over, he would retrieve his things and walk quietly
home to his quarters in the Normandie Hotel. Oddly
enough, his very reticence marked him out as especially
noticeable.

Mancinelli was fond of Italian wine and, after the
performance, he would always go to the same corner
table in the Normandie's café, call for the same waiter,
and order a bottle of the same vintage wine. It was an
expensive wine, costing nearly five dollars the bottle.
Mancinelli never troubled to order from the wine-card.
He simply told his faithful waiter what he wanted. Af-

ter months of regular attendance in the café, Mancinelli learned one night that his favorite waiter was ill, and had to satisfy himself with the services of someone else. Being a man of fixed habits, even so slight a deviation from regular routine disturbed his evening's relaxation. But when the bill was presented to him, he was still more disturbed. His regular bottle of wine was charged at one dollar and a half. Mancinelli called for the card, and found, for the first time, what his choice vintage really cost. His "favorite" waiter had regularly been pocketing the difference.

A different type of conductor was Alfred Hertz, in charge of Conried's German repertory. He was as naturally explosive as Mancinelli was naturally quiet. Hertz could do nothing without emphasis and vehement gestures. He put such hard physical work into his conducting that he had to make a complete change of linen after every act. When the artists retired to their dressing-rooms to change their costumes, Hertz hurried off to put on a fresh shirt and collar.

For a time, Hertz caused some dismay by arriving just a little late in the orchestra pit. The delay was not over-important; perhaps a minute or two. But the signal for the conductor's appearance would be given, the House lights would go down, the men would stop tuning their instruments to receive the conductor in silence, the audience would be keyed up by these preparations for the start of the opera—and always an extra moment or two would pass before Hertz showed himself. This caused a slight tension of expectancy and when he did appear, at last, he was greeted by prolonged applause. Polite managerial remonstrance was made; Otto Weil even pointed a humorous finger at the situation by hanging in Hertz's room a sign which read:

"Am I not always on time?  Yes, I am not!"

But the late arrivals continued.  Finally, the technical director, Mr. Castel-Bert, lost patience.  At that time, some of the European opera houses had wooden hoods covering the orchestra pit, so that neither the men nor the conductor could be seen, and full attention was directed to the stage.  Without offering any definite "reasons why," Castel-Bert suggested to Conried that the Metropolitan might do well to follow the example of the European houses in regard to the hood.  At last Conried agreed to try it.  The hood was set in place, and the next time that Hertz made a delayed entrance, there was neither tension nor applause.  Nobody knew whether he was late or early.  After that, all performances began strictly on schedule.  After a time, it was found that the hood tended to muffle the sound of the orchestra and it was taken away.  But the prompt arrivals continued.

Hertz was a magnificent musician, though, and put himself completely into his work.  His very zeal once led to an amusing happening.  He was on the stage rehearsing *Siegfried,* and lost himself in the ardors of acting out the business of the principals.  Off in a corner, the two property men who managed the Dragon were getting this monster ready, lighting up the eyes, settling themselves inside it, and practising the synchronization of their motions.  Somehow or other, they wiggled themselves across the stage and came directly behind Hertz, who was still entirely occupied with his instructions and gesticulations.  Everyone else on the stage noted the progress of the Dragon; only Hertz did not. Presently, then, he turned around and found himself within a few feet of the gnashing jaws and the murderous eyes. With a cry, he wheeled about and fled. From that time on, the Property Department had no further doubt but what the Dragon carried conviction.

Shortly after his retirement, Hertz came into the House as one of the audience, for a performance of *Walkuere*. He had been visiting in the wings and reached his seat just as *Bruennhilde* advanced to the vantage-point of her rock on the stage. Hertz was somewhat short-sighted, and had had no time to examine his program.

"Who is the *Bruennhilde?*" he whispered to his neighbor.

"I'm not sure," came the reply, "but I *think* it's the lady standing on the rock!"

In addition to the credit accorded him as a distinguished and versatile artist, Andreas Dippel won a special popularity from the fact that he was always ready to fill any sort of tenor cast replacement, in any bill, at a moment's notice. Cartoons of thirty-odd years ago show him sitting in his dressing-room, surrounded by the costumes of two dozen operas, waiting quietly to be called for any one of them. In one season, Dippel appeared in sixteen different parts. When a replacement was announced from the stage, humorous rumor had it that only the name of the rôle needed to be mentioned; the audience could supply "the part will be assumed by Mr. Dippel" without being told.

On one occasion, Alois Burgstaller was taken ill during the First Act of *Tannhaeuser* and could not go on with the performance. With the opera under way and the audience waiting, an immediate substitution was necessary, and Gerber set off, post haste, in a cab, to look up Dippel, and fetch him straight to the opera. So sure was the management of the tenor's unswerving amiability in such matters, that Max Hirsch made the announcement from the stage that Dippel would continue in Burgstaller's part, even before the cab was well started on its way uptown. (The excitement had its effect upon Hirsch's command of English, and he announced that Dippel was "already being prepared," which sounded as though some sort of surgery awaited him, and the audience expressed its appreciation in roars of laughter.) By luck, Dippel was at home, in his apartment in the Majestic Hotel. He had company, a hearty dinner lay behind him, and an exciting game of pinochle was in progress. Gerber told breathlessly what was wanted, and the party around the table looked stricken. All but Dippel himself.

"Did they get through the First Act?" he asked.

"Just about! But there's not a moment to lose . . ."

"Oh, yes there is. If they've got as far as the first intermission, a few minutes more won't harm. I'll come—but first we're going to finish this hand."

And he turned back to his cards, and his guests. Four thousand people waited that night, while Dippel finished a round of pinochle. After an hour's delay, then, the performance went on.

Conried's love of realism once brought about a minor panic on the stage. The performance was *Tannhaeuser* again, but this time the excitement did not proceed from any of the principals. The Second Scene of the First

Act represents a hunt. Normally, this is indicated by
the presence of a few veteran stage horses and a property stag tied to two poles. But Conried wanted something more. The audience was not merely to see the
hunt, but to feel its very atmosphere. Accordingly, he
borrowed a pack of trained fox-hounds from the Long
Island estate of one of his friends. The dogs arrived
in a special truck and in the charge of special keepers.
They were as genuine as even Conried could have desired; lean, keen, hungry, ferocious—altogether in the
pink of condition for action in the field. They strained
at their leashes, barking, yelping, and striking terror
into the hearts of the actors and stage crews. The
vocal huntsman of the evening, whose duty it was to
lead them on, declared that he would sooner resign his
contract than go near those dogs, and one of the
keepers had to put on a costume and bring them out on
the stage. Even then, everyone connected with the hunt
drew back from them, and their barking cut across the
sound of the orchestra. It was a noble gesture towards
realism, but the scene was completely spoiled. After
that, Conried contented himself with the standard
properties.

The great atelier of Kautsky, in Vienna (which then
furnished the opera's costumes), sent its representative,
Mr. Winternitz, to New York one season, and Conried
went to considerable lengths entertaining him. The
facilities of the House were put at his disposal, of course,
and during the day, Conried asked Gerber to show the
visitor the sights of New York. Automobiles were just
beginning to supplant horse-drawn carriages, and the
tour was made in Conried's electric coupé, beginning
with the Tombs, the Brooklyn Bridge, and the Stock

Exchange, and ending, at last, with the theatrical district in the upper Forties. Gerber inquired whether there was anything else that might interest the guest.

"Yes," said Winternitz thoughtfully, "I should like to make the acquaintance of an American ice-cream soda."

Gerber took him to the Astor Hotel, where they were later to dine, and Winternitz made the acquaintanceship he desired.

"It is remarkable!" he exclaimed. "We have nothing like that in Vienna. I must have another."

Another tall soda was brought, and then Mr. Winternitz proceeded to his dinner. Throughout the duration of his American stay, the Viennese gentleman regularly consumed two ice-cream sodas immediately before dinner. And when asked what had pleased him most in his visit to New York, he answered promptly,

"The American ice-cream sodas."

Max Hirsch, then Box-Office Treasurer of the company, never lost an opportunity to play a joke. One of the bassos at that time was Ludovico Viviani, who always seemed to draw hidden possibilities from Hirsch because of the somewhat lofty airs he gave himself. He was a charming person, though, and he and Hirsch were the best of friends. Viviani was an Italian nobleman and entitled to style himself "Count," which he never failed to do, except, of course, in the opera programs. The company was on tour at this time, and the opera train arrived late in the evening in Chicago. Viviani gave up his luggage to the hotel porter, with the exception of a fine leather silk-hat case, which he kept close beside him. He strode up to the desk, asked for a room, and announced himself grandly as "Count Ludovico Viviani, member of the Metropolitan Opera Company." The young room-clerk was visibly impressed by this list of distinctions, all belonging to the same individual. Viviani took up the pen to register and set his hat-box close at hand while he wrote. Hirsch, though, came up behind him and gave the box a shove, hoping to upset the Count's dignity a bit, by making him chase after the rolling box. Hirsch was the most surprised of all, then, when the hat-box not only fell and rolled, but flew open —revealing, instead of a lordly silk hat, a complete and neatly-packed set of cooking utensils, which bounced over the stone floor of the lobby with considerable clatter. The Count was more than a little embarrassed, but the hat-box had a salutary effect on the peace of mind of the young room-clerk, who recovered sufficiently to present Viviani with the hotel's printed rules forbidding cooking in the apartments.

The battle of the cook-stove was always a grievous issue between the hotel managements and many of the foreign artists, who found existence unbearable without their native fare. Regularly they smuggled their little plate-burners and other kitchen equipment in with their clothing; regularly they slipped out at odd hours, an over-night bag in hand, to do marketing; regularly the tempting aromas of tomato sauce and meat gravies betrayed them via the key-holes; and regularly they were requested to betake themselves to other quarters—where the same warfare would begin all over again. It was not economy which prompted these domestic interludes, but an unconquerable distaste for foreign food in general and foreign hotel meals in particular. Long before the day of kitchenette suites, one hotel in New

York swept in the patronage of practically the entire foreign contingent of singers by openly allowing cooking in the rooms. Then there were great doings. Many of the artists brought their own chefs along with them, together with their accompanists, secretaries, and valets. A certain German prima donna was regularly to be seen, an hour after her performances, hurrying into the lobby with her arms full of brown paper bags. And the wife of one of the Italian singers, herself a famous cook, brought new joy into the lives of her compatriots by preparing her meals in mass production, setting up card-tables in her splendid hotel parlor, and accepting paying table guests!

Otto Weil was another prankster, but once, at least, the joke turned its point against him. The company was again on tour, this time in Philadelphia, just after America's entrance into the war. Those Philadelphia visits were memorable affairs. Mr. Walter H. Herring, of the Globe Ticket Company, lived there and gallantly appointed himself as host to the company every time they came. He would have a fleet of automobiles at the station, waiting to speed the male members of the company to the Union League Club, on Broad Street, where Mr. Herring entertained them at dinner. His dinners were notable, too. This night, the menu included terrapin soup, a rare delicacy in those war-time days, when ordinary potatoes and onions were referred to as "Rockefellers." Mr. Gatti looked at the cup of soup placed before him, savored its aroma, and plunged his spoon into it before the guests at the other end of the table had been served. Then he leaned back again with a gratified expression.

"It is good," he observed in a whisper to Weil. "What is it?"

Thinking it a capital joke for turtle soup to go unrecognized by the company's chief, Weil whispered back,

"Lamb stew. Philadelphia style."

"Ah?" said Gatti. "You don't say! This is a complete novelty."

Whereupon he went back to his soup, finished it, and called for a second serving! In some confusion, then, it developed that but one cup had been prepared for each guest, and there was no more. To hide his burst of humor from the ears of the host, Weil gave Gatti his own cup, saying that he did not particularly care for "lamb stew." But he cast wistful eyes towards it while the chief again made laudatory mention of the superiority of Philadelphia cooking, and the other guests seasoned their soup with the added sauce of mirth. Never again did Mr. Gatti find lamb stew that so completely tickled his palate.

It was after one of these Philadelphia visits (an earlier one, though, before the war), that two members of the company got lost. The performance was over, the dressing-rooms had been cleared out, and the singers were in the station, boarding the special train back to New York, when it was discovered that Burgstaller and Goritz were missing. The train was held while inquiries were telephoned to the opera house and to the various hotels, but the singers did not appear and no one had any news to give of them. At last someone suggested that they might have taken a sudden notion to drive back, and the train started without them. Next morning, inquiries to their homes were anticipated by anxious calls from the singers' families, begging to know what the management could possibly have done with Alois and Otto. By that time, there was serious concern, and the police were notified. The hours dragged by and no word came. Towards late afternoon, then, Police Headquarters made an official report. Burgstaller and Goritz had been found. At that moment, they were on a ferryboat, heading in from Jersey City. Still in their evening clothes and opera hats, they were singing sentimental ditties to a delighted group of truck-men and boot-blacks, who were heartily urged to join in the choruses. Philadelphia hospitality had proved so alluring, that the two set out, after the performance, to investigate it further, in a series of visits to beer-gardens which left them entirely cheerful if somewhat the worse for wear.

The soul of generosity resided in the person of Otto H. Kahn, of the Board of Directors, and later Chairman of that Board. He was a type of *bon vivant* who enjoyed the good things of life and was perfectly ready to share them. During the season of 1910, the House staff were the recipients of a startling offer. The staff of the Boston Opera Company challenged them to play a game of baseball, to be held in the National League Grounds of Boston, and to be attended with all possible pomp and ceremony. The invitation was more than enticing, and everything was in readiness except the matter of ways and means. So Mr. Kahn came to the rescue. He advised the staff to accept the challenge, and gave Earle Lewis a blank check for all expenses. The season's most ravishing opera held no excitement to compare with that! Outfits were measured, equipment

was delivered to the stage-door, tickets for the trip were
reserved on the *S.S. Harvard,* and every available moment was devoted to practise. The team included
Lewis, Hugh R. Brown, Gerber, and members of other
departments, now gone from the House. The Metropolitan team arrived in Boston, was entertained by the
Boston team, and the next afternoon the game was on.
The Mayor of Boston was present, and the grounds
were as full as ever they were for a big league contest.
The Metropolitan nine was ignominiously beaten.

Then, in the hilarity of the supper that followed, it
came out that the Bostonians had played a little joke.
A professional pitcher had been put in, not so much to
win the game as to "put one over" on the New York
visitors. Everyone took the joke in good part, especially Mr. Kahn, who immediately demanded a return
game, again at his expense. Again there was a fine
reception dinner (in the Opera House lobby), and again
the time came for the game to begin, this time in the
Polo Grounds. Not to be outdone in chicanery, Frederick Rullmann provided professional aid for the Metropolitan team, bringing in not merely a pitcher, but a
battery from the National League. This time the
Metropolitans won. And so the score was even and the
trickery was even—but everybody had had a rousingly
good time.

It remained for two baritones, one an American and
the other an Italian, to present the reverse side of the
generosity score. During a given season, the American
gentleman had gotten more than usual aid from one of
the property men. The man was always ready in the
wings to hand the singer his sword, or lyre, or cup; and

he also played opposite the baritone as the animating spirit within the Dragon, an office which required patient and difficult rehearsal. Though the various House staffs are on regular salary, it is a sort of unwritten law that especially personal services be personally rewarded. The property man had performed many such faithful services for the baritone, and when, at the close of the year, the singer paid him a special visit, the man made no attempt to conceal his pleasure.

"Charlie," the baritone began, "you've been a wonderful help to me this season."

"Thank you, sir. I'm glad of it."

"Especially with the Dragon, you know. I'd have muffed many a scene without your aid."

"Thank you, sir."

The appreciative comments filled ten good minutes of pleasant speechifying. At last, then, the singer came to the point.

"And so, Charlie, I've brought you a little something to show my appreciation."

And he reached into the pocket of his splendid coat and drew forth—three unwrapped oranges.

The Italian gentleman asked Gerber to get for him three general admissions for a performance at the Brooklyn Academy of Music. Gerber, who represents the Metropolitan Opera Association at the weekly performances in Brooklyn, readily gave him the admissions, and the singer asked whether he owed him anything.

"Nothing for the tickets. Just the war tax."

There was a tax of ten cents on each admission, and the Italian baritone paid it. Early the next morning, then, as Gerber was opening his desk, there came a hurried step down the corridor and the baritone appeared.

JEAN DE RESZKE, AS "TRISTAN"

FEODOR CHALIAPIN, AS MEFISTOFELE

"Did you have a good time last night?" Gerber inquired.

"Oh, yes. Fine. The performance was beautiful. But—look here. One of my guests couldn't come. The admission ticket is quite unused. See, here it is. You give me back my ten cents, yes?"

The greatest generosity, though, involves the giving, not of one's goods but of one's self. At one time, Emma Calvé lived at the Plaza Hotel. On the same floor with her, lay a gravely sick man. He was a prominent surgeon, a cancer specialist, who was dying of the dread disease to which he had devoted his active years, and knew it. Those close to him reported that his thoughts were not on the suffering that lay ahead of him, but on the life of the active world, from which he was slipping further and further away. He spoke of the theaters, the opera, all the things in which he had once taken pleasure. These reports reached Calvé's ears, somehow, and she asked permission to visit the stricken man. Leave was readily granted, and the appointment was set for eleven o'clock on a Monday morning, the very hour of the fashionable morning musicales. Calvé took as much pains with her toilette for this visit as ever she did for a stage appearance. She wore a rose-colored concert gown, and her finest jewels. She came to the dying man's bedside like a draught of the life for which he so longed, and sang for him a complete program of arias and songs.

Richard Crooks once undertook a similar act of kindness, although Crooks, strictly speaking, has no place among the records of the older stars. In the vast mail he receives after his radio broadcasts, Crooks noted that the name of the same correspondent appeared over and over again. It was a woman's name, and her letters revealed such a sympathetic insight into matters musical, that Crooks responded, first with the not-unusual autographed photograph, and later, with letters of sincere appreciation. Crooks had no idea of who the writer was, her age, her condition, or anything about her; still, they became epistolary friends. The letters were postmarked from a little town in California, and when Crooks' concert tour next took him to a nearby city, he sent his unknown friend a pair of tickets for his recital.

On the day of the concert, an urgent telephone call was put through to the tenor in his hotel. There came a woman's voice and it seemed agitated. She explained that she was the mother of his correspondent. The writer herself was a girl of eighteen, a hopeless invalid, who had never walked, and whose sole pleasure was the music she heard over the radio. She had hoped to be carried into the concert hall for Crooks' recital, but the excitement had been too much for her feeble strength, she was ill, and disappointment was making her worse.

"Tell her not to worry," said Crooks briefly over the wire.

That afternoon, and during the traditional rest period before a performance, Crooks first sent a grand piano out to the invalid's home, and followed by motor, with his accompanist. At the sick girl's bedside, he went through the entire recital program.

Long before the question of nationality entered into the consideration of an artist's abilities, a young American tenor came to sing an audition, and made so splendid an impression that he was engaged for the

Metropolitan before he left the House that day. His name was Riccardo Martin, and he was hailed as "the second Caruso." Just this irked Martin, who admired Caruso so sincerely that he felt any comparison with him to verge upon sacrilege. At his audition, Martin had sung several arias when one of the Administrative Staff present asked him to sing the *Vesti la Giubba,* from *Pagliacci.* Eager as he was to make his audition satisfying in every way, Martin hesitated.

"Don't you know it?"

"Oh, yes. I know it perfectly. But I'd rather not sing it *here.* I have too much respect for Mr. Caruso!"

Caruso and Martin became excellent friends, and their friendship led, indirectly, to an incident which caused Caruso the greatest amusement. Martin was scheduled to appear one night and took sick at the last moment. Caruso was seldom called upon for a cast replacement—the longer in advance he was announced, the better the sale of seats—but, hearing of Martin's indisposition, he offered to appear in his place, "for Dick." Without disparagement of Martin's abilities, that night's audience was in a rapture of enthusiasm. Tickets for Caruso's regular performances were nearly impossible to obtain, and here the people had come to an "ordinary" opera, to find Caruso in the cast! But one patron hurried to the box-office.

"I want my money back!"

"Because of the change in cast?"

"Yes. I bought my ticket for an advertised cast, and I don't want any of your last-minute substitutions."

"But—you're getting *Caruso!* It isn't as though you'd bought a seat to hear Caruso and someone else were taking his place . . ."

"I don't care who's taking whose place. I paid my money to hear what you people said I was going to hear, and if I can't hear what I paid for, I want my money back!"

A refund was made him, and his single ticket was eagerly pounced upon by a waiting line. But Caruso never tired of telling of the time when the circumstance of his presence in a cast caused one patron to demand his money back. This was entirely characteristic of Caruso. So many incidents of warmth and humor and kindliness are entirely characteristic of him! If one personality, of all the galaxy of vivid folk who have come and gone, could be chosen as the *most* glamorous, it would be his. A more human man never lived.

# Chapter VII

## CARUSO

### 1.

A LESS peculiarly endowed singer who devoted as much time and care to the preparation of his rôles as did Caruso, would have emerged with a noteworthy reputation as a music scholar. Caruso did not depend upon the sheer opulence of his voice to carry him through. He realized that, as a mature artist, he needed to build for himself all that his background and training had lacked; and he set himself to this task with purpose and zeal. He studied books on opera plots to improve his English and to acquaint himself with rôles and works which had no relation to his own performances. As his vocal surety developed, he spent more and more time on perfecting his stage business; on details of make-up; on the authenticity of his costumes. Each successive season showed notable progress along such lines, and it was due entirely to his own searching efforts. As the great Caruso, who was idolized as perhaps no other stage personality has ever been, he would eagerly learn from some assistant conductor or secondary singer who came new to the House and brought new ideas with him. Because his voice was naturally robust and dramatic, he set himself to mastering distinctly lyric parts—parts which hardly showed his vocal powers to their fullest advantage. If *Aida* and *Pagliacci* came naturally to him, he put extra effort into drawing the full lyric mean-

ing from the rôles he played in *Butterfly* and *Bohême*.
One of his most poignantly unforgettable moments occurred at the close of the First Act of *The Girl of The
Golden West,* which ends with a hauntingly lovely tenor
aria, sung to slowly closing curtains and touching the
greatest heights of the opera. Caruso put every ounce
of his energy into his rôles. At the end of a performance of *Pagliacci,* he frequently had to be assisted, robust as he was, up the flight of steps that leads to the
tenor's dressing-room.

He was severe in judging of his own work. He studied
such adverse criticisms as he got with care and never became blinded by the peculiar adulation that met him on
every hand. He was especially sensitive about the artistic value of his phonograph records. His revenue from
these was immense; from the standpoint of popular demand he could have made more discs than he did; yet
he never approached the business of recording without
misgivings. He believed that, of all his discs, only a
half dozen offered a faithful reproduction of his voice.
The others, he often said, were "not too bad to hear,"
but might have been made by almost any tenor at all.
At his apartment one night, Caruso volunteered to play
his newest records for a group of guests. The records
had not yet been released, he explained; they had been
heard only by himself; and now he wanted the candid
opinion of the others. The machine was put into motion
and presently a fine tenor voice filled the room with the
melodies of Italian folk-songs. The guests compli-
mented Caruso enthusiastically. These, they declared,
were his best recordings to date; no one but he could
achieve such a splendid outpouring of tone, such spon-
taneity, such fire.

"No more—please!" Caruso cut in. "It makes me too sad. These are not my records at all. They were made by an unknown tenor who is not even included in the catalogue of the better artists!"

In his public work, too, Caruso never lost the shrewd suspicion that nine-tenths of a singer's fame rests upon his name and public glamour, rather than upon the actual merits of his work. And even though he, as "the Great Caruso," derived only advantage from such a critical system, he deplored it. He begged to be told "the real truth" about his performances, and never tired of inventing little schemes to prove that he was being judged as a name rather than as a serious artist. One night, at the start of a performance of *Pagliacci,* he rushed into the dressing-room of Albert Reiss, the possessor of a good if limited tenor voice, whose part in the opera included the singing of a serenade off-stage.

"Look, Reiss," Caruso burst out, "I have something in my mind. You do me a favor, yes? You let me sing that serenade to-night?"

Reiss agreed, though not without surprise. It is not routine procedure for a first "star" to clamor for tasks which leave him unseen and creditless. When the cue came, Reiss stepped aside in the wings, and Caruso sang the aria, putting his best efforts into it. It was over, at last, and Caruso waited with breathless expectancy. Not a ripple of applause was to be heard in the House. Nor was there any comment, the next day in the press, to the effect that Reiss was suddenly developing unexpected vocal powers.

"You see," observed Caruso, with a sort of sad triumph, "it is not *Caruso* they want—it is only the knowledge that they are hearing Caruso!"

For such reasons, the unusual circumstance of a derogatory criticism held special charm for him. He talked long and delightedly of a less-than-favorable notice he had received at the hands of a conservative critic in Boston.

At his first Metropolitan performance of *Lucia,* Caruso's voice rang out with such tremendous power in the sextette, cutting through the orchestra and the other five voices, that a policeman, on duty in the lobby, rushed into the House demanding to know the cause of the commotion.

"Aha," commented Caruso later, "I sing too loud! I must look out for that."

But for all his sincere efforts, a reputation for mere study never seemed to attach itself to him. Great as his work was, with Caruso there was always something greater. That was his irresistible, expansive human warmth. In the end, it overshadowed every other quality he possessed—even his unmatched voice. To those who knew him, it always seemed strange that this man, of all men, should be marked out by a greatness which set him apart. Apartness was not in him.

The laurel-wreathed bust of him, which stands in the main lobby, serves its chief use to-day as a meeting-place. Intermission appointments are generally indicated by "I'll find you at Caruso's 'statue,'" a convenient spot in dense crowds. Those he left behind him might often wish to see his likeness regarded as a thing to be revered in its own right. But to Caruso himself, perhaps, such an arrangement would have been highly satisfactory. To have people about him and in some way to serve them were the things in which he most delighted.

2.

On the nights when Caruso sang, the standees' line began to form by ten in the morning. By early afternoon, it extended down Broadway to Thirty-ninth Street and around the corner to Seventh Avenue. When Caruso came in to call for his mail, he would look at that line and say,

"Ah, I feel sorry for those people! All day they stand, and those on the end won't get in anyway."

Often, then, he would go around to the box-office and buy a hundred standing admissions. These tickets are not allowed to go on sale until half an hour before the performance, but when Caruso asked for them, the powers had an idea of what was afoot, and nobody refused to give them. With his hundred tickets, then, Caruso would go back to the end of the line and present the admissions himself. Never could a secretary perform this particular office for him.

"Here—with Caruso's compliments. And I hope you enjoy!" He himself derived greater enjoyment from the people's amazement than they did from the gift.

Caruso never asked the management for complimentary tickets for his guests. He always bought them himself. That was quite a ceremony. Days before the performance, he would appear at the box-office with a carefully prepared list—so many seats downstairs, so many in the Dress Circle, so many in the Balcony. He selected each location himself, thoughtfully consulting the House plan, and marked down the names of his guests on the envelopes.

"These are for Joe (the bell-boy of Caruso's hotel)

. . . these, for Toni (his tailor) . . . you sure they can see and hear good?"

Caruso spent hundreds of dollars on tickets every time he sang. Only once did anyone take advantage of his generosity. This day, a man came to the box-office, held up a pair of tickets, and asked if the locations were desirable. Mr. Lewis looked at them and replied that they were among the finest seats in the House.

"I wanted to make sure," said the man. "I've just bought them, from a speculator outside, and he told me they were Caruso's personal seats."

Mr. Lewis had the matter investigated, and found that one of the guests for whom Caruso had so carefully chosen the seats, had sold them to a street speculator and pocketed the proceeds. When Caruso heard of it, the tears came to his eyes—but before his next performance, he was back again at the box-office, selecting further hundreds of dollars' worth of guest tickets.

As Caruso's fame increased, he was literally deluged with request-letters of all sorts. His morning's mail at the House was vast enough to vie with the entire post-office turn-over of many a small town. Quantities of these letters were signed with the name Caruso (the name is not an uncommon one), and in all of these there was a claim of kinship of one sort or another. Without attempting to investigate such claims, Caruso regularly sent the petitioners whatever it was they desired of him, whether the requests were for free opera tickets, or the capital necessary to set someone up in the coal-and-wood trade in Ohio.

"Maybe he *is* my cousin," Caruso would say. "I don't know. I guess he doesn't, either. But anyway, give him what he wants." There was a time when many

Italian families derived their chief support from Caruso.

There is danger that anecdotes concerning Caruso must suffer from repetition. Most of them root into the amazing generosity of the man. It made no difference to him that the recipients of much of his kindness were strangers to him. The company never visited Atlanta but that Caruso would go out to the Federal Prison there, and ask leave to sing to the prisoners. And for years he improved upon the bread-lines in New York.

During these years, he had his apartment in the Knickerbocker Hotel, and became a close friend of Mr. James Regan, the proprietor. As Caruso entered the hotel late at night, after his performances, he noticed a line of shabby men forming outside the side door. At once he inquired who they were and what they did there, and learned that, as the dining-rooms closed, Regan would have the kitchen left-overs distributed to the needy who applied for them.

"Ah, that is fine, Jimmy! What do you give them? What do they get to eat?"

"Whatever happens to be left over that can't be saved. Mostly bread and soup and stew."

"Never any beefsteak?"

"No, Mr. Caruso. I'm afraid not. Beefsteaks keep, you know."

"Yes, sure. But those men should have beefsteak. They are poor and cold, and steaks would be good for them. I tell you what, Jimmy—to-night, you give them good thick beefsteaks instead of the stew, and send the bill to me."

Thereafter, there were regular nights when the menu of that line included the finest steaks from the Knickerbocker larders.

There was actually no limit to Caruso's generosity toward those whom he knew and loved. It was enough for a friend to admire anything that Caruso owned, to find it immediately his own property. Caruso once ordered for himself a new and richly designed stick-pin, and talked freely of the pleasure he anticipated from the new possession. The first time he wore it, he encountered Earle Lewis in the House corridors.

"Is that the new pin?" Lewis asked, purposely to please him. "It's a beauty. I never saw such a handsome one."

"Ah, you like it?" Caruso cried, his hand already at his cravat. "Then you must take it. Please! I want you to. I can get another easy." And nothing would do but that Lewis accept the jewel.

(Some time after this, Gerber, in all innocence, chanced to admire the cravat pin worn by another member of the company; whereupon the gentleman clutched at his tie with one hand, waved off all appreciative comments with the other, and shouted, "No! No!" in frantic tones.)

Caruso was extremely sensitive about having these spontaneous offers refused. Knowing how sincerely he meant them, he put greater stress upon the spirit of the gift than on the object itself, and felt deeply hurt if the recipient failed to follow him. At rehearsal one day, a member of the Property Department admired a handsome diamond ring that the tenor chanced to be wearing —Caruso was always on the best of terms with these stage workers, and jokes and personal comments of all sorts were quite the order of the day. Caruso's only answer was to take the ring off and hand it to the man. But the stage-hand refused to accept it.

"No, how can I? It is too much! Never did I mean you to give it to me when I admired it . . ."

Caruso insisted and the man insisted, and in the end Caruso was seriously offended.

"Very well, then. You refuse my gift. You hurt my feelings. I tell you only this—you will never again have the chance to refuse a present from me. Not at Christmas time, not ever!"

Caruso was as good as his word. This particular worker never again received a gift from him. But at holiday times, at the end of the season, and often for no reason at all, elaborate parcels found their way to his wife and family. After which Caruso would gleefully exclaim,

"You don't have to refuse any present from me now, do you?"

Caruso loved the toy "billikins" which were much the vogue at one time (he declared that he looked like one himself), and fashioned many models of them which were then cast in bronze. He gave these to his friends as intimate souvenirs, and the workman of the diamond-ring-tragedy was anxious to have one. But Caruso never gave him the toy, reminding him of his pledge to lay himself open to no more refusals. During Caruso's last illness, this stage-hand visited him, saw one of the billikins on a table, and, more by way of amusing the patient than in earnest, threatened to steal it. Caruso bade his valet hand him the thing, and put it under his pillow, where he lay heavily upon it, much pleased at his own astuteness. After Caruso's death, his widow presented the workman with one of the cherished billikins, assuring him that Caruso had intended it for him all along, had set it aside with the man's name on it, and had postponed giving it to him when he asked for it, just to annoy him a while longer.

No one could perform the least service for Caruso without reaping a reward many times its value. On one occasion, Caruso was besieged for autographs on the stage, just as he was leaving it after a performance. He had no pen with him, of course, and borrowed one from the nearest person at hand. It chanced to be one of the electricians, who gladly handed the tenor his new pen, of which he was exceedingly proud because it had cost all of five dollars. Caruso signed a number of programs and then, in the confusion of greetings and after-opera reactions, he absently put the pen in his pocket and went on to his room. The electrician saw him go, and sent after him a glance of regret for his five-dollar pen. The next morning, a package was left for the electrician at the stage-door. In it was his pen, carefully wrapped in a twenty-dollar bank note.

Another time, Caruso came down to the House to try on some new wigs. He was an extremely busy man, there were many calls upon his time, and he used this hour of comparative leisure in his dressing-room, to settle a number of business matters. One of those who came to see him there, was a business official who brought with him a part of the tenor's extra-operatic earnings. He brought the sum in cash, and laid a number of five-hundred-dollar notes on the dressing-table. The elderly wig-man stared at them.

"Such a lot of them!" he exclaimed. "Why, if I had only one, I could take my wife home to Europe for all summer, to see our folks!"

Caruso made no reply; the wig-man went on with his fitting and adjusting and curling, bending close over

the tenor and then stepping back to note the effect; and
the matter of the bank notes was forgotten. When the
fitting was over, the wig-man returned to his room.
Putting his hand into the pocket of his smock, he was
horrified to find a five-hundred-dollar note there. He
rushed back to Caruso's dressing-room, distressed by the
thought of what Caruso would assume when the loss was
discovered. He met the tenor making ready to leave
the House.

"Mr. Caruso—there was *this* in my pocket . . . I
just found it and I don't know how it got there . . ."

"I do," said Caruso. "I put it in while you were so
busy with the wig. You said you could take the missus
to Europe if you had one of those bills. So now you
have it and you shall go!"

During the Christmas season, Caruso was in his
element. Every day of that festive week, he would come
into the House with his pockets bulging with gold pieces,
and hand them about to everyone he met. In addition,
he would plan special presents for the various House
groups. For the chorus men there might be stick-pins,
for the women, bracelets; the administrative staff had
gold watch-charms designed with an interweaving of
the initials EC; the ballet had pins or lockets. Before
Christmas really came, everyone had had a number of
generous tokens, and for none of them would Caruso
accept thanks. For his personal friends in the House,
he prepared individual gifts and spent weeks trying to
discover what they most wanted, with an elaborate sur-
reptitiousness that was more revealing of his purpose
than a direct question. One year, Gerber bought a set
of new cuff-links which he prized. Washing his hands
one day, he removed his cuffs with the new links in them,

and left them on his desk.  When he returned, both
cuffs and links were gone.  He searched for them, inquired about them, tried to discover who could have
entered his office during the few moments of his absence,
but all to no avail.  On the day before Christmas, then,
Caruso brought him two separate packages.  One contained the missing cuffs with their links; the other, a
handsome stick-pin, designed especially to match the
links.

"I want to make sure I get the pattern right," Caruso
explained with great gusto, "so I swipe cuffs and all
while you were away, to show to the jeweler!"

On his first concert tour, Caruso arrived in the city of
Scranton, to find that there had not been raised sufficient funds to meet his guaranteed fee.  It is customary
for such fees to be paid in advance—the theory being
that it is too late for a singer to take back his unpaid
"merchandise," after—and Goerlitz, who managed that
tour, refused to permit the tenor to appear, even though
Caruso gave strong signs of offering to sing anyway and
collect later on.  According to the terms of his contract,
Caruso was fully entitled to claim that night's fee, since
the cancellation of the concert was in no wise due to
any lapse on his part.  When the tour was done, though,
Caruso ran his pencil through the Scranton entry and
refused to accept payment for it.

"I don't see why it should be your loss," he observed
to Goerlitz.  "I can stand it better than you can."

Ever after, though, Caruso rolled the r's of
"Scr-r-r-ranton" with special significance.

For all his voluntary generosity, Caruso hated to be
imposed upon.  Nothing pleased him better than driving a creditable business bargain in a business way.

To my best friend
Aime Gerber
from Enrico Caruso
N.Y. 1913

ENRICO CARUSO

THE METRO-
POLITAN
OPERA HOUSE
STAGE

During a tour to the West one year, he made a short visit to a mining town, inspected the mines, and was much interested by a handful of nuggets which one of the miners showed him.

"How much for the lot?" Caruso asked.

The man weighed them carefully in his hand and said he'd take three hundred dollars for them. Caruso bought them on the spot, and brought them back to New York, to be mounted into watch-charms to give away to his friends. Gerber wears his still. Caruso took them to his jeweler's to be mounted, and asked the clerk who served him to give him an exact appraisal of the value of the nuggets. After an hour of careful weighing and adding, the man found them to be worth two hundred ninety-nine dollars and thirty-seven cents.

"Ah, you see!" cried Caruso in delight, "that man did not cheat me because I do not know! He keep for himself only sixty-three cents profit. That is good. But if I know his name and address, I send him more!"

### 3.

Caruso chose his friends strictly according to his own inclinations. Position, dignity, or glamour had not the slightest weight in tipping the scales of his favor in either direction. The "little people" about the House—stage-hands, property men, choristers—came to be his close associates, when he liked them. So did the celebrated "stars"—when he liked them.

One evening, Caruso gave a little dinner party at his apartment, for half a dozen of his cronies. The guests included Scotti of course, Amato, De Luca, and Philip Crispano, who is still the company's Master of Properties, and whom Caruso especially loved. The dinner hour had been set for seven. Shortly after six, Crispano telephoned to say that he could not come.

"But why not?"

"A hurry-up job over at the House."

"Well, that won't take you all evening, will it?"

"No, but a good two hours. I couldn't possibly get over before eight, and that'd be too late . . ."

"Don't talk nonsense! It wouldn't be too late at all. You come along whenever you can."

The other guests arrived, and the moments passed. Toward seven-thirty, Scotti grew restless.

"Look here, it's way past seven, and I'm starved. Where's dinner?"

"Not before eight," said Caruso. "Filippo is delayed. We'll wait till he comes."

And the company's "stars" had to wait with their dinner until the property man had finished his work.

It was Crispano's duty to go about town and seek out plain, unpretentious little Italian eating places, where Caruso could dine at his ease, enjoying the national dishes he loved without being spotlighted by the groups of admirers who never failed to surround him whenever he showed himself in public. Crispano would report on his investigations, and then Caruso and his oddly-assorted friends would go forth "for a party," into the back room of some little delicatessen shop in Carmine or Elizabeth Streets, where the floor was sprinkled with saw-dust, but where the cooking spoke of Naples.

Though Caruso delighted in the public recognition accorded him, he hated having to "act grand" in appreciation of it. On the company's tours, when there was no time to search out the smaller restaurants where he

felt most at home, Caruso would take his meals in the
dining-rooms of the great hotels, without in any way
altering his manner—except to conduct himself with
even greater prankishness.  The chefs of these hotels
were always on their mettle when word came that Caruso was dining in the house.  A friendship sprang up
between the tenor and the chef of the Lenox Hotel in
Boston, and Caruso would regularly be invited down to
the kitchens there, to superintend the preparation of his
favorite spaghetti.  Such visits enchanted him.  As soon
as the dish was ready, then, he would hurry upstairs,
ahead of the waiter, to the dining-room.  Knowing
himself to be the cynosure of all eyes there, he would
behave badly on purpose, savoring his spaghetti, winding it around his fork in great rolls, turning up his eyes,
and emitting loud "Ah's" of gustatory satisfaction.
The more amazed his fellow-diners appeared, the better
pleased he was.

Crispano lives in a small town in New Jersey, and one
Sunday, Caruso drove to that vicinity to visit other
friends close by.  In the midst of a game of quoits in the
back-yard, he suddenly remembered the proximity of
his dear Philip, and set out at once with his hosts to pay
him an impromptu visit.  When the party arrived at
Crispano's, Philip was out.

"Where did he go?"

"To a ball-game.  He'll be terribly disappointed to
miss you."

"Oh, but I'm going to wait!  You send someone to
fetch Philip."

The quoits game was resumed in a neighbor's yard—
every Italian household contains the facilities for it—

and an hour was passed, waiting for Philip to come home.

It was well known that Crispano ranked among Caruso's intimates, and it sometimes happened that the property man's good offices were sought as a wedge into the favor of the tenor. Caruso never undertook many concert tours, and when he did, there was hardly a town in the country that did not apply for an appearance. Only the smallest proportion of all the offers could be accepted, and there was considerable rivalry among the various cities as to which ones would "get" Caruso. During the opera's tour one year, a Chamber of Commerce official came to Crispano, offering to pay him two thousand dollars if he could succeed in inducing Caruso to sing a concert in his town. Crispano, of course, went straight to Caruso with the strange proposition.

"But how can I say whether I'll go there or not?" cried Caruso. "That's entirely in my managers' hands. I just go where I'm routed." Then, after a moment, "But look—you lose two thousand dollars because of this, don't you?" Immediately he drew out his checkbook and wrote Crispano a check for the amount he stood to forfeit. Crispano took the check, thanked Caruso heartily for it—and tore it up.

Had Caruso never sung a note, he would have made himself known as a cartoonist. It was entirely a natural gift. He had no training in it, but took the greatest delight in it, sketching in and out of season, on menu cards, old envelopes, rehearsal slips, anything that came to hand. His strokes were broad and generous, and his likenesses, ludicrously faithful. In this work too, the nature of the man stood revealed; no matter how

ridiculous he made his subjects appear, there was
never a trace of malice in
Caruso's cartoons.

A leading New York
newspaper offered Caruso
a contract to serve as one
of its cartoonists, at a
salary of fifty thousand
dollars a year, and with
the understanding that the
work should not interfere
with his vocal engage-
ments. Caruso refused the
offer.

"That sort of thing I do
only for the pleasure of
my friends. My money I
make by singing. But—
I'm very glad you like my
drawings."

Seriously as he took his
singing, Caruso always
had time to spot the ri-
diculous. In *Pagliacci,* a
donkey is brought upon
the stage, and twice out of
three times, the animal
would sit down, refuse to
go on, and upset the per-
formance by making the
audience laugh. It could
have brought serious dis-

AIMÉ GERBER
*By Caruso*

turbance to the opera's dignity, but Caruso took a different view of the matter.  Often as he sang in that work, he would regularly announce,

"I said a special prayer to-night that the donkey would behave bad.  Then the people can laugh."

On one occasion, at least, a joke was turned against Caruso.  It didn't happen often.  During a spring tour, more than thirty years ago, the company played a few performances in Washington, D. C.  This night was particularly warm, the tenor part in the opera required no change of costume, and Caruso spent the between-act interval in the long alley outside the stage-door, cooling off and telling jokes to one of the porters.  Suddenly, the door-man's head appeared from inside the theater.

"Mr. Caruso," he began with a stage-whisper and a broad grin, "the President is here and would like to meet you."

Caruso saw the grin and interpreted it after his own fashion.

"Sure," he called back, "on a hot night like this!  You tell him to wait, please, till I get through out here.  Then I come."

The door-man retired and Caruso felt pleased not to have been caught in the sort of joke he would have been only too happy to play on someone else.  The interval wore on, Caruso enjoyed the fresh air at his leisure, and went on with his funny stories.  As call time approached, then, and he re-entered the theater, something happened.  Caruso often told of it, with many gestures and grimaces.

"I nearly die, then.  Inside by the door-man, stands—who do you think?  T.R. Himself!  He stands there, he is hot, he is not in a dress-suit, he smile his fine smile at me, and grasp my hand. 'Mr. Caruso,' he say, 'I hear you are ver' busy in the alley, so I wait for you!' What can I do? 'Mr. Presidente . . .' I stammer, but I can say no more. My heart aches. All the time I am acting foolish in that alley, I could have been talking to T.R.! I think they make jokes with me and what happen? I make the joke on myself. There is not even someone to blame!"

Caruso had his wicked side. Up to the moment he went out to the stage, he would stand in the wings, his valet beside him, spraying out his throat with a huge, foreign-looking atomizer full of gargle preparation. Anything that savored of "high hat" annoyed him, and if, in those moments of waiting, he noticed members of the cast becoming important or "upstage" in manner, Caruso would manœuvre his way across to them, choke "accidentally" in his gargling, and spray quantities of the lotion upon the offender.

"There is nothing like a leetle of the bad-smelling throat wash," he would say, "to take down the too-big height."

No one—except Nordica—took offense at Caruso's antics because, like his cartoons, they pointed drolly to truth and were entirely without malice. In his good moments and in his bad ones, Caruso's every action was founded on an essential bigness. He had faults aplenty. His sheer prankishness often carried him to lengths which could be interpreted in various ways. But never in his life did Caruso do or say a mean thing.

# Chapter VIII

## THE NEWER PERSONALITIES

C ARUSO seems like a bridge between the old days and the new. This is not said in an historical or critical sense. From any such scholarly points of view it is probably inaccurate. There are events which mark a modern operatic era more exactly than the absence of a single singer. But for all that, those who have lived long in the House feel that the old times ended and the new times began with the passing of Caruso. It remains entirely a matter of feeling. Dates have no part in shaping it. Whatever the forces responsible for the things we call "modern," they must have been asserting themselves in a more or less quiet gathering of power, long before any given day called to them to show their faces. There are no prompters' cues for the entrances of trends of thought. Even personalities are of small avail as boundary-posts in fixing such a line of emotional demarcation; for some of the artists who sang with Caruso are still with the company.

The only reasonable explanation for the feeling is that, given the tremendous force of Caruso's personality (of which he was less conscious than any who observed it), a new "fashion" in operatic personalities came into vogue. Hearing this and that about Caruso, the public gradually arrived at some vague notion that the tricks and the pranks and the antics were associated less with the individual and more with the job. Thus, one began to expect from opera "stars" something "different" from what one looked for in painters or writers or doctors—"different," even, from what one had expected of de Reszke or Plançon or Sembrich. At all events, with the decline of the older "stars" (who seldom made "copy" outside the pages of musical criticism), and especially with the passing of Caruso, a new type of operatic personality came to be desired.

In the old days, it was easy to talk about the artists. Printed accounts of eminent musicians stressed those qualities which made them eminent; which set them apart from the rank-and-file citizen who, whether through lack of talent, magnetism, effort, or sheer good luck, seldom rises to eminence in any field. Articles may be unearthed in the magazines of thirty-odd years ago— popular magazines, too—in which an artist is permitted to speak seriously of his work, his training, his intensive study, his conflicts of spirit, the ways in which he penetrates to the deepest meaning of his parts. An interesting series of such a nature appeared under the name of a then-young journalist who ranks to-day as perhaps the most sensitive literary artist this country has yet produced. The name is that of Willa Cather. But all that has been changed.

It would seem that the public no longer desires a musician (who must work for eminence at every step, if he hopes to survive at all) to identify himself openly with the very qualities which make him artistically acceptable. He must give no evidence of his moments of torment. He must conceal the fact that he works over a scene or an aria or a trill weary hours at a time. He must be "smart." He must be "dramatic." He must go to many parties and become their life. In short, he must be a "regular guy," exploited in terms of those traits which will grapple him closest to "the man in the street," quite regardless, apparently, of the fact that if he *were* like "the man in the street," he would not be a musical celebrity.  Recently, an editor refused to print a story about one of the artists' ideas on costuming.

"*That* wouldn't interest the public," he explained. "But let him get into a fight at some night club, and I'll send a man over to write it up.  *You* know—something *human.*"

The human communicativeness which Gatti stressed, has been asked to give proof of its existence in a series of "stunts."  It is a source of satisfaction to report that most of the singers—and all of the artists—look with a sort of thoughtful wonder upon the newer demands made of them, preferring, in the end, to cling to the worthier standards.  But again, it all depends upon the point of view.

Because Caruso gave satisfaction to both points of view, spontaneously unstudied in his "stunts" and severely mindful of his art, he stands as the bridge between the two periods of public receptiveness.  Yet accepting such a division, it is difficult to begin the "new days" with Caruso's death, for many of his co-workers, who began their careers under the standards of an older day, are still active among us; and those who are no longer active are familiar, at least, through personal acquaintanceship rather than remembered tradition.  They belong to the newer personalities as much as to the older ones.

When new artists come into the company, their first rehearsal brings most of the House staff to the back of

the orchestra rail, to observe, all unseen in the dark
auditorium, the accounting they give of themselves.
House people have very definite opinions of the newcomers' abilities long before the critics begin to exert
themselves upon them. Early in the first season of
Gatti's directorship, a new Italian conductor began rehearsing *Butterfly*. The usual group stood there at the
back of the House to listen and, familiar as they were
with the score, the new conductor had not got through
the First Act before they realized that they were hearing this music for the first time. Thus did Arturo
Toscanini make himself known.

Toscanini's methods of conducting without score and
heaping fiery abuse upon the men for the least mistake,
are history to-day, but they were new then and they
made a sensation. Never had there been anything like
that. The men of the orchestra did not know quite
what to do about him. One day, the rehearsal gave
some trouble, and the conductor's expressions of
opinion flew with more than ordinary fury. Presently
the men grew resentful. They laid down their bows
and their instruments and refused to go on with the
work. Some of them even threatened to go to Mr.
Gatti about it. There was considerable uneasiness on
both sides, and finally Toscanini left the orchestra pit.
He came back at last, and Mr. Gatti came with him.
In his dry, dignified way, Gatti spoke to the men. Toscanini had told him all about the unpleasantness, and
he wanted to know if the men would go back to work
if an apology were forthcoming. The men said they
would.

"Then," said Gatti, "I am authorized to ask you to
accept the Maestro's sincere apology."

The men cheered. It seemed a wonderful thing for Toscanini to have "told on himself." The rehearsal went forward with zeal, and from that day on, there wasn't a man who wouldn't willingly have cut off his right arm for Toscanini. That was the only time that the Maestro ever gave an apology for or an explanation of his actions.

The men were conscious of the fact that something special was afoot when Toscanini wielded the baton. There was always something immensely impressive about the man. Quiet, dignified, and scholarly in manner, he had the art of making other people feel important. Those who met him for the first time came away with the surprised discovery that he hadn't said a word about himself. He made them talk, gave the impression that he was far more interested in them than they could possibly be in him.

Toscanini's prodigious memory once led to an incident that was amusing at the time, but which ultimately opened the doors upon a new conception of opera. In the old days, the long works, and especially those of Wagner, were given with cuts so that the performance might fit into the normal limits of theater time. Toscanini held to the idea of giving the music exactly as it was written. When he began rehearsing these longer scores, he conducted them as he knew them while the men played the notes before them. When the cut passages came due, Toscanini suddenly heard something entirely different from what he expected. He stopped, rapped for silence, and began all over again. Again the same queer mistake! Toscanini was furious.

"But you do not play your parts!" he cried.

"But we do!" the men objected.

After much bewilderment then, the truth came to light. The notes Toscanini wanted had been struck out of the men's parts.

"True, true," he said. "You play what is written—only it is not what the composer wrote. Let us open up those cuts, now, and hear the music as the composer intended it to be."

To-day, the uncut performances of Wagner are the chief attraction of the repertory.

In those days, the fad that took the place of the cross-word puzzle was the "Bughouse" puzzle. This was a little glass-covered box marked off into compartments, with bits of lead that had to be fitted into these spaces beneath the glass, entirely by external manipulation. It was very popular and very tricky, and derived its name, no doubt, from the fact that the manipulator could easily go crazy trying to piece it together. Gerber had one of the things, and one day he showed it to Toscanini.

"Look, Maestro, you've had a lot of experience piecing scores together. See what you can make of this."

Toscanini took the puzzle and began jiggling it. They were standing in the Press Office, off the Thirty-ninth Street lobby, at about eleven in the morning, just when the day's busiest work begins. Toscanini leaned on the desk and studied the puzzle. Gerber watched him for a while and then he was called away. Duties piled up, puzzles (which bore no relation to House routine) were whisked from his mind, and it was well into the afternoon before he chanced to pass through the lobby again. There was Toscanini, still leaning on the desk, still jiggling the puzzle in his sensitive fingers, and concentrating his keen glance upon it as though nothing else in the world mattered. Possibly nothing else did; here was something that held his attention.

"Look," he called in delight as Gerber entered the room, "you are just in time. I've got this thing at last!"

And sure enough, the bits of lead fitted perfectly into their grooves. Toscanini had stood there the better part of the day, neglecting his lunch and the hundred calls upon his time. But he had done what he set out to do. The fact that it was only a silly puzzle didn't enter the question at all.

One of the sincerest tributes to Edward Johnson's art was expressed without a thought to musical values. As a matter of fact, every rôle which Johnson assumed came to bear the imprint of his personal cachet; so much so that now, since administrative duties have claimed him, it is difficult to present the operas which were so definitely "his." One night, as Johnson was leaving the stage after a performance, a group of friends descended upon him, congratulating him warmly upon his splendid outpouring of tone, the subtle poetry of his portrayal. Off in a corner of the wings, one of the ballet-girls overheard the praise.

"Voice and poetry," she observed, "may be all very fine, I'm sure, but Heavens! Didn't anybody notice his *legs?* That man should've been a *dancer!*"

The eminent Friedrich Schorr is an artist who seems congenitally incapable of publicizing himself. He comes, he works, he ranks as the foremost of Wagnerian baritones, and has not a word to say of himself. One night, during the season of 1935, Schorr came in to sing *Wotan*, in *Die Walkuere*, with the air of a pleasant secret upon him. There were those who demanded to know what was making him so especially cheerful, but Schorr only laughed and went on to his room. A few days later, then, Gerber met him in the House and this time Schorr could contain himself no more.

"You remember that night of *Walkuere*, when you asked what tickled me so? Well, it was my two hundredth performance of *Wotan*. I didn't say anything because I didn't want any fuss. I thought no one knew about it but myself. But Johnson knew! Goodness only knows how he dug it out, but he came to my room after the Second Act and gave me a gold pocket-knife, engraved for the occasion. We had a long talk, he and I together, and—well, I can't tell you how it touched and delighted me!"

Geraldine Farrar left behind her the impression of independent courage. Whatever she did was motivated by a driving desire to accomplish something according to her own ideas of fitness. If the results were sometimes spectacular, that quality was quite accidental, and made very little difference to Farrar herself. With her, the important thing was to see the project through according to her plans, which were always sincerely and thoroughly worked out—another instance of a naturally magnetic personality that "made copy" without in any way resorting to deliberate effects. Miss Farrar's realistic stage portrayals often called forth comment, notably when one of her colleagues demanded medical attention after the "fight" scene in *Carmen*. And such an event, of course, could not fail

to make spectacular news. But to Farrar herself, her
deportment was the only logical result of her honest
conception of *Carmen*. At no point did she seek the
sort of "differentness" that is assumed merely for the
sake of being "different." The same driving desire to
carry through her own ideas sometimes resulted to her
disadvantage. In one of her performances of *Tosca*,
Farrar's wig caught fire from a lighted lamp. In
a moment, the front of the artificial hair was burn-
ing. The prompter, down in his box, reached for a
fire-extinguisher and made to throw it to her, but Farrar signed to him not to do it. A modern fire-
extinguisher, she explained later, had no place in the
development of *Tosca*. Turning her back to the audience in the "big scene" she had to herself, she invented
completely new stage business, clutched at her hair as
though in a gesture of dismay, and beat out the fire
with her hands. The mishap was righted so quickly
that only those sitting close to the stage were aware of
anything wrong. Painful injuries resulted, but not
for an instant did Farrar lose track of the way she had
planned that scene to go.

It is a curious circumstance that, for all the striving
after "differentness" and "glamour," the genuine article
is frequently misinterpreted. When Miss Farrar
announced her retirement from operatic activity, voices
were heard to brand the news as a gigantic "stunt." It
seemed inconceivable that the most colorful figure at
the Opera should withdraw at the very zenith of her
popularity, for no other reason than that she had arrived at the age where many another just begins to
find herself. "How soon," asked the doubters, "before
she comes back?" At a perspective distance of a decade

and a half, we know that Farrar did not come back; that what looked like a "stunt" was another instance of her working out a plan according to her own ideas.

Around 1931, Rose Heylbut was sent as representative of a national magazine to approach Miss Farrar on the subject of a "ghost" story. A "ghost" story is nothing more spectral than the result of that singular cooperation between the owner of a glamorous name and a professional writer, whereby the writer produces an article and the celebrity signs it. Miss Farrar's name was wanted for one of a series of such stories, and the reporter's instructions were to get the use of it, in exchange for publicity value if possible; otherwise to work up to the offer of a considerable sum of money.

Miss Farrar was at her country estate at the time, and arranged for the visit there, writing minute directions for trains and station changes in her own bold hand. After a half-hour of pleasant preliminaries, the reason for the visit was broached, and Miss Farrar's blue eyes grew enormous.

"But I never give my name to anything like that!"

At last the matter of the considerable sum of money was brought up. Farrar laughed.

"I don't mean that the *terms* are wrong. Simply, I don't earn my money that way. I won't put my name to anything I haven't created myself." Then, after a moment, "I'll tell you what I will do, if you wish it. I'll give you the story and you can print it 'By Geraldine Farrar, As Told to Rose Heylbut.' And of course I take no pay."

Those were the only terms she would consider.

The magazine did not favor "As Told To" collaborations; had never used them and was loath to make a beginning. Still, they did want Geraldine Farrar to appear in the list of contributors. There was an exchange of telegrams. In the end, Miss Farrar won her point. Her story appeared last in the series of six— the only one with the "As Told To" addition.

The sense of buffoonery that has established Leo Slezak as the "hit" of certain current Viennese motion-pictures, was already well developed when he sang classic tenor rôles with the Metropolitan Opera. In those days, of course, it had to be kept within bounds, at least as far as the audience was concerned. It is pleasant to see Slezak building a second career from the wealth of native material that he used to have to hold in check. Slezak's tricks were entirely vocal. He never *did* anything spectacular, but how he would chatter! He spoke poor English and became utterly fascinated by American slang. The result had to be heard to be properly grasped. After assiduous study of the comic strips, Slezak would hail the House errand-boy:

"Hello, sugar beauty! Tell me, honey love, iss the *Aida* rehearsal going to be holded on the roof-stage, lovey bunch, dear-ling?"

The expression "nuts" is not so new at all. Twenty-five years ago, smartness of that kind was expressed through the word "peanuts." The modern term may enjoy a wider connotation as to nut variety, but it is not startling in its novelty. "Peanuts" came to be Slezak's favorite expression. He used it in and out of season, inscribed it upon photographs he signed, and treated it, both vocally and in writing, as though it

were spelled "pienatz." His nonsensical chatter, accompanied by the same grimaces and snortings which
are earning him attention to-day, would continue uninterrupted through rehearsals, in the wings, and up to
the moment when the giant tenor made his impressive
entrance upon the stage . . . "dear-ling, honey love,
pienatz!"

Emmy Destinn was a true Bohemian, by temperament as well as by nationality—Bohemian in the best
sense of the word. She was impulsive, simple-hearted,
and generous. Destinn's generosity was of a special
sort. She gave wonderful parties, but seldom invited
the company's "stars." Her guests were the "little
people"; choristers, secondary singers, assistant conductors, prompters, orchestral players—men and women who are serious and studied artists, but who, for
one cause or another, have failed of celebrity, and are
therefore seldom included in the more imposing gather-
ings. Destinn judged them on their personal merits,
felt at home with them, and made them feel completely
at home under her hospitable roof. An excellent cook
herself, she planned her dinners according to Bohemian
fashion, whereby the courses are not only numerous but
manifold—several kinds of fish, a variety of fowl, half
a dozen different meats, a pastrycook's exhibit of
sweets. Besides the fine food, there would be at each
guest's plate a souvenir of practical value—warm
gloves of superior make, comfortable mufflers from the
finest haberdasher's, things that no one else would have
thought of buying for the "little people." Destinn enjoyed these parties even more than did her guests.

Frieda Hempel, like Caruso, required the better part of a season to come into her own with the New York public. The sea trip over had upset her, she sang too soon after it, and made her first few appearances as just another interesting soprano. Then, as she grew more acclimated, it became evident that here was an artist of the calibre of Sembrich. Hempel had an indefinable charm, built of extreme good nature, the suave delicacy that inspires just the right thing at just the right moment, and her own Saxon *"Gemuetlichkeit."* In those days, the company's tours—never too comfortable a campaign, of long train trips and short bivouackings in hotels—were enlivened by Hempel's hearty charm. Her drawing-room on the train came to be the meeting place for the entire troupe. After tramping miles of corridors, and staring out upon hundreds of whirling fields, the artists would come to a halt outside Hempel's door, and be sure of finding the right mood just inside. There was conversation, chess games, card games, and impromptu choruses of old German folk and student songs, in which everyone joined in. A record of *Ach, du lieber Augustin,* as it was sung on those tours by Hempel, Homer, Ober, Gadski, Caruso, and half a dozen more, would have made a sensation. At the small station stops, Hempel would lead the group out to the platform, there to entertain the wide-eyed country folk with further outpourings. But it was the colored people throughout the South who especially interested her. Often she would urge them to sing their melodies for her—negro spirituals had not yet come into "fashion"—repeating the plaintive strains after them.

Louise Homer was a charming artist who brought the greatest integrity and fidelity to her work, without ever seeming actually to belong to the world of the theater. She was essentially the housewife and mother, and her first interests belonged to her husband and children. Mrs. Homer—she preferred being called *Mrs.* to *Madame*—once said that the most difficult part she played was that of the *Witch* in *Haensel und Gretel.*

"Not that the rôle is difficult in itself," she explained; "*Brangaene, Ortrud,* or *Orfeo* are much harder. It's the emotional strain after!"

Then it developed that this children's opera was the only one which her own children were then permitted to attend, and the dreadful aspect and deportment of their mother upset them. The ultimate casting of the *Witch* into the stove—at which all the other children in the audience screamed their delight—reduced them to such a state of wretchedness, that it took days after the performance to bring back normal calm to the Homer nursery.

Lucrezia Bori, consummate artist and able executive, brought distinction to a name which her father requested her to assume in order to avoid carrying to the stage one of the oldest and proudest names of Latin aristocracy. Her real name is Borgia, and she is directly descended from Lucrezia Borgia. Though forbidden to bring the Borgia name to the stage, she brought there the essence of aristocracy, in her work as well as her person. Convent bred and carefully reared, Miss Bori's private thoughts were enflamed by the stage ever since the days when she "played opera" with her dolls. When she was ready for her operatic début,

as *Micaela* in *Carmen,* she lacked the means with which
to buy a professionally designed costume, and made
one herself, during what leisure hours she had in a
crowded routine of rehearsing, practising, and coaching. Established as one of the great singing-actresses
of the world, she clung to that simple costume, and used
it in the last performance of *Micaela* she gave, because
of the associations it brought her. At the height of
her powers, Miss Bori became stricken with a throat
ailment that left her voiceless, and it seemed that the
career which had progressed so auspiciously had been
suddenly snuffed out. Dauntless of spirit, she retired
to her native Spain, and began to build a new life for
herself from her memories, her books, and the simple
pleasures of country life. While out on mule-back one
day, she was thrown by the animal, and fell with a jolt
upon a stony mountain road. After she recovered from
the shock of that jolt, she found that her voice had returned. It is not often that the waywardness of a mule
makes musical history.

Artur Bodanzky gives forth from the conductor's
chair precisely what Caruso gave forth from the stage.
After a performance of *Tristan,* Bodanzky is as near
exhaustion as so vigorous an energy as his can be. His
first need is for a breath of fresh air, and he usually
takes it outside the stage-door, playing with his little
dog, which is always sent along in the car to call for
him.

Bodanzky gives all to his work—and requires all
from his co-workers. He is just, understanding, and
kindly, but has no patience with stupid mistakes. Once
his ire is aroused by unintelligent slips and errors, his

verbal ferocity can touch Jovian heights.   Bodanzky
once summed up his creed;

"I know how to deal with a mean man, and I can
handle a bad man—but Heaven preserve me from a
stupid one!"

When Bodanzky conducts, the orchestra feels the
same sure strength that came from Toscanini.   The
men respect him for his erudition, his artistic integrity,
and his complete and compelling sincerity.   They are
on their mettle to give him their best.   For all his professional discipline, though, once he is safely removed
from the dangers of musical stupidity, Bodanzky is
genial, impulsive, zestful, possessed of trigger-quick wit
and ready, vital humor—a typical son of Vienna.
Bodanzky got his professional start in musical comedy,
ranking as the youngest, the most popular, and the best
salaried conductor of operette in the Danube capital.
He was regarded as definitely "queer" when he gave
up his coveted position to cast in his lot with a strug-
gling and insecurely financed grand opera venture in
Germany, for the sole reason that he wanted to devote himself to serious art.   On his becoming the Chief
Musical Director of the Ducal Theater of Baden, however, the reputation for "queerness" departed.

During the days of prohibition, Bodanzky was
frankly homesick for the delights of good beer.   In
those days, Gerber's "home brew" had earned what
might be termed stellar reputation in the House.
Bodanzky heard of it, sampled it, and declared that he
must cultivate its acquaintance further.   Whereupon
an agreement was entered into.   On the nights that
Bodanzky conducted, Gerber would regularly have as
many bottles of beer as there were acts in the opera,

cooling outside the window of his fifth floor office. The
moment the act was done, Bodanzky would rush upstairs, and take his place at the long pay-roll table.
Then the beer would be tested for temperature, poured
at just the right speed, allowed to settle to the orthodox
degree of frothiness, and the intermission became a
period of relaxation and nostalgic savor for the tense
conductor. As call time drew near for the next act,
Bodanzky would compare his watch with Gerber's.

"The Second Act ends at nine-forty-one—look for
me by nine-forty-three at the latest!"

The business of broadcasting has had no appreciable
effect on House life—from the viewpoint of the radio
engineers there is a different story to tell—but once, at
least, this modern mechanical miracle caused something
approaching a sensation. Lawrence Tibbett was singing *Amonasro* in *Aida* on the same night that he was
scheduled to broadcast a non-operatic program from
the studios of one of the great networks. Since
*Amonasro* does not appear until the middle of the
Second Act, there was time enough to fulfill both engagements; the only problem was the difficulty of getting back to the House from the studio in time to
apply *Amonasro's* exacting make-up. The rôle of
the Ethiopian King requires few garments beside a
leopard's pelt, but, to compensate for that, it needs a
generous application of brown paint and glittering
decorations to the regions where a leopard's pelt does
not reach. Furthermore, Tibbett is a tall man. He
solved the problem by coming down early to the House
and making up before he went on to the broadcast.
Thus did the sensation come into being.

At a little before eight o'clock, into the midst of the densest theater crowds, there strode from the Opera House doors a singular apparition, brown of face and extremities, appalling of expression, and wearing a Bond Street top coat, a woolly gray wig, thonged sandals, a barbaric crown, ear-rings, and an altogether interesting variety of tiger-tooth necklaces. People stared. People gasped. People followed the apparition's waiting motor car. A uniformed policeman had to be taken along, to effect an unimpeded passage through traffic; yet despite this reassuring presence on the front seat (which was doubtless misunderstood to signify the arrest of an entirely new type of criminal), every traffic stop brought its own little harvest of startled stares, pointing fingers, and bewildered screams. But the baritone's two musical appointments were faithfully kept.

If radio has failed to alter the tenor of House life, another modern development affected it materially. That was the depression. Many of the artists who had been most prosperous were suddenly reduced to the point where they had nothing to fall back upon for the next season's living expenses, except that delicate little mechanism inside their throats, and the business acumen of their managers. Those who took their losses with philosophy (and who found engagements) made a fresh start and presently worked their way back into the happy state of prosperous existence. But there were those who fell to brooding, found their voices affected as a consequence of their mental attitude, and were at last completely sucked under by the whirlings of that vicious circle in which they could not sing while they worried about financial insecurity, and could not

become financially secure until they were once more
able to sing.  Miserable stories came out which never
reached the public's ears, and which are better left un-
told.  Two depression case-histories, though, can safely
be given.

It sometimes happens that an opera singer is
genuinely thrifty, and such a phenomenon adorned the
House.  Though not a first "star," this gentleman
earned a most adequate salary, and saved the largest
part of it.  He lived frugally, avoided taxi-cabs,
patronized only the more moderate restaurants, bought
one cigar at a time, budgeted his expenses down to the
last postage stamp, and bought his way, by gradual
payments, into one of the government annuities of
France.  His dream was to retire one day and live
comfortably, if modestly, on his savings.  Then he was
invited to sing in Chicago.  There he listened to the
miraculous tales of quick profits from quick speculative
turn-overs, and found himself the butt of ridicule, for
his participation in anything so meager and cautious as
a government annuity plan.  In time, the virus did its
work.  The gentleman could not get back the money
he had already invested, of course, but he determined
to send no more abroad, thus reducing the amount of
his annuity policy.  He, too, began trafficking in
utilities and industrials and all of their bright brethren.
Then came October of 1929.  The gentleman's fine
profits were swept away to the land of non-existing
things, where they were joined by all the taxi-cabs and
Havana cigars he had been denying himself.  Further,
the Chicago Opera closed its doors.  From this point
on, the story loses its moral tone.  The gentleman was
not reduced to impoverished repentance.  There still

remained that scorned little annuity in France.  He is living upon it to-day—and its current purchasing value makes his existence quite as comfortable as it would have been had he continued his investments towards a larger premium yield!

The other case is that of an artist who bought himself into an annuity, the terms of which contracted for payment only so long as he was without employment. The result is that, for fear of losing the value of the funds he has already invested, he dares not accept an engagement.  Thus, he lives comfortably enough—except for the knowledge that his career is over.

Another modern development which caused some dismay in the House is advertising.  A large tobacco enterprise came to one of the minor workers with a "proposition."  He was to get statements from the various artists as to the brand of cigarettes they either used or served, and whenever there was a happy coincidence between the singer's choice and the company's output, the investigator was to be rewarded.  It proved to be interesting and fruitful research.  The desired brand was named often enough for the investigator to add up a total number of rewards that exceeded six months' salary.  The work was completed at last, the results handed in, and the reward bestowed.  Presently, then, the artists were startled by the appearance of entirely authentic statements to the effect that Signor X . . . and Madame Y . . . used Summer Breeze Cigarettes exclusively, because they benefit the vocal cords.

But to return to personalities.  The amazing Madame Flagstad is little publicized; her tastes and habits are unbelievably simple; there is about her an old-world quaintness which, according to the best standards of modern salesmanship, should wilt outright before the methods of Hollywood. And yet she has accomplished what few others have been able to do. In her person, she has revived opera interest; without "stunts" she has captured the imagination of the American public. It roots back to the qualities that made history in the old days. She is absorbed, not in Kirsten Flagstad, but in building the finest art that effort can produce. The things that happen to Kirsten Flagstad as a result, be-wilder her. One of the choice blooms at the Flower Show was named in her honor, and Flagstad objected:

"But you can't do that," she said, "it wouldn't be sensible. In my country, they name flowers only after important people!"

Flagstad's present eminence comes somewhat in the nature of a second career. Upon her marriage some years ago, she retired from her operatic activities in Norway, which were found to be entirely worthy but not world-rocking. An emergency call to fill in for a soprano who had become indisposed at the last moment, brought her once more into contact with professional duties, and her coming to New York was largely an accident. She tells one frankly that she looks forward to retiring again to the privacy of home life, home chores, and home companionship. Cordial and kindly of manner, Flagstad is not at all the party type of "good mixer." She enjoys playing solitaire, reading, looking into shop windows, drinking sodas at drug-store fountains, talking over the details of home and business with her husband, and knitting dresses for her young daughter. She rehearses entirely in full voice, sparing herself no effort and sending out her magnificent tones at a first piano rehearsal with exactly the same fervor and intensity as though a full House were listening to her. She rehearses more than company assignments require, and then thanks the conductors for taking so much "trouble" with her. During those parts of the opera when she is not needed on the stage, Flagstad seldom goes to her dressing-room to rest. Instead, she sits on a battered old piano-stool in the wings, sipping a cup of warm tea, and watching the work of the others in the cast. This, she tells one, keeps her in close touch with the spirit and pace of the opera.

Richard Crooks, one of the best beloved of the operatic forces, lacks nothing of the alertness and efficiency of the modern day, and harks back in his art to the dignified traditions of the Golden Age of song. His popularity roots into the personality of the man as much as in the eminence of his art. A professional press-agent once told Crooks that there was no hope of doing anything for him—he was entirely too normal, too sane, too typically American ever to make "good copy." Precisely these traits cause him to stand out. Crooks is unspoilable. The glamour of success after the hardest kind of beginnings has been unable to swerve him from his own wholesome standards of fitness. His one dread is lest the theatrical paraphernalia of wigs and trappings make him look "like a sissy." Yet his loathing of the "sissified" is never expressed through boisterousness.

A group of newspaper people, one woman among them, came to Crooks' dressing-room one night, and the lot of them got to joking. One man—the representative of a large daily, who was in a position to do much towards inclining popular opinion for or against a public singer—told a story that was rather off-color. Some of the men laughed; others held back to see how Crooks would match the tale. Crooks didn't seem to have heard it. Pointedly, he turned to his dresser:

"Well, Angelo, how's that kid of yours? Did he get over his grippe in time to be promoted at school?"

There was a moment of silence. When the joking was resumed, there was a conspicuous absence of off-color stories.

Crossing the stage on his way to rehearsals, Crooks often stops to give the scene-shifters a hand with the back-drops. At his first performance each season, there usually occurs a demonstration comparable only to the things that Caruso used to inspire. The entire stage-crew troops up to his dressing-room, to decorate the place with toys, mottoes, vegetables, all manner of amusing things, just to please him. On one of these occasions, a property man had the inspiration to festoon the room with garlic, and the idea was so well received, that the man was encouraged to let his fancy roam to even more spectacular levels, and ended by hiding Crooks' suspenders. Crooks discovered the loss only after the opera was over, took it in excellent good nature, and pieced himself together as best he could for the journey home. (The tenor lives in a small seashore town in New Jersey, because he prefers country life, and commutes to his performances.) The next time he entered his dressing-room, forty pairs of suspenders were hung about there, to greet him.

It is always hazardous to make comparisons between artists. Yet there are those in the House, caring

nothing for such dangers, who associate Crooks with
Jean de Reszke. In his distinction of person, his
artistic zeal, and his consideration for others, this clean-
cut young American shows traits which no one else
combined in quite that degree, except Jean. Crooks
has the same painstaking care for detail.

It is not impossible to see an artist come rushing in
at seven-fifteen to make ready for an eight o'clock curtain, shrieking out for the wig-man, the make-up man,
the dresser all at once, regarding nobody's business but
his own, and getting everyone into a nervous flurry.
Never with Crooks. He is at his dressing-table by six,
and if ever he feels a spasm of foot-light agony, nobody
sees it. Printed statements in the press often refer to
Crooks' magnificent stage appearance. He bestows as
much care on smoothing down his own hair which does
not show under the wig, as he does on his vocalizings.
It is the all-absorbing enthusiasm which Crooks brings
to the least detail of his work, that comes through in his
performances.

One of this genial tenor's greatest treasures is the
vest which he wears in *Manon* and which formerly belonged to Caruso. It has special associations for him.
When Crooks first came to New York for serious
study, he lived in a furnished room with four other
boys from his native Trenton, used the eighty dollars a
month that he earned as clerk for the Aetna Insurance
Company to pay for singing lessons at twenty dollars
each, ate only when financially convenient, and took his
amusement standing up in the Metropolitan Balcony
to marvel at Caruso. An interesting subject for
an idle hour is speculation upon the potentialities of
the Opera's standees. Caruso's performance of *Des*

*Grieux* in *Manon* afforded Crooks especial delight. He assures one that, in those days, he looked upon a person who sang at the Metropolitan as being formed from special clay; not at all the ordinary human variety. Also, he assures one that he has changed his opinion since. To-day, *Des Grieux* is one of his own most successful rôles, and he never adjusts the Caruso vest without making a mental journey back to the boy in the standees' enclosure of the Balcony, whose enthusiasms were fortified by a supper of crackers and milk. Crooks likes to talk about those lean years of his.

He often lunches at a little Italian restaurant, where the same waiter always serves him. The papers announced that Crooks was to sing certain Italian arias at one of the Sunday night concerts, and the waiter became ecstatic. Crooks gave the man a pair of tickets. A day or so later, when he returned to the restaurant, he found the waiter utterly disconsolate. Extra work had come up, his employer had refused to give him the promised evening off, and he had not been able to attend the concert. He had missed both Crooks and the Italian arias.

"We can fix that," said Crooks.

Whereupon he left his table, conducted the waiter into the little restaurant's back room, and repeated the program for him alone.

Crooks is at his best when he takes a group of men down to his fishing shack on Barnegat Bay. There he relaxes in a pair of old khaki trousers, and an ancient flannel shirt with the sleeves hacked out. He makes up the bunks for his guests, washes the dishes, and gives thought to no art save that of casting. And, like as not, eleven-year-old Dick Junior is a member of the party. It tells much about a man when his "stag parties" include his little son.

Limitations of space make it impossible even to touch upon the traits or habits or doings of all the personalities who have shed, and are shedding, brightness upon House life. No one who has ever worked there has failed to leave some impression or other. But those who have been mentioned will induce a measure of sympathy, it is hoped, with the belief current in the House that the people make the glamour.

*Part Three*

THE "FACTORY"

CHAPTER IX

SETTING THE SCENE

**1.**

THERE is an interesting exchange of curiosity constantly flowing across the footlights, between the active group on one side and the audience-group on the other. These two unite to make the performances possible at all, and each maintains a wholesome interest as to "how the wheels go 'round" in the opposite camp. The layman out front likes to know what goes on behind the curtain; what life is like in the dressing-rooms; how the "show" is prepared; what happens when a dozen different "stars" all begin to shine at each other simultaneously. On the other hand, the House people often wonder whether those out front, who come solely to be entertained by some three hours of singing and acting, realize the amount of sheer business and working energy that must be delivered before that entertainment can come off; the number of people engaged in contributory jobs of one kind or another; the hours of work they put in; what they do, and how they do it.

The normal Metropolitan performance schedule includes five regular subscription performances a week, one popularly priced subscription series on Saturday nights, and one Sunday night concert. When there are Tuesday night performances in Brooklyn, Philadelphia, or Hartford; and when special non-subscription performances are given at matinées, the weekly total may amount to ten. Ten units of sheer entertainment value which, through the conversion medium of the Box-Office, become the means of providing labor outlets and livelihood for more than five hundred and fifty regular workers in the "factory" backstage. Perhaps half of these are engaged in the visible, familiar aspects of grand opera. The other half punch time-clocks; sit at typewriters or adding machines or sewing machines or paint frames; wield dusters or scrub-buckets or hammers or color palettes or dye-baths or night-sticks; carry luggage or properties or scenery; work out travel schedules; report that "all's well" between midnight and morning; prepare pay-rolls and income tax reports; copy scores; and build the Opera House into one of the few business enterprises where activity goes on for twenty-four hours a day, every day.

The opera differs from the ordinary theater in that it is a repertory enterprise, involving a complete change of cast, bill, and equipment for each consecutive performance. This, in its turn, calls for fresh preparations by way of rehearsing, setting, lighting, and costuming, for every opera given. Further, opera is conceived along larger lines, and "larger," in this sense, implies more than comparative stage footage. Operatic bills are composed almost entirely of "standard" works, in the presentation of which there must be observed a certain fidelity to tradition. The most elaborate theatrical production can be settled in a series of conferences between the playwright, the producer, and the scenic artist, whose chief task is to present a clear picture of the thing they have originated themselves and concerning which there may be criticism, certainly, but no comparison. The least operatic production calls for a

faithful and stylistically accurate reproduction of a
scene and an atmosphere created anywhere from thirty
to two hundred years ago, plus a watchful glance towards inevitable comparisons with the methods of Paris,
London, Vienna, Rome. *Meistersinger, Aida, Norma,
Samson et Dalila* cannot be mounted in quite the same
way as "Act Three—A Library."

The preparation for a single performance of opera is
a sort of House-That-Jack-Built activity that centers
about the great stage. The Metropolitan Opera House
stage measures one-hundred feet from left to right, and
seventy-eight feet from the rear wall to the footlight
line; extends in length from Thirty-ninth to Fortieth
Streets; is approached by sound-proofed entrances
from both sides; and can be crossed while the performance is in progress by means of a narrow, steam-pipe-
lined corridor at the extreme rear. The musical work
that is chosen, the talents of the singers and orchestral
musicians who rehearse and perform it, the costumes
that are repaired and pressed and carried to the various
dressing-rooms, the properties that are assembled and
overhauled, the scenery that is carted in from the storehouses and touched up by painters and carpenters, the
scenic blue-prints that are posted in the wings for each
set of each scene of each opera, the lighting that is
plotted hours in advance of the performance on the master switch-board under the prompter's box, are all
aimed at the proportions of, and the effects producible
from, the stage. All of these tasks, which can be told
off but singly (owing to that deficiency of language
which precludes the fugue form of construction) are
carried on simultaneously, together with a great deal of

administrative and sanitary routine. But the main thing is always the stage.

The best time to begin an inspection of the stage (although the stage crews might hold a different opinion as to the desirability of such a choice) is the morning of a two bill day. Let us suppose that *Tristan und Isolde* is being given as a special matinée at one-forty-five, and *Aida* in the regular subscription performance at eight-fifteen.

There is a vast blank stage and it must be dressed. Its equipment involves the preparation and carting of the scenery; the setting of the stage; the packing of used sets while the performance is in progress; the striking (or dismantling) of the stage; the setting of the new scene; the clearing away of the scenery at the end of the opera; and the recarting of the used sets by the night crew. These steps require the services of forty-five men —six carpenters, nine men in the storehouse gang, nineteen regular stage-hands, and eleven in the night crew. These are permanent House employes; more help may be taken on when needed. All of them are skilled, experienced workers, accustomed to reading plans, making repairs, following instructions, and rising to any emergencies (all within scheduled time limits), with military precision.

The "snake," or long, narrow play-bill of the week's repertory, is posted in each of the four storehouses. The storehouse crew has the stage sets ready to be carted out the day before the performance for which they are needed. The storing of the scenery calls for ingenious planning. The sets must be grouped, as far as possible, as inventoried operatic units; further, ordinary storehouse expediency must be observed so that the massive

pieces (*Isolde's* ship, the throne platforms for *Aida* and
*Tannhaeuser,* and the bridge for *Carmen,* etc.) are
ranged behind the smaller pieces, regardless of opera
classifications; and all of the sets must be arranged in
such positions that they may be withdrawn from storage
at a day's notice and with enough space for last night's
sets to be brought in and to-morrow's to be carted out at
the same time.

The carting routine, in charge of the night crew, is
arranged so that the same trucks which carry the used
sets from the House directly after the performance,
bring in the scenery for the next day's opera. Each
piece is stamped on the back of the canvas with the name
of the opera and the number of the scene and act in
which it is used, together with abbreviated indications
of the place it occupies in the ground plan. "Tannhaeuser, Act I, Scene II, RH" tells the stage worker a
complete story, involving the right side of the set. The
whole array of back-drops, flying scenery, set pieces,
and massive properties is loaded into the House
through the great hatchway on Seventh Avenue (which
opens directly from the rear of the stage into the street,
thus obviating the need of turning corners and mounting stairs), and is housed about the back of the stage
overnight, until the day crew of scene shifters comes in,
the next morning, to sort the pieces, and dress the stage
for its next activities, whether these be a rehearsal or a
public performance. The mass of material is subjected
to the most careful checking and re-checking by the
Head of the storehouse that sends it, the Head of the
night gang that delivers it, and the Master Mechanic,
who receives it on the stage.

The first step in the actual setting is to prepare the

stage itself. The blue-print for the scene is posted, and the floor is marked off, according to the architect's measurements on that plan, so that each piece may be placed exactly where it belongs, with a maximum of accuracy and a minimum of "fitting." Certain scenes—especially "indoor" sets—have individual floor-cloths, permanently marked to accommodate the standing scenery; but for most of the sets, the floor of the stage is freshly marked off in chalk. When the scenery is assembled and the stage ready for its reception, the setting begins.

This work is done according to strict schedule, and is accurately timed. The Master Mechanic stands to the front of the stage, watch in hand, giving the signals for the adjustment of the various pieces, and supervising progress. Each man is assigned to his own place, knows just where he must begin and what he must do. The men wait for the signal and then fall to work on the back-drops, which are unrolled, fastened to their frames, and raised into place. It takes just so many minutes. The Master Mechanic, watching his time-piece and directing the work, counts the requisite time and then gives the signals for the next pieces—the "flies," the sets, the big equipment, working always from the larger units to the smaller ones. The timing is infallible, as it must be, for the exact calculation of between-act intermissions and the end of the performance. The programs permanently filed by the Administrative Department, are marked with the time at which each act ends. Such records are valuable to the staff in calculating production plans, to the singers who may have further calls on their time, and to the patrons who wish to order their motorcars to call for them.

At setting time, the stage resembles nothing so much

as a freight ship while it is being loaded. There is an incomprehensible scramble of carting, shoving, stowing, unwrapping, unfurling, hammering, shouting, signaling, and pulley-squeaking, and then, suddenly, order prevails. The stage is set. *Isolde's* ship has been put together, moved within the limits assigned it, and stands there, big enough and firm enough and authentic enough in detail to take out upon the Hudson River. The stage crew's immediate work is done, and the time consumed in that particular setting of the stage is marked down among its predecessors, from which it varies by not so much as a second.

When the stage is entirely ready, the signal is given to the stage-directors in the wings, who group the singers in their initial positions on the set. Warning bells are sounded in the dressing-rooms of the ensemble groups, and call-boys make the rounds of the principal artists' rooms. The House lights are darkened, the foot-lights go up, the "ready" signal is flashed to the orchestral players in the pit who stop tuning up their instruments and wait in silence for the conductor to come down, and the performance is on.

The Head of the Stage Department is Frederick Hosli, who is responsible for delivering the stage, perfectly set and equipped for work, to the stage-director and the singers. Hosli entered the House some thirty-six years ago, as errand-boy. He was brought up in the opera neighborhood and had been a school-mate of Gerber's. When Maurice Grau permitted his office-boy the luxury of an assistant, to take care of outside commissions, Gerber suggested his friend Hosli. What recommended Hosli especially was the fact that he owned a bicycle. Because of the rigid economy which Grau

maintained in the matter of extra expenditures, the
errand-boy was allowed no carfare for commissions lying
within the area bounded by Twenty-third Street on the
south, Fifty-ninth Street on the north, Fifth Avenue on
the east, and Eleventh Avenue on the west. No carfare
meant that the errand-boy would have to walk, and this,
in turn, meant a loss of time. But Hosli's bicycle solved
both the problems of economy and speed. For errands
lying beyond the limited area, however, carfare was allowed, and this Hosli was permitted to keep, to cover
wear and tear on his bicycle. It proved altogether a
satisfactory arrangement. It was discovered, in time,
that Hosli had a nice ability for painting, and he was
transferred to the Property Department, whence he
emerged to enter, as ordinary stage hand, the department he now heads.

The work on the stage is rigorously departmentalized.
The stage crew proper is occupied exclusively with the
setting of scenery. Repair work or construction jobs
(such as the putting together of the larger pieces, like
*Isolde's* ship) are in the hands of the carpenters; while
the adjustment and wiring of lighting fixtures is left to
the electricians. In some of the scenes (as, for instance,
the First Act of *Traviata,* where there are the regular
sets to be placed, steps to be nailed together, and table
lamps to be wired), all three groups of workmen are
busy at the same time.

The moment that the curtains close, and while the
singers are still bowing their acknowledgement of the
applause, the stage crew begins striking the scene and
setting up for the next one. Each man is assigned to
his particular post, exactly as mates on shipboard are

stationed at their life-boats. The stage crew pulls down the sets, and the property men hurry in to carry off the "props." Again, all is done according to timed and scheduled signals; while the work is handled as expeditiously as possible, haste is quite unnecessary. The used sets are carried away through the back of the stage and the coming sets are brought down through the right and left wings. Again the blue-print is posted, again the floor is chalked, and the second set of scenery is moved into place. Directly the new set is placed, the used scenery is inventoried, re-rolled, re-packed, and sandwiched against the wall, in unbelievably ship-shape space limits, later to be hauled out and re-carted to the storehouses. This work is done while the opera is in progress. At the end of the performance, only those sets which are in actual use on the stage remain to be packed.

When a single act calls for two scenes, which follow closely upon each other without intermission, thus allowing no time for a complete resetting, the stage is generally set in sections. In the First Act of *Faust,* for example, the full depth of the stage is set for the Kermesse Scene, with its houses and musicians' boxes, and back-drop of distant hills. Across the front of this set, as a curtain, is hung the back-drop of *Faust's* Study, where the First Scene is played, in a space no more than a quarter of the actual depth of the stage. When the Study scene is done, then, this back-drop is raised, the scanty properties are removed, extra tables and benches are set out for the Kermesse merrymakers, and the Second Scene is ready to go forward in less than two minutes' time.

As the scenery is taken out, every piece is inspected

for the unavoidable wear and tear made by carting and handling. All needed repairs are made, on the stage during the morning hours, before that particular set is due to be used again. No piece is in defective condition at curtain time. Large-scale scenic overhauling (together with the preparation of new sets, the refreshing of properties, the polishing of armory, etc.) is done before the operatic season begins. Constant retouchings are expected and provided for, but no serious repairs are needed once the season is on.

Half an hour after the final notes of the *Liebestod* have died away, the *Tristan* scenery has been cleared, packed, and placed ready for re-cartage. The stage and the auditorium are taken over by the cleaning women and refreshed for the evening's performance. By six o'clock, the entire business of plan-reading, floor-marking, and stage-setting begins all over again, in exactly the same routine. By six-thirty, the stage crew may be spared for a supper pause (during which the watchman makes his rounds; the stage is never left unguarded), and the House is ready for *Aida*. When *Aida* is over, the crew that carts away both sets of scenery, delivers the scenery for the next night's bill. The beginning of to-morrow's job has been made, and the sets of three operas have been handled.

The most popular operas from the stage crew's point of view, are *Madama Butterfly*, *The Barber of Seville*, and *Traviata*, requiring, as they do, few changes of setting and no massive scenery. The most dreaded are *Don Giovanni*, *Romeo and Juliet*, and *Goetterdaemmerung*, where the shifts are frequent and cumbersome.

JOSEF NOVAK AT WORK ON THE PAINT-BRIDGE

property men, as soon as the stage crew is ready with
the setting. Meanwhile, the smaller "props" for the
evening's performance are looked up in the inventories,
collected into hampers, and inspected for repairs which
are made during the regular working hours of the day.
They are then distributed according to their use; stage
properties are placed upon the set, the properties used
by the principal singers are delivered to their dressing-
rooms, while those for the chorus, ballet, and supers
are assembled in the wings or hallways, where they can
be taken up as their users approach the stage. In *Faust,*
for instance, the armorer looks up the number of choristers appearing as soldiers, counts out the requisite
number of swords, and leaves them in a hamper at the
foot of the stairs leading from the chorus men's dressing-room. The choristers come down empty handed,
take up their swords on their way to the stage, and put
them back into the hamper when the sword scenes are
over. The armorer immediately recounts them, takes
them back to the armory room, where they are inspected
and polished, the following day.

During the performance, a representative of the
Property Department sits in a cubby-hole off stage,
with a basketful of such "props" as will be needed during the scene, but are not carried to the stage at its
beginning—letters, documents, writing materials, party
ingredients, daggers, small bouquets. As the time for
their use approaches, they are handed to the singers in
the wings. Small properties that might be mislaid in the
scramble of scene-shifting, are always duplicated.

The use as well as the care of the properties is super-
vised by the Property Chief. An hour before curtain
time, he makes an inspection of all hampers, and all

dressing-rooms, to assure himself that ensemble groups and principal singers have been provided with the correct number of correct accessories, to take to the stage. Properties which are definitely called for by the opera's libretto (such as the fan and mirror in *Butterfly,* or the snuff-box in *The Bartered Bride,* which have their part in the action as well as in the general scenic effect), are carefully checked over with the artists. Even when the "props" are privately owned, the Property Master is responsible for their use.

The moment a scene is struck, the property men hurry in, on the heels of the stage crew, to carry off the used "props," to dress the scene with the new ones, and to call for the things from the dressing-rooms. The complete array of properties from Act One is sorted and returned to the proper cubicles while Act Two is in progress on the stage. At the end of a performance, only those properties used in the last scene remain to be housed. When the rooms are locked for the night, every least property is back in its place. Only in one case are properties left unstored and unlocked. That is when they are eatables. In the *Bohême* scene, to name but one, real bread and fruits are provided by the Chief Property Man, and the clearing away of such items is always the signal for hilarity among the workers.

The wines, liquors, and poisons consumed on the stage are usually weak tea or ginger ale, the exact nature of the liquid always being determined by the singer who is called upon to drink it, since different voices are individually affected by different beverages. When Miss Bori sang *Mimi* in *La Bohême,* a dish of ice-cream was always provided for her. Others in the cast have preferred to feast from a pyramid of cotton-wool, lest the milk content of ice-cream cause phlegm. Not all stage eatables are genuine, however. The sausages in *Die Meistersinger,* and the stuffed peacocks in *Sadko* are distinctly "props," made of *papier maché.*

### 3.

While the stage crew is setting the stage and the property men complete its dressing, to follow the House-That-Jack-Built pattern of progress, the scenic artist goes about touching up all evidences of wear and tear occasioned by hauling and carting. Josef Novak and two assistants keep stage-rocks, grass, and baronial halls looking fresh. Men with buckets and brushes may be busy on the set at any time, but the headquarters of the Scenic Department are on the paint frame, or bridge, which connects the Thirty-ninth and Fortieth Streets wings of the House, four stories above the open stage. Here are stored the supplies of paints, varnish, putty, brushes, oils, and the like. Here, too, are undertaken the more detailed scenic repairs. When completely new sets are designed and painted in the House —which is sometimes if not always the case—the scenic staff may be increased. Such sets are the creations of Novak.

### 4.

While the stage is set by the crew, dressed by the Property Department, and touched up by the scenic artists, the wardrobe people, on the fourth floor, are making ready the costumes. A staff of twenty workers, further departmentalized as dressers and sewers, are kept constantly busy in the wardrobe rooms, under the direction of N. L. Lanzilotti. The Metropolitan Opera owns all the costumes used by the ensemble groups, and some used by the singers; the wearers are given their "own" robes each time they appear. Most of the principal artists provide their own wardrobes. These robes are stored, under the names of the operas in which they are used, in long galleries on the fourth and fifth floors, one set reserved for men's wardrobe, and one for women's. The privately owned costumes of the principals are stored in trunks in the baggage and wardrobe rooms during the season, and cared for by the House department. Many of the garments are designed by Lanzilotti, who ranks among the most expert of theatrical tailors.

Costumes are taken from their racks during the morning of the day on which they are to be used, pressed, and delivered to the various dressing-rooms. They are hung against the closet doors; and when the singers arrive, they find their complete wardrobe ready for them, together with the properties which have been left on the table. The garments are collected immediately after the performance, and left in the wardrobe room in hampers. The following morning, they are inspected, cleaned, and repaired. Operatic repairs include anything from mending a torn bit of ruffle, to setting new "jewels," or dyeing a length of silk to make a fresh bodice for a skirt that is still usable. No costumes are hung away until they are in condition to be worn at a moment's notice. Costumes used only for rehearsals are put through the same inspection routine.

Some half dozen expert dressmakers sit at their machines all day, in the sewing room, working on the hundred-odd costumes that come in every night. The

Wardrobe Department keeps on hand a considerable stock of silks, materials, gauze, jewel-colored stones, dye-stuffs, ribbons, and the like, for immediate use. When new productions are scheduled, the House Wardrobe Department may be called upon to make the costumes. An interesting angle of costume preparation is that the colors are chosen for their effect under the spotlights. A robe which is desired to appear as green in a scene where the light is yellow, will be cut from goods which shows more blue than green in daylight.

Besides preparing and caring for the costumes, the Wardrobe Department is responsible for the dressing of the singers. Where artists have their personal maids or valets to assist them in dressing, the Wardrobe Department's responsibility is confined to a careful inspection, just before curtain time, by the Wardrobe Master. He enters all dressing-rooms, requires the "stars" to walk about before him, mannequin-fashion, and puts his final stamp of approval upon the hang and fit of the robes. Where singers have no privately provided assistance, and in the dressing of the ensemble groups, the Wardrobe Department sends its dressers to the various rooms to help the singers into their robes and to adjust the fit. The Wardrobe Chief inspects the attire of every performer who appears on the stage.

During the season of 1936, Richard Crooks ordered a new costume for *Faust*. The costume was to be used in the First Scene of the First Act, in which *Faust,* under Mephistophelean auspices, becomes transformed from a world-weary old philosopher into a dashing young beau. *Faust* dresses the scene in his young-man's outfit, slips the old man's robes over it, and removes the outer layer on cue. Normally, this sloughing off is accomplished under cover of *Mephisto's* flowing cape. Crooks, however, had something different in mind. He wanted a robe that would fall from him so quickly that no covering would be necessary. The change was to take place in full view of the audience, thereby heightening the illusion. Crooks came to be measured, and brought with him a tall, typically American young man. Crooks outlined his ideas and Lanzilotti reflected upon them. While the reflection was in progress, the tall young man gave forth some remarkably practical hints as to how such a "quick change" costume could best be made. Whereupon Lanzilotti retired into even deeper reflection, with an air that might have been interpreted as meaning, "does a young man, obviously not of the operatic world nor yet of the world of the *couturiers,* issue directions for the creation of a Metropolitan costume?" The young man noted the air, but continued with his hints.

"The robe must fall from him quickly . . . like this!"

And raising his hand, he drew forth a dollar-bill from Lanzilotti's nose. Lanzilotti blinked and the imperturbable young man went on with his talk about concealed ravel-strings, pointing each sentence with more dollar-bills, which appeared from Lanzilotti's ears, his collar, his coat-lapels. At last the Wardrobe Master could stand no more.

"All right," he cried, "I make the costume just like how you tell me!"

Then the tall young man introduced himself as John Mulholland, of the American Society of Magicians, who had designed Crooks' costume along strictly magical lines.

## 5.

While the scene-shifters are preparing the stage, and the property men are getting ready the "props," and the Wardrobe Department is pressing and hanging the costumes, the Make-up Master and his two assistants are busy with wigs and beards and grease-paint. Senz (his given name is Adolf, but he has seldom been known to use it, officially or privately), is an expert at his craft, and his services are frequently required by theatrical, motion-picture, and radio performers, who wish to be especially well made-up for special photographs. Senz makes the opera wigs, cares for them, and supervises the make-up of the performers.

Some three thousand wigs are handled during the operatic season, and about two hundred new ones are made every year. The wigs designed for the principal singers may cost anywhere from seventy-five to three hundred dollars each. They are designed according to the period of time and individuality of country indicated by the libretto. The exact color of the hair, unless definitely specified, is decided by the artist who wears the wig and the stage-director who supervises the opera, so that the harmony of effect between the individuals and the ensemble groups on the stage, may be at its best.

Wig and beard routine is similar to that of the costumes. The principal singers generally furnish their own, while the House provides those of the secondary singers and group performers. Wigs and beards are delivered to the dressing-rooms just in advance of each performance, to be found in readiness when the singers come to dress. Each chorister is measured for his own wigs, which are marked inside with his name and control

number.  The chorus wigs are delivered on a large tray,
and distributed to match the numbers on the dressing-
tables.  Wigs and beards are collected immediately after the performance, and are refreshed with new hair,
cleaned, and recurled the next day.

Senz begins his tour of inspection an hour before
curtain time.  He visits each dressing-room, approves
the adjustment and dressing of the wigs, and supplies
the final touch to elaborate coiffures.  Wigs are treated
with the same dignity as human hair.  They are combed
out and well brushed on the wig-stand, but are generally re-coiffed on the head of the wearer.  Wigs that
hang loosely about the face, like *Aida's* or *Azucena's,*
are a source of delight to the Make-up Department.
The long flaxen braids of *Marguerite* and *Elsa* offer no
particular difficulties, although they must be carefully
woven, from absolutely equal strands of hair.  But the
authentically Japanese top-knot of *Madama Butterfly*
and the elaborate head-dress of *Manon* require much
time and the minutest attention from the maid, or wig-
man, at work on the structures and the prima donnas
who sit beneath them.  Men's wigs, especially "character" wigs, can be equally difficult to dress.  *Samson et
Dalila, The Tales of Hoffmann,* and *Manon* give most
activity to the Wig Master, while *Siegfried* and *Die
Walkuere,* from the wig point of view, are the easiest
operas of all.

Wig inspection includes make-up inspection as well.
The artists make themselves up as a rule, although some
prefer to deliver themselves over entirely into Senz's
hands, from the first application of cold-cream to the
final adjustment of a built-up nose.  Make-up also includes disguising the moustaches of those artists who

ated by remote control, by means of radio tubes and reactors.

The lighting proceeds from 176 reactors set under the stage, like a number of huge radio sets, and grouped according to those sections of the House to which light is to be furnished.  Separate reactors control the first and second rows of border lights, the stage pockets, the bridge lights, the spotlights, the lights thrown down from the fly-floor, the main chandelier in the auditorium, etc.  The system is built to furnish white, amber, red, green, and blue light automatically, while all further desired colors are supplied by sliding specially tinted gelatin frames in front of the white-light lamps.  The reactors are connected to the master control-board, also under the stage, which is equipped with contactors, and the intensifiers that regulate the actual supply of light.

The board is about eight feet high and twenty-two feet long.  It is arranged in sections to correspond to those of the reactors, and each section is further sub-divided according to light-color.  These sections of the control-board are marked with tiny electric bulbs, one for each of the fixed colors, and each is regulated by its own intensifier.  Thus, if a gradually deepening green light is desired in the second row of border lights, at the same time that a fading amber light is wanted on the fly-floor, a single motion from Werber, at his post under the stage, regulates the intensifiers of the green lamp in the border-light section of the board, and of the amber lamp in the fly section.

The control-board can be pre-set, to the extent of three scenes.  But, as the fourth scene can be prepared as soon as the first is over (and before the second and third scenes begin), it is possible to set the lighting of an entire opera some hours in advance.

The control-board is further connected to a console, which looks and operates like that of an organ. The console stands in a special observation-booth, directly beside the prompter's box. Werber's routine is to set the board, three scenes ahead, from the directions in the charted light-plot; to transfer this setting from the board to the console; and, finally, to follow the light-plot on the console, in changing the colors and intensities of light during the progress of the opera. Some of these pre-set effects (such as the Magic Fire in *Die Walkuere*) are released on musical cue, indicated to Werber by assistant conductors on the stage, who follow the beats of the conductor in the pit.

Besides the countless colors and intensities of "regular" light, special effects must be prepared for certain operas. In some of these, the lighting effects are an integral part of the stage action. In *Walkuere,* to name only one such work, some of the dramatic moments upon which the continuity of the plot depends (*Siegmund's* seizure of the Sword, and the spell of the Magic Fire) are projected to the audience almost entirely by lighting. The sword effect, in Act One, is produced simply by throwing a concentrated spot-lamp, of golden-amber hue, upon the highly polished hilt of the sword. *Sieglinde's* torch is a three-foot cylinder, shaped like a funnel at the upper end. Inside the funnel's hollow is a small electric motor, equipped with fan-shaped blades, which blows a number of narrow silk ribbons in an upward direction. These ribbons are illuminated by amber flashlight bulbs, fed by batteries inside the cylinder. To produce the famous Magic

Fire, long flame-shaped pieces of silk are blown by high-powered exhaust fans grouped behind the scenery, and are illuminated by spotlamps and reflectors equipped with color-frames of golden-amber gelatin sheets. Real steam is turned on in front of the blowing ribbons, to give the illusion of smoke; and the effect is further heightened by a special process of light-dimming, which must be gradual as to timing and irregular as to intensity.

In *Rheingold,* the illusion of the bottom of the Rhine is made by using lengths of green-blue painted gauze, upon which water effects and ripples are projected, in suitable angles and intensities. The water-effect device is a round, thin mica disc, about two feet in diameter, and painted with small waves or breakers. A small electric motor revolves this disc in front of a series of projecting lenses, fitted to a high-powered spotlamp. The ripple device has square mica discs, is moved vertically instead of in a circular motion, and is painted with fine, uneven lines. The gold in the Rhine is made visible by turning on a five-hundred-watt incandescent lamp, mounted inside a rock-shaped box that is lined with crumpled gold leaf. The proper color and intensity of this lamp create the desired illusion. In the Second Scene of *Rheingold,* the sulphur vapor is made by throwing spotlamps, through green-purple gelatin colors, upon live steam. In the Third Scene, the disappearance of *Alberich* is effectively accomplished by means of a narrow steam-curtain, turned on at a cue in the score. The steam completely covers *Alberich* as he steps from its shelter, behind a black velvet curtain, alongside. The Rainbow, at the close of this opera, is projected by specially constructed prisms which are placed in the exact focus of a high-powered spotlamp. This spotlamp is equipped with the proper projecting lenses, and is so constructed as to admit of regulating the desired curvature of the rainbow.

For sun effects (used in *Iris, Coq d'Or,* and *Wilhelm Tell*), a group of large incandescent lamps is mounted in a round metal pan, some four feet in diameter, and covered with heavy transparent white silk. The pan is then hung diagonally on two parallel piano wires, so arranged that the complete device can be raised or lowered, according as the routine calls for sunrise or sunset. In sun effects, the lamps are of frosted white glass. In moon effects (used in *Die Meistersinger, La Gioconda,* and *Der Freischuetz*), the same procedure is followed, except that the lamps are of light-blue glass.

The fireflies, in *Madama Butterfly* and *Haensel und Gretel,* call for small light-blue lamps, hung on thin black electric wires, on a supporting cable. These lamps are connected, in a staggering circuit, to a small switch-board, and as the different switches are pressed, the different groups of "fireflies" light up. All of these special effects, once they have been set up, are operated from the master control-board, and in full view of the operator in charge.

The Electric Department is also responsible for special sound effects, which cannot be supplied by the instruments of the orchestra. Thunder, for example (again, in *Walkuere*), is produced in two ways. Distant thunder is made on a regular thunder-drum, upon which is mounted an arrangement of hammers, driven by motors in such a way that they strike upon the surface of the drum in irregular beats. Crash thunder comes from a huge square box, as large as a fair-sized room, set up on the fly-floor, four stories above the stage. The box has a double floor, of hard wood. On the topmost floor are placed large wheels with gear-shaped edges. The wheels are revolved by motors, and driven against the hard wood. The faster they are revolved, the louder the "thunder." In vaudeville and radio work, thunder effects are often supplied by a phonographic record of actual thunder, amplified in intensity. This device is not practical for operatic work, however, where the thunder must fit into the musical score, and must come on exact cue, both as to time and intensity.

### 7.

Straight scenic "effects" are prepared by the Technical Department. These effects include the raising and lowering of the various traps, for sudden appearances; scenic demolitions, transformations, and the like. The demolition of the Temple in *Samson et Dalila* is always an effective scene. To accomplish it, the large round columns beside the altar are set up in movable sections, one above the other. A heavy flexible cable is run through the center of these sectional structures, fastened solidly to the floor of the stage below, and held taut at the upper end, to keep the columns straight. At the proper musical cue, *Samson* pushes one of the movable sections of each column aside, and the cables are slackened from above, causing the columns to collapse. At the same moment, stage-rocks are dropped upon the scene from overhead. These rocks are fashioned from thin wire frames, covered with suitably painted muslin. They are very light in weight and could do no harm even if they were to strike someone on the stage.

As the columns collapse and the rocks fall, the lights are dimmed to a glow, and the crash sound effect is put into operation.

For scenic transformations (as used in *Parsifal, Don Giovanni, Goetterdaemmerung,* and *Le Prophète*), all set pieces and hanging scenery are equipped with double canvas coverings. The outer cover is painted to represent the desired scene (walls, trees, houses, etc.), and is fastened to the top of the scenic pieces with specially constructed snap-hooks. The inner canvas is stretched across the scenery and painted with exactly the same scenic picture as the outer cover, except that it is represented in a broken, demolished condition. At the proper cue, the snap-hooks are released, the outer cover drops quickly to the floor, and the inner painting is exposed. The transformation process is also accompanied by quick changes of light and by crash sound effects.

## 8.

While the various workers are busy with stage sets, properties, paint brushes, costumes, wigs, and lighting effects, Mr. Lionel S. Mapleson, the Chief Librarian, makes ready to send out the scores for the night's performance. The orchestral players sit in pairs, two to a desk, and each desk is furnished with its own part of the score, before the players come to take their seats in the pit. The separate parts are sometimes printed, but often copied, in manuscript, from the complete orchestral score. Mr. Mapleson and his two assistants are responsible for copying such parts, distributing them to the proper desks, and filing them away again after each performance or rehearsal. Further, the House Li-

N. L. LANZI-
LOTTI AT
WORK IN THE
WARDROBE
ROOM

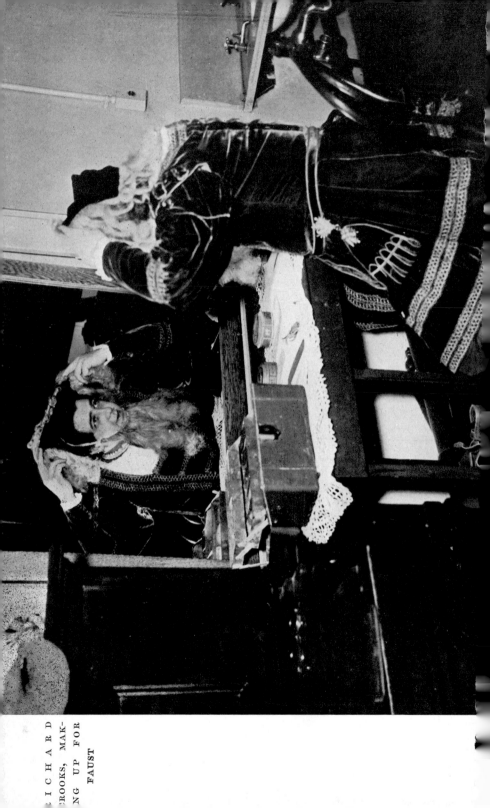

RICHARD
CROOKS, MAK-
ING UP FOR
FAUST

brarian edits the scores, according as the conductors mark new cuts in the operas, or replace cuts which have been observed in previous performances. Scores are repaired and refreshed in the House library.

The courtly and dignified Mr. Mapleson is thoroughly conversant with operatic routine, possibly because it "lies in the blood." Since 1740, the Mapleson family has served in the capacity of Music Librarians to the Kings of England. Various members have also won distinction as singers, actors, and impresarios. Lionel S. Mapleson has been with the House some forty-five years. His uncle, Col. Henry Mapleson, gave New York its early seasons of grand opera, at the old Academy of music; and offered serious competition to a new venture which was destined to survive as the Metropolitan. Colonel Mapleson was among the first impresarios to bring opera to this country. Adelina Patti was among his "stars." Mr. Mapleson's office at the House is a veritable musical museum, containing family records in the form of autographed photographs, and personal letters from Meyerbeer, Verdi, and other great musicians of the eighteenth and nineteenth centuries, asking the Mapleson gentlemen for scores, or acknowledging receipt of them.

### 9.

The setting of the scene backstage, however, presents only part of the picture. The other part, charted by the boundary line of proscenium arch, deals with preparing the front of the House for the reception of the opera patrons. The "setting of the stage" in the auditorium devolves upon Hugh R. Brown, the House

Superintendent, whose varied responsibilities include attention to everything that makes the patrons comfortable, from assigning the contract for new carpets, to dealing with the City Building Department authorities, testing the fire apparatus, and drawing the plans and specifications for the Opera Balls. The Superintendent's department includes a staff of porters, coachmen, footmen, cleaning-women, carriage-call men, program-boys, matrons, stage-door men, watchmen, and elevator attendants. Opera patrons are familiar with Brown as the sartorially immaculate guardian of the main Orchestra entrance, the only one to wear an opera hat. His appearance there gives no evidence of the numerous and detailed tasks he assumes before the House doors open. Brown is a Scotchman by birth, a construction contractor by training, and a designer of ship models by avocation.

The daily cleaning of the House gets under way towards six o'clock in the morning. The crew of scrubbing and cleaning women begin with the offices and the stage and the lobbies, so that the working parts of the House may be ready for business routine and rehearsals by nine-thirty. Thence, they progress to the auditorium, where every trace of last night's activity (with its wake of crumpled programs, torn ticket stubs, turned-down seats, cigarette ends, bruised flowers, and foot-marks) must be cleared away before the stage rehearsals begin. Occasionally, though, there is a bit of overlapping, and then the cleaning women, with cloths over their heads, are careful to work quietly towards the back of the House, while world-famed voices are coached and drilled up front, on the stage. Both groups are in the House for work, even though the nature of their work

lies at opposite poles, and they exchange dignified greetings when they encounter each other in the half-lit corridors. Here and there, some homesick foreign singer
may discover that one of these women comes from his
own corner of the world, and then there is a moment of
joy that quite wipes out any disparity which might be
thought to arise from a rich fur cloak on the one hand,
and a dingy checkered working apron, on the other. After rehearsals, the House is again inspected and set to
rights. The cleaning staff generally goes off duty towards one o'clock, except on matinée days, when both
stage and auditorium are cleaned again, between performances. Before the opening of the doors for the
performance, and while the "front" staff of attendants
are taking their stations at ticket-boxes, doors, aisles,
elevators, rest rooms, and libretto and program tables,
the auditorium is sprayed through with disinfectant.

The twenty-two ushers offer mute testimony to what
a love of opera may do to a tired business man. Only
the fewest of this staff are "professional" ushers. Most
of them have regular commercial employment during
the day, and hasten to don their House uniforms at seven
o'clock, for the sheer glamour attendant upon functioning as an integral part of the Metropolitan Opera season. The day-time occupations of these men cover a
wide range of diversity. Among them are bank clerks,
salesmen, ledger workers, customers' men in brokerage
houses, music students, beginner-vocalists with great
zeal and few engagements, and embryo politicians. One
of the ushers is an officer in the Court of General Ses-
sions, and another sells lots in a cemetery! Some of the
older men have been with the House upwards of twenty-
five years, and are familiar with the names and the seat

locations of each night's regular subscribers, with whom they exchange very expert opinions on comparative cast values, between the acts.

Thus the stage is set, the sets refreshed, the properties assembled, the costumes prepared, the wigs made ready, the lights pre-set, the scores delivered, and the auditorium made comfortable—all of which serves as but the frame for the work of the operatic performers themselves. The logical moment to turn to the activities of the musical personnel is the time of their entrance into the House for the auditions which decide their membership in the company.

# CHAPTER X

# THE CAST

## 1.

TO JUDGE by the inquiries that reach the House staff, there is one piece of information more eagerly sought, perhaps, than any other. Its form may vary, but its essence remains the same: How does a singer "get into the 'Met'"? The answer is simple enough, even though it may involve considerable tension among those personally interested in the process of selection. No singer appears on the Metropolitan stage without presenting sound and well-investigated recommendations, and without submitting to a series of auditions, conducted by the General Manager or his representatives.

Normally, auditions are held on the Metropolitan stage. In the case of established foreign artists, who may be fulfilling engagements in opera houses abroad, however, this is not possible. Under such circumstances, the necessary "recommendations" are supplied by the artist's public standing, while the "auditions" are conducted by a representative of the Metropolitan, who visits the foreign opera houses, and judges the candidate by his performances. Mr. Johnson makes annual scouting trips of this kind. Sometimes the management deputes certain of its conductors to report on a possible "find."

Favorable accounts of a singer are regularly followed

up by personal inspection, so that the candidate may be judged, not merely as abstract vocal material, but according to the individual needs of the Metropolitan. A singer who makes an excellent record for himself in one of the smaller opera houses of France or Italy, might scarcely be heard in the vast auditorium in New York.

When regular auditions are scheduled, and the candidates come to be heard, curiosity is always rife in the House, whether *this* is the one who may assert himself as "the second Caruso." The management is as eager to make a "find" as the candidates are to be "found"; it is governed in its choice by the ability of the candidate and by those needs in which he might make himself most useful—never by a desire to "keep someone out."

Throughout the year, the management receives countless requests for auditions. No such request remains unconsidered, although the candidates' own statements of preparation and experience may render it inexpedient to grant a Metropolitan audition. The General Manager files the most promising applications for future action, and when enough have accumulated, he sets aside a number of days for hearing candidates. There is no fixed season for auditions; they may be called at any time during the year, at the discretion of the management. Possibly a dozen candidates may be heard on the same day.

Caruso once attended an audition, and came away with an awed look.

"If I had to go through *that*," he observed, "even now—to-day—I'd certainly lose the job!"

At the appointed hour, the candidate is escorted to the stage, which is left bare, except for a piano and a

single light beside it. In front, is the glare of the footlights. Beyond the proscenium arch, the auditorium
looms vast and dark and empty; and somewhere in it,
possibly under the blacker shadow of the overhanging
boxes, there sit the General Manager and his invited
staff of co-judges, foregathered to decide which candidates shall be asked to enter the Metropolitan Opera,
and which shall be "excused." The candidates never
know exactly who attends the auditions, or where they
are listening.

If the candidate does not bring an accompanist with
him, one of the assistant conductors plays for him. He
announces the list of songs and arias he is prepared to
sing, and shows what he can do, counting himself fortunate if he is allowed to continue after the first number.
If he makes an especially good impression, however, he
may hear a voice out of the darkness ask for some
special aria. But even such a request serves as nothing
more than an indication of interest. Only rarely is a
candidate engaged on the strength of a single hearing.

When the audition is over, the candidate departs
without a word of either criticism or decision. The
judges then confer among themselves, from notes made
during the audition, and decide which candidates de-
serve a second trial. A second audition definitely raises
the hopes of the candidate, although a third and even
a fourth trial may be required before the ultimate decision is given. Among the most successful auditions
heard in the House were those sung by Riccardo
Martin, Paul Althouse, and Richard Crooks, all of
whom were engaged after a minimum number of trials.
The recently instituted "Auditions of The Air" follow the same routine of recommendation and testing,

permitting the radio audience to listen to the candidates, along with the House judges. Unsuccessful candidates are simply not invited to come back. Successful ones are given contracts with the Metropolitan Opera.

## 2.

In the House files, artists are listed not merely as "sopranos" and "tenors," but according to the type of rôle they sing, and the number of parts they have at their command, ready for use at a moment's notice. At the end of each season, the management outlines the repertory for the coming year and assigns the rôles which the artists must be prepared to sing, when they return to the House for work. In the case of the leading artists, these assignments are fairly definite. Among the secondary parts, however, the same rôle may be given to several singers, the ultimate cast choice waiting over until rehearsals begin. By such a system, the management is able to vary its casts, while the performers are given an opportunity of enlarging their repertories and working out new rôles under expert guidance. Lillian Nordica mastered dozens of rôles which she was never called upon to use, partly as a means of development, and partly to "be ready for anything that might happen." Since the House has no system of understudies, it is as useful to the management as it is to the singers, to have the same rôle firmly lodged in several hands. The ability to step into a part at a moment's notice often gives a fledgling member of the company his "big chance."

Artists are engaged for leading or for secondary parts. The term "secondary parts" is an uncomfortable one to use, suggesting, as it may, an absence of first-rate material on the part of the singer. This is anything but the case. Secondary work requires consummate artistry, and often stands as the test of a well-rounded performance. Indeed, there are singers of secondary rôles, especially "character" parts, who portray them with such marked success that they find themselves limited to them purposely, because of their value to the company in their proven field. Lawrence Tibbett was cast entirely for secondary parts, until he asserted himself as stellar material.

Cast rehearsals, on old parts and new, are begun some two weeks in advance of the season's opening, and continue until the day before the final performance. Rehearsals are held on the stage; on the roof-stage above the fifth floor; in dressing-rooms; in the private offices of the conductors and stage-directors; in the foyers and the buffet; and in the rest-rooms of the auditorium—where richly-gowned ladies will give the final touches to their hair, just before the performance begins, and wonder what a grand piano can possibly be doing there, because no one from the audience, certainly, would think of sitting down to play during a presentation of *Goetterdaemmerung*. There are nineteen pianos in the House, and all of them may be "going" at once.

Operatic rehearsals are vastly different from dramatic rehearsals. In the theater, a single rehearsal period is designated, during which the same new play is learned by a cast which expects, at least, to perform it as a unit as long as it runs. In the opera, the nightly changes of bill are further complicated by variations of cast. Three performances of *Aida* may bring three entirely different casts, and each must be rehearsed as though it were for a new production. The presence of a single new artist (or stage-director or conductor), makes it necessary to begin fresh rehearsals of an opera with which all of the performers are perfectly familiar, so that the individual working-methods of the complete cast may be properly co-ordinated. When Gertrud Wettergren made her first appearance as *Amneris,* in *Aida,* full rehearsals were ordered—even though Mme. Wettergren had won fame in the rôle in Stockholm, and the other artists were accustomed to working together at the Metropolitan.

Because of the constant rehearsals of one kind or another that go on in a ten-performance week, the planning of the rehearsal schedules is one of the most important parts of House routine. These schedules are prepared by the company's Musical Secretary, Giuseppe Sturani. Maestro Sturani consults with the various conductors and stage-directors as to times and places that shall not conflict, and works out his "time tables," which are sent on to the Rehearsal Director, Jules Judels (who holds the same position in the company which his father held, forty-five years ago). Judels records the rehearsal schedules for reference, and assembles the various casts, in the proper rooms at the proper hours. Rehearsals are announced to the singers by printed slips, left in the House mail—and the private engagements of all company members are contracted with one eye upon the mail-rack, where the familiar blue envelope may appear at any moment to challenge the "freedom of the artist's life." The singers are on rehearsal call at any hour of the day or night. Rehearsals are frequently held on the roof-stage while a performance is in progress; and House people are entirely accustomed, as they make their way through the building, to hearing Verdi on the ground floor, Massenet on the second, Wagner on the third, Puccini on the fourth, Bellini on the roof, and a blending of all upon the stairs. That is one of the reasons why opera folk lead such a colorful existence.

The first rehearsals of any work begin with the musical score. The artists are summoned singly, to go through their rôles with one of the assistant conductors, who supplies the missing orchestral and vocal parts on the piano, and convinces himself that the singer is perfectly sure of all the words, music, and cues of his rôle. Next, the parts are gone through again with the conductor who will direct the performance, and who indicates the exact colorings and climaxes he wants. At such times, an operatic rehearsal sounds like a vocal lesson, with the conductor lifting high an essentially non-singing voice to demonstrate the desired effect, and the artist repeating it after him, three times, four times, a dozen times. After the individual parts have been thoroughly mastered, the singers come together to work through duets and ensemble passages (exclusive of the chorus' music), to time their cues, and fit their performances to each other. Ensemble rehearsals are taken scene by scene, sometimes in regular order, sometimes in the order of musical difficulty, and sometimes according to the parts that need most polishing. All of these preliminary workings-out take place in the rest-rooms or the dressing-rooms.

While the musical routine is attaining a state of fluency, the stage-director is busy with scene-plots, light-plots, and costume-plots. Although indications for the musical and dramatic progress of an opera are set forth in the score and the libretto, each conductor and each stage-director who mounts a performance, colors it with very definite conceptions of his own. Consequently, the artists must be made aware, not merely of notes and gestures, but of those details—of color, tempo, emphasis, and intensity—which will bring forth the clearest projection of the directors' ideas. The stage values of a performance depend upon the stage-director exactly as the musical values depend upon the conductor.

Dramatic rehearsals follow the same general routine as the musical drill. The stage-director meets the members of the cast first singly and then in groups; explains the quality of the performance he wishes; and coaches the actual dramatic "business." Dramatic rehearsals are not only acted out but sung, so that the stage work may always be gauged to the best vocal effect. Operatic acting differs vastly from "regular" acting. Singers must keep the demands of their vocal mechanism uppermost in mind, and cannot permit themselves postures or expenditures of energy which would mar the production of good tone. Further, they have not nearly the freedom of an actor on the dramatic stage. The actor may vary his performance from night to night—quickening his tempo here, inserting a telling pause there—and the play as a whole loses nothing by it. The operatic actor may assume no position on the stage from which he cannot observe the conductor's beat. And the performance admits of no variation. Its every moment must be regulated and timed by that all-important beat down in the pit, and must run with the same precision of a locomotive on time-table schedule.  And the audience out front must notice nothing of the stringency of these extra demands.

While the principal singers are being coached in their musical and dramatic routines, the chorus and orchestra have rehearsals of their own, in the buffet or the foyers, or on the roof.  An opera may be in rehearsal a week before the cast approaches the stage.  The performance is not gone through as the complete whole which the audience will witness until the final, or general, rehearsal.  Before that, the acts are worked over in any order, and scenes that need polishing are gone through again and again and again, with interruptions and suggestions from conductor or stage-director. Stage rehearsals are avoided on matinée days, because no human power can tell in advance how long they will last.  A rehearsal that begins at ten in the morning may be out at one; it is just as possible that it will continue until after four.

Until the orchestra is added to the complete ensemble, stage rehearsals are accompanied at the piano by one of the assistant conductors.  The chief conductor sits on a chair directly before the prompter's box, with his score before him, and frequently raps on his music-stand for the correction and repetition of this or that passage.  The stage-director moves among the singers, altering a bit of business here, emphasizing the effects of the chorus-group there.  In the wings stand the assistant conductors and chorus masters, carefully marking their scores from the conductor's indications. These directors are at their posts at all performances, to send the singers out to the stage at the proper moment, and to transfer the conductor's beat to the performers off-stage, who cannot see the pit.  Often, they stand upon ladders so that they may be clearly observed by all in the wings. Each performance is thus "conducted" by at least four different men.

At ordinary rehearsals, the stage is dressed with only those sets and properties that are actually necessary for the calculation of distances, stage positions, or dramatic drill. Non-essential properties are supplied either by "make-believe" or by the battered chairs that the curtain-boys and the stage hands use. The artists work in their street dress, and rehearsal attire is an individual affair. Some of the artists elect to appear in the newest Paris creations, while others have regular working gear, in the form of old-vintage sports dresses, which may be comfortably fallen down in, without cause for palpitation. The men usually remove their coats and their collars, and roll up their sleeves. And everybody's hair becomes most unglamorously tousled. During preliminary rehearsals, some artists sing in full voice, while others, preferring to conserve their vocal energies, mark their parts in half-voice. Once, after a brief indisposition, Caruso whistled his way through a rehearsal.

The auditorium is dark and empty. The General Manager and members of his staff visit rehearsals, to observe the working-methods of the artists and to check up on the progress of the opera. When new productions are in preparation, the heads of the Stage, Property, Scenic, Electrical, Wardrobe, and Make-up Departments come to the auditorium, to confer further with the stage-director, and chart or amend the routines which will remain the standard indications of procedure for subsequent productions of that work. But visitors are rigorously excluded. Only those of the cast actually at work are permitted upon the stage. Those waiting to be called, sit in the front rows of the dark orchestra, and chat among themselves of cabbages and kings. A bare wooden runway of unpainted planks extends from the left side of the stage down to the auditorium, for the singers to use when called, and for the stage-director to cross on his frequent trips "out front" to observe the effects as the audience will see them.

The general rehearsal is always a great affair, and all House members try to be on hand to witness it. Then, for the first time, is the performance gone through as a complete opera. For new productions, the general rehearsal becomes a dress rehearsal, with the stage fully equipped and the cast made up and in costume. It is the desire of all concerned that the final rehearsal shall be as free from error as possible, but it sometimes happens that adjustments still have to be made. For that reason, the general rehearsal is held several days in advance of the performance. Caruso used to say that after the final rehearsal was over, only two things remained to be done: to look back over the weeks of work, and to look forward to three days of prayer.

For performances proper, most of the artists arrive about an hour before their call-time, to warm up their voices, dress for their parts, and be ready for property and wardrobe inspection. Since, in a company of nearly a hundred solo singers, it is impossible for each performer to have his private dressing-room, these rooms are assigned according to rank. All the leading sopranos use the same room on the nights they sing, Mme. Flagstad occupying it for Monday's *Tristan und Isolde,* and Miss Mario for Wednesday's *Pagliacci.*

The first tenor's room still has an aura of sacredness about it, as the room that Jean de Reszke and Caruso used. The men's dressing-rooms are in the Thirty-ninth Street wing of the building, and the women's in the Fortieth Street side. In the corridors outside, are hung placards in four languages, publishing the intelligence that dogs are not allowed, that bouquets may not be received over the footlights, and that visitors are requested to delay their appearance until after the end of the last act.

The dressing-rooms are spacious and comfortable, but wholly unadorned. There is a plain dressing-table, a piano, accommodations for washing, a couple of chairs, and a full-length mirror equipped with stagelights. Each room has a number of wall closets, one of which is assigned to each artist who uses the room, for the storing of make-up and the like. Some of the singers—but in the Fortieth Street wing only!—supply decorations of their own, to make the rooms beautiful as well as habitable. The prima donna's maid is sent to the House, during the late afternoon, with a complete array of curtains, draperies, portières, slip-covers, pillows, and monogrammed towels, all of which must be put into place before the artist arrives—and removed again before she departs, as the cleaning women must find all rooms ready to be prepared for to-morrow's occupant. Normally, this is all a part of operatic routine, but an interesting scramble can result on matinée days, when one set of decorations must be removed after five-thirty, and the second set adjusted before six.

When the singers arrive, they find their rooms unlocked, lighted, provided with costumes and properties, and tested as to temperature. The temperature-testing of Rosa Ponselle's room takes on a form all its own. Miss Ponselle feels at her best when the room is cold, and all windows must be open and all heat turned off hours in advance of her coming. The singers' arrival in their dressing-rooms marks the best time to observe their idiosyncrasies. Some suffer horribly from stage-fright, and must be talked to and amused by their dressers. Others permit not a word to be uttered. Some bring light lunches along, to sustain them through a normally dinner-less performance. Some tone up their muscles by dancing. Some set up holy pictures before their dressing-table mirrors. Some establish character dolls on the chairs. All of them warm up their voices, while they dress, with *vocalises* and scales; and the air in the corridors throbs to an assortment of world-famed organs, going through their exercises on different syllables and in different keys.

The first step in dressing is the make-up. The performer wraps himself in a plain washable robe, binds a towel about his head at the wig-line, and sets to work. False eye-lashes. Grease paint. Rouge for the cheeks and lips. Crayon lines for sunken cheeks and wrinkles. Eye-shadow. Powder over it all. Then the towel comes off and the wig is adjusted. The women generally bind their own hair back in a silk-mesh net, so that the wig may fit firmly. Then the robes are put on and the accessory ornaments adjusted. Then the inspections begin. Presently, the call-boy makes his rounds, tapping at the doors and announcing "ten minutes before the overture." Not a note of the performance is heard through the sound-proofed doors which separate the stage from the rest of the House, and the call-boys make frequent announcements of the progress of the opera to those performers who are not needed at its start.   Artists are summoned to the stage five minutes before their cues.   The call-boy announces that "We are ready for you, Madame!" and the "show" is on.

### 3.

The opera's chorus numbers, at present, ninety-four regular members (forty-four women and fifty men), under the direction of two chorus masters.   The majority of this group have been with the House for many years, and the musical level of the chorus is maintained by annual individual audition tests.   There are no "contingents" among the choristers, the same personnel singing all the operas, in all languages.   The preparation of the operatic chorister is far more detailed than that of the average chorus man or girl. Members of the group are required to give evidence of vocal ability, musical knowledge in the matter of reading scores and directions, repertory, diction, stage business, and languages.

The Metropolitan chorus presents a colorful group of Americans, Frenchmen, Belgians, Austrians, Russians, Italians, and Germans, all united in the greatest cordiality.   Many of them are fully capable of solo performance.   Indeed, "bits" of stage business and musical work are frequently given into the hands of selected choristers, often with recognition in the printed program.   Then there is great rejoicing in all departments of the House, the management offering special congratulations, the dressers and make-up men taking special pains with the adornment of the individuals thus honored, and the artists remaining in the wings, to observe and applaud. Many of the choral group made their first long-ago entrance into the House as aspiring "stars," who wished to stay "only for a season or two," to earn, to learn operatic routine at first hand, or simply to mark time until the big opportunity should present itself. Minnie Egener began as a chorister, graduated into a versatile artist, and, at one time or another, assumed most of the secondary rôles in the soprano repertory. One of the most satisfying delineations of the part of *Silvio,* in *Pagliacci,* was offered by Mario Laurenti, who entered the House as a chorister. One of the greatest occasions in chorus history was the night when the daughter of two members of the group, both on the stage, made her début as prima donna of the evening. She was Claudia Muzio, a veritable "child of the opera," who often came, in pig-tails and socks, to wait in the House while her parents rehearsed, and whom members of the staff remember carrying about (and occasionally spanking).

The chorus begins its rehearsals some four weeks in advance of the opera's opening. New parts are distributed for study, and familiar parts are reviewed. Chorus rehearsals are held in the foyers or the buffet— the only rooms large enough to accommodate the group without marring the effect of full-voiced singing. The men's chorus and the women's group are drilled separately, until the work goes smoothly enough to fuse. One of the chorus masters coaches all rehearsals, to piano accompaniment. During the preliminary stages of pattern shaping, he often beats time with his baton against the metal music-stand, sharply marking the rhythms and indicating the emphases. When the parts have been blended and the musical routine is sure, the choristers are taken to the stage for further coaching by the stage-director and the conductor. As in the case of the principals, choral rehearsals are called for the stage when a new singer or director takes part in a thoroughly familiar work. Much of the life and motion of the operatic scenes is secured by adroit bits of "business" on the part of the choristers, who are directed to walk about in groups in the background, or to talk among themselves, thus bringing an illusion of everyday activity into a moment which might otherwise be fairly static.

Dressing-rooms in the Thirty-ninth Street wing are reserved for the men of the chorus, and in the Fortieth Street wing for the women. The long dressing-tables that line the walls are subdivided into individual units, each marked with the name and control number of its owner. The choristers take their own places, and find their costumes and wigs in readiness for them. They are inspected as to wardrobe and make-up, and are summoned to the stage by bell signals before the beginning of the scenes in which they are to appear. At such times, the wings are crowded with monks or lords or villagers or soldiers, waiting in orderly formation to be "sent on." During those scenes in which the chorus is not on the stage, great sociability gets under way in the dressing-rooms. The monks or lords or villagers or soldiers take their ease, playing cards, conversing, or, on two-performance days, trying to snatch a brief nap amid the noise; while their feminine counterparts wipe their hands clean of make-up to make progress with a bit of sewing or knitting. Great points of musical and general philosophy are settled. Off-stage choruses (as in the First Act of *Madama Butterfly* or the final act of *Aida*) are conducted by the chorus masters and assistant conductors, mounted upon their ladders at a point in the wings from which they can observe the pit and transfer the conductor's beat to the singers. When, as in *Aida,* an off-stage chorus is the final task of the evening, the group is permitted to change back to street clothes after its last visible appearance, and to return to the wings for the closing passages, "out of character." The stately chant proceeds from a group in hats and mufflers and overcoats, and then there is a rush for the doors.

### 4.

The Metropolitan orchestra numbers eighty-five players, who will be referred to as the men of the orchestra, even though one of the harpists is a woman. This group of carefully selected musicians is as thorough an organization as can be found anywhere in the world. Most of the men have had their training in ranking symphonic and operatic orchestras, and some have had solo careers, while many are the sons of older Metropolitan players, now retired, who bring their preparation straight from home. Among the "celebrities" who have emerged from the House orchestra are Victor Herbert, at one time first 'cellist; Nahan Franko, violinist, who became concert-master and later conductor; Mr. Franko's nephew, Dr. Edwin Franko Goldman, distinguished band-leader and composer, who played cornet in the House; Josef Pasternak, of radio fame, the only orchestral player to come in to his work in a silk hat; and Simone Mantia, solo trombonist in the band of John Philip Sousa and at the Paris Exposition, who serves at present in the dual capacity of first trombonist and orchestral manager.

The orchestra is by far the busiest unit of all House departments. There are no cast variations for these men. Although all operas do not require the full complement of instruments, the same men play at all performances, keep hard at work during every moment of the performances, and are on rehearsal call during the morning hours. Singers may have three to four performances a week; and the chorus has brief rest periods when it is not needed on the stage—but the orchestra goes on forever!

The orchestra begins its rehearsal period two weeks before the season's start. New scores are worked out and old ones refreshed. The orchestra's rehearsals are directed only by the chief conductors. Each of the half dozen conductors brings his individual conceptions and directing methods to his work, and the men must adjust themselves to all. During the working hours of the day, when the stage is in the hands of the various scenic departments, the orchestra often rehearses on the roof-stage.

Many of the operas require additional musicians in the stage band. As many as twenty extra brass players are used in this band in *Aida,* while *Norma* and *Lohengrin* come in as close seconds with sixteen each. The stage band members are competent musicians, who don costumes and appear as part of the acting personnel.

The orchestra's quarters lie under the stage, and directly adjoining the sunken pit where the men play. This section of the House is known as "fiddlers' alley," and here it is that the men congregate between the acts to smoke and talk and rest. Often enough, the players take a busman's holiday, and spend their scanty leisure up in the wings, threshing out the musical philosophies of the coming act. In the long "band room" in "fiddlers' alley," each man has his locker, for the housing of his street gear and the storing of instruments. A bell summons the men from their room to the pit, and a signal advises them of the moment when the conductor starts on his way down to join them. Then the tuning of the instruments ceases and the men watch expectantly for the rap and the down-beat that begin the opera.

### 6.

The floating population of the operatic world is supplied by the "supers," who neither sing nor act, but provide the stage with its background of crowds and its feeling of motion. One of this group defined a super as "a gentleman who merely walks on." The walking-on needs of the different operas vary greatly. *La Traviata* (with its party scenes), *Cavalleria Rusticana* (with its village square), *Lakmé* (with its bazaar), *Die Meistersinger* (with its guilds), and *Aida* (with its great triumphal march) require from fifty to a hundred and fifty supers each. Because of these varying needs, the House maintains no permanent staff of ladies and gentlemen to walk on.

The supers are supplied by the Rehearsal Director. By means known only to himself, Mr. Judels has accumulated a vast list of names and addresses of persons who have served as supers, could serve as supers, and would like to serve as supers if they got the chance.

The list numbers more than five hundred candidates, and is constantly in a state of flux, old names dropping out and new ones taking their places. As the repertory is announced for rehearsal, Judels looks up the number of supers regularly used in the different operas, and sends out postal cards summoning the ladies and gentlemen for their walks. If fifty supers are wanted for a given performance, eighty cards will be sent, so that the management may not be left in a difficult position, should any of those summoned fail to appear. The exact hour for their appearance is indicated, and the first fifty who present themselves are engaged. No one may pass the stage-door guardian without his card.

Where possible, the same supers are used in the same operas, to avoid confusion as to costume-fitting and stage deportment. Supers are carefully matched in height for processions of soldiers, and just as carefully varied for the ordinary group scenes. The House maintains two "regular" supers on its permanent payroll, to act as leaders of the group. These leaders are veterans, who are thoroughly familiar with the routine of all the operas; can execute business that demands more finesse than a mere walking on (as, for example, the business of the café waiter in *La Bohême*); and can drill their less experienced colleagues in the routine they must follow. Even then, supers have been known to fall victims to acute stagefright during a performance, no matter how well they have been coached. The surest test of stagefright among the ladies and gentlemen who walk on, is a falling out of step in the Grand March. As soon as a super takes the accented beat with his right foot instead of his left, one may know that his emotions have become seriously involved.

The supers dress in large rooms in the basement, the men in the north wing and the women in the south. They are assigned lockers for the housing of their gear during the performance; and costumes and wigs are placed upon long tables in the center of the rooms. Dressers are sent to help them with their robes and their make-up. The supers are summoned to the stage by bell signals in advance of their scenes, and must be kept out of the way of the other working units about the wings.

During those parts of the opera when the supers are not needed on the stage, their rooms are the gayest spots in the House; for, in addition to the normal pleasures of cards and conversation, this floating population savors the adventure of making new acquaintanceships. No super ever knows who his neighbors may be. Among them are music students, teachers, recluses from the Mills Hotels, writers or artists in search of "copy," music lovers eager for a "close-up" of Mme. Flagstad or Mr. Crooks (whom they never fail to ask for an autograph), society folk from Park Avenue who want a "thrill," and out-of-work actors who look forward to the thrill of feeling pay between their fingers again. Talk is lively and varied in the supers' quarters. Serious business men still go in for the fun of walking on, and one prominent subscriber gives away his seven dollar Orchestra chairs whenever he and his wife can get into the supers' line. Especially interesting is the group of Negro performers used as the captives in *Aida*. They take keen delight in being dressed in their robes—even though the costumes of the captives are far from glamorous—and respond to the music and the stage spectacle with the most sensitive

pleasure. The same people have worked for the House
for years, come in from their regular employment a
good two hours before they are due, and wax more excited over their share in the "show" than if they were to
witness the performance from box seats.

Considering the unprofessional background of most
of the supers, it is always a source of pleasant surprise
that so few mishaps occur with them. Of late years, the
deportment of the supers has been as poised and regulated as that of veteran showmen. But oddities have
happened! In the very old days, an arrangement was
entered into between the management and certain of
the local institutions of learning, whereby college boys
were permitted to work as supers for the educational
benefits attendant upon a close and personal inspection
of grand opera. All went well until the night when
Nordica so stirred these youthful pursuers of culture
that the lot of them broke forth into a heartily spontaneous but somewhat disconcerting cheer of the "Rah!
Rah!" variety, in the midst of *Lohengrin.* Another
time, one of the college boys (whose educational privi-
leges entitled him to climb up to the paint-bridge and
gaze down upon the performance from aloft) let fall
a lighted cigarette upon the gauzy decorations below.
No damage was done to the set, but from that time forward, the management decided that the educational aspects of grand opera could be best (and most safely)
appreciated from out front. Since then, the supers
have, by and large, remained supers. However, a super
who was *not* a college man let fall his trousers during
one of the most stirring moments of Liszt's *Saint Elizabeth.* Tension was high until the walking gentleman
cast aside his spear with a loud clatter, and retrieved

his vestments in time to go on with the march. Those
are positively all the stories that can be told against
the supers themselves. But a moment of mirth was
slipped into a certain long-ago performance of *La
Bohême* when, to the surprise of all, Caruso walked on
as the waiter in the café scene.

### 6.

The ballet is no longer a department of the opera's
management. Since 1935 it has functioned as an independent group, The American Ballet, under management of its own, using the opera building for its
practise and rehearsals and engaging to take part in
those performances which require dancing. Before
that time, though, the ballet ranked as one of the regular
House units. Conried used to devote much anxious
energy to the problem of getting the ballet girls to arrive punctually for rehearsals and performances. He
tried posted notices and personal lectures, but to no
avail. Finally, he hit upon a system of reward and
punishment. Girls who had a perfect record were
presented, at the end of the season, with gold pieces and
laudatory speeches. Late-comers were subjected to a
system of fines, calculated on a graduating scale that
began with ten cents for five minutes' tardiness, and
soared up to a dollar. The fines were allowed to ac-
cumulate until the end of the season, when the punctual
girls got their reward. Then Conried's heart smote him
and he divided the amount equally among all the
dancers, sheep and goats alike.

"But anyway," he observed, "it will be a good lesson
for them!"

7.

Two of the assistant conductors serve as prompters, one for the Italian and French repertories, and one for the German works. These gentlemen attend all rehearsals and familiarize themselves with the cues, the entrances, and the general tempo of the opera, all of which they mark in their scores. At the performances, they take their place in the prompter's box, in the front center of the stage, and visible to the audience by its hood. This box is actually an opening in the floor of the stage, supplied with a platform fixed at such a height that the prompter, when seated, can be plainly seen by all the performers. Directly beside him, on the open stage, there is placed a small mirror, which reflects to him the conductor's beat. The prompter follows from his marked score, and "prompts" the first phrase of each line to be sung. Experienced artists seldom forget their lines, but should such a moment occur, the hapless performer would not have to wait until his predicament were made known to get help. Throughout the opera, there is a constant murmur from the prompter's box.

The entire musical personnel of artists, conductors, assistant conductors, stage-directors, chorus masters, choristers, and orchestral players numbers two hundred-eighty-eight. When the full complement of supers and stage band players is on the stage the count rises to four hundred-fifty-eight.

# CHAPTER XI

# CERTAIN MATTERS OF ADMINISTRATION

## 1.

THE dressing-room caller is hardly invited to inspect the books of the Metropolitan Opera Association, and the problems and policies of administration have no place in a visit backstage. To a limited extent, however, it is interesting to know of some of the questions with which the Management has to contend.

When the artists have been given their contracts (a procedure that reaches beyond salaries and rôles to include such details as the type of travel accommodation that shall be provided for the singers, both on sea and on land), and when the other House departments are in working order, the Management settles down to the season's business of producing opera. All matters of artistic policy are under the direct supervision of the General Manager. The full repertory for the coming season is chosen during the previous spring, from among standard works, less familiar classics, and such modern novelties as warrant production by an organization that lays no claim to functioning as an experimental laboratory. It may be known, for example, that *Aida* will be given; *Norma, Madama Butterfly, Don Giovanni, Tannhaeuser, Tristan und Isolde,* and *I Pagliacci;* but the exact number of performances of each cannot be determined in advance.

The detailed planning of the repertory and the casting of the parts is as sensitive as a seismograph to the fluctuations of public preference as well as to those of internal economics. To a certain extent, the rotation of the operas depends upon the availability of the principal artists, some of whom are not under contract for the entire season, and none of whom normally appear more than three times a week. Further, the greatest care must be exercised that all patrons be given the works they want; that all be afforded an opportunity of hearing the casts they want; that the most popular works and casts be distributed among all the subscription performances; that the same work be never repeated in the same subscription series during the entire season, or in any one week's list of regular performances; and that a certain amount of variety from among the Italian, French, and German works be infused into the schedules for each week. The demand for certain operas, the rotation of all the operas, and the working capacity of the artists are like a juggler's three balls, which must be kept spinning symmetrically throughout the length of the season. The execution of a task of such delicacy is immensely facilitated by Mr. Johnson's personal experience in practical operatic procedure, and by Mr. Ziegler's long familiarity with both critical and managerial demands.

The normal intricacy of keeping the balls spinning in the air can be further complicated by occasional startling requests. During the season of 1936-1937, the Management received two letters, both from subscribers, and both couched in unmistakably definite terms. One correspondent complained that his subscription contained entirely too many Wagnerian works.  He expressed his readiness to make a cultural obeisance before the new popularity of Wagner (if it had to be) ; still, he felt that the tastes of the non-Wagnerites deserved consideration, too.  He had paid to be entertained by operas other than those of the heavy German repertory, and *would the Management kindly do something about it?*  The other gentleman complained that his subscription contained entirely too few Wagnerian works.  Wagner, he held, ranks as the supreme master of music drama; the newspapers were ablaze with enthusiasm for the Wagnerian operas that *other* subscribers were getting; he had paid to be entertained by something richer than "Italian tinklings," and *would the Management kindly do something about it?*

After the most careful ball-spinning possible, all this fell as something of a blow.  A preliminary investigation of the subscription books showed that both indignant gentlemen were registered to appear for their operatic fare on Friday nights.  Obviously, somewhere, something was wrong.  Then further probings brought to light an interesting fact: both gentlemen had split their subscriptions, using their seats only on *alternate* Fridays, and selling the remaining tickets to friends.

The weekly list of operas is determined some ten days in advance of performance.  Then the casts are assigned.  Then the rehearsal schedules are planned.  Then the stage departments take the preliminary steps in requisitioning the necessary scenery and properties from the warehouses.  Then the stage band players are engaged.  Then the supers are summoned.  Then work begins in good earnest, with rehearsals in progress throughout the House, and scenic and property repairs

undertaken on the stage or in the departmental headquarters.  Out in the lobby, the tickets are being sold.
And in the General Manager's office, where the wheels
of this intricate mechanism are set in motion and kept
lubricated, every buzzing of the telephone may herald a
piece of news that can bring all the activity to a stand-
still.  The prima donna is ill and cannot appear.  The
tenor has come down with grippe, and even if the fever
abates, he cannot possibly sing by Wednesday evening.

The repertory listing of the artists is such that a cast
replacement can generally be made at short notice,
after a great deal of anxious telephoning, last minute
rehearsals, and the printing of slips announcing the
substitution in the programs.  Cast replacements are
never imposed upon the singers, whose private working
schedules must be considerably adjusted to the demands
of the occasion.  The Management regards it as an act
of courtesy for one artist to step into a colleague's
place, so that the "show may go on."  But even such a
gesture of good-will fails to lift a cast replacement
above the level of an anxious emergency.  Only one
cloud looms blacker upon the managerial horizon.
That is the last-minute necessity of a complete change
of bill, and all humanly possible steps are taken to avoid
it.  If a freak of chance—or of influenza—strikes several members of a cast, or if substitutes cannot appear,
it may happen that "the show goes on" in the form of
a different opera, which occasions frenzied and vex-
atious activity to every least member of the House
staff.  A new cast must be gotten together; the warehouses must assemble new sets and properties; the stage
crew must tear down the scenery already in place; new
costumes must be fetched out and distributed; different

SCENE ON THE METROPOLITAN STAGE DURING A PERFORMANCE
OF "LA TRAVIATA."

OFF - STAGE
CHORUS DUR-
ING A PER-
FORMANCE

wigs sent about; new scores delivered; arrangements must be made with the extra performers of the stage band and the supers' group; while prospective patrons in the Box-office line may find that the substituted opera does not match the mood which impelled them to come. The brief, calm announcement that the opera has been changed offers small indication of the turmoil behind it.

Of all the House departments, the Box-office is in most constant and most direct communication with the public. What the opera's patrons like or do not like about performances and casts, is sooner or later reported there. The most obvious way in which patrons make known their preferences is, of course, through their purchases of tickets. When all the seats for *Tristan* have been sold less than five hours after being put on sale, it is a fair assumption that *Tristan* is "popular," and may be reported as such when later performance schedules are being prepared. But the ticket sale is by no means the only way in which the Box-office keeps its finger upon the pulse of popular demand. Since his youthful days at the Family Circle window, Mr. Lewis has made it a point to note down the wishes, inquiries, and suggestions of those people who take sufficient interest in the opera to come at all. Where the General Manager may receive a dozen letters of suggestion (normally written only in a moment of special ardor), Lewis and his staff interview hundreds upon hundreds of patrons, in an effort to learn exactly what it is that the public wants. Patrons come with all sorts of suggestions and requests, and careful note is made of all, for the subsequent scrutiny of the Management.

Since the Box-office is also the source of the opera's revenue, it might seem that the Management regards such reports chiefly for the sake of their "Box-office value." This is not the case. Certainly, every responsible management wishes to close its season with as large an intake and as small a deficit as is possible, without sacrificing the standards of the institution. The management of the Metropolitan is no exception. The Metropolitan, however, stands definitely as a non-profit-making enterprise. Its purposes are artistic and educational, and the best it can hope for is to "keep out of the red." Any possible profits that might accrue would be turned back into production. Still, the earning of expenses is not the sole reason for giving attention to the reports of popular taste. Equally important is the desire to maintain the good-will of the public. The position of the Metropolitan is such that it must do more than try to "keep out of the red." It must continue to stand in the public mind as the foremost operatic establishment of the country. Verdi's advice to the young Gatti, to "keep the house full," carries an implication farther-reaching than one of dollars and cents. If a house is to be kept full, the people who fill it must have a regard for it, over and above a willingness to pay an occasional entrance fee. Operas or artists which should persistently fail to please the public, would harm the institution to a greater extent than could be calculated in terms of a deficient intake on the nights they were billed. They would tend to lower the attraction-powers of the house, and keep people away as a matter of habit. During the years of its existence, the House has often presented special-cast performances or Sunday Night Concerts, at prices which hardly netted expenses, but which definitely impelled the public to come—and coming, to hold the House in esteem. Similarly, the House has often experimented with less-than-popular works, sheerly for the sake of an artistic principle. A case of this kind was *Pelléas et Mélisande,* which was regularly offered for its musical and educational value, even though it was "popular" with but a limited proportion of the opera's patrons. "Pleasing everybody, all the time" is a difficult order for any organization to fill; on the whole, however, the Management does its utmost to offer productions which people *want* to hear, not only as a means of "staying out of the red," but of maintaining the faith, the interest, and the good-will of the public. That the public's pleasure and the public's payments often coincide, does not alter the fact that they exist as two separate factors, both of which are necessary. In this sense, Mr. Lewis' carefully prepared reports are valuable as a direct barometer of public taste which the administration offices might never discover—and the shabby little clerk, who saves all winter for a visit to the opera, and uses his lunch hour to wait in the queue for a Balcony ticket, may have a hand in shaping the repertory policies of the Metropolitan.

## 2.

Mr. Lewis and his staff of assistants begin their work in the Box-office with the issuance of the season's subscription tickets. Each of the five regular performances and the one popularly priced performance of every week, stands as a single subscription unit. Before the season begins, the subscription books are open, old subscribers renewing their tenure on seats, and new subscribers applying for locations. Once these books are closed, Lewis knows exactly how many seats have been taken up by subscriptions, and how many remain to be offered for single-performance sale. The tickets are then printed, subscription admissions bound into booklets and delivered to their purchasers in advance of the opera's opening, and the single seat admissions printed "loose" and sold one week before the performance for which they are valid.

The tickets for the various performances are regulated by a thorough control-system of numbering, and their House location is indicated by color. A white stub marked Forty-one, for example, tells the doorman that its holder shall be admitted to the Orchestra on the night of the season's Forty-first regular subscription performance.

Since the tickets go on sale a week in advance, the Box-office is constantly handling at least eight different sets of tickets (and answering at least eight different sets of questions) for different performances, with different casts and different curtain-times, in different locations, and at different prices. The tickets for each performance are arranged in separate racks, according to their color. No matter how many ticket windows are open or how many Box-office attendants are conducting sales, a glance at any rack shows the number of Orchestra, or Balcony, or Dress Circle seats still available for any performance. Standees' tickets go on sale one half-hour before the start of each performance. Since the number of standees admitted to the House is limited by the City Fire Department, especially attractive productions draw these purchasers to the doors by nine-thirty in the morning, the earliest comers often standing in the ticket line some ten hours for the privilege of standing four hours more at the "show." A special Box-office staff is detailed to the care of the mail orders, of which there is a vast amount. Only rigid system could avoid confusion among the thousands of tickets handled each week by the various Box-office departments.

The ticket-sellers get their share of curious questioning. A scientist of scholarly distinction, whose photographs made him recognizable on sight, appeared in the line one day, to purchase tickets for a performance that was already sold out.

"I'm very sorry," said Mr. Lewis, who attended the gentleman himself, "but we've no seats left."

"Not one?"

"Not even one. Every last one's sold."

"*Every* one?"

"There's nothing left at any price. We've been sold out since the first day the tickets were offered."

"But," the scholarly gentleman went on in imperturbable calm, "haven't you got two good ones in the center of the Dress Circle?"

### 3.

During the season of 1913, an interesting article appeared in the old *New York Herald,* wherein an able reporter sought to make known to the public the mysteries involved in "paying off the opera's hands." To the credit of all be it said that the reporter asked no impolitic questions, the Paymaster revealed no impolitic House news, and the article turned out interesting without telling too much of what should not be told. The able reporter is to-day in a position where, in all modesty, he can appreciate the journalistic discretion he exercised in 1913. He is Edward Ziegler, the Assistant Manager of the company, in whose keeping lie all the secrets of salary scales and wage rates, which the news-hawks of a hardier age try to pry out—and fail to secure. The business of paying off the hands of grand opera is in the charge of the genial Frank Garlichs, Treasurer of the Metropolitan Opera Association, and of Aimé Gerber, the Paymaster. The facts of who gets how much are not for public consumption. Suffice it that the offices are busy six days a week.

### 4.

An important part of managerial activity (of which the local public is scarcely aware) is the organization of the opera tours. Throughout the regular season, the company makes a fixed number of visits to the nearby cities of Brooklyn, Newark, Philadelphia, and Hartford. These visits are arranged for Tuesday nights, when no performances take place in New York, and the schedule sometimes falls out so that operas are given in two cities on the same evening. On such occasions, separate carloads of scenery, properties, and costumes are sent ahead, separate casts and conductors are transported there, while the orchestra is divided and then rounded out by a group of players known as "regular extra men," who have played with the organization for years and are thoroughly familiar with operatic routine.

Though the Brooklyn Academy of Music is a delightful house to play in and the reception of its public is heartening, the Brooklyn performances have come to be associated with the dread of a "jinx." There it was that Caruso was overtaken by his last illness. There it was that the impromptu choral "show" had to be staged when *Lohengrin's* truck broke down in the snow. In a week of stormy winter weather, the worst night is sure to be a Brooklyn Tuesday. And other happenings of a more or less diverting nature have delayed their appearance, it would seem, until the company visited Brooklyn.

Andrea de Segurola, who never appeared anywhere without his monocle, once entered the Brooklyn house, on his way to dress for the performance, and stopped a moment in the lobby to exchange greetings with Gerber. A strikingly handsome young woman came up to join them, and Gerber presented de Segurola to her. In the flurry of meeting the distinguished-looking "star," the young woman let fall her vanity bag, the contents of which went clattering over the stone floor of the lobby. In an access of gallantry, Segurola went after the things, stooped too precipitously, and dropped his monocle into the midst of them. The glass broke into a hundred pieces, and de Segurola, who was somewhat dependent upon it, had to accomplish his dressing and make-up "by ear."

Another time, one of the tenors adjusted a false moustache, took up some scissors with which to trim it to the ultimate degree of attractiveness, and cut a deep gash in his lip. There was much blood, much confusion, and much superstitious dread on the part of the wounded Italian, as to the outcome of a performance that revealed so inauspicious an omen even before it began. Dr. Henry F. Bruning, who chanced to be present in the theater, was hastily summoned backstage; a dressing was applied, the make-up man brought his arts to bear upon the glaring white plaster, and the terrified tenor was plied with restoratives, after which the performance got under way to a nine-fifteen start. Inquiries were put through to Mr. Gatti, whether the performance would have to be cut.

"Nothing will be cut in the opera," replied Gatti, "except, perhaps, the lip of our tenor."

In the face of such happenings, only one comment is offered:

"There's nothing one can do about it—it's the Brooklyn 'jinx.'"

For outlying performances, private railroad cars are provided to carry the complete "show" out and bring it back to New York. It is for these occasions that Mr. Judels has devised the astute system of announcing outgoing trains seven minutes in advance of their actual departure. Return trains are sent out immediately after the performance, "heads are counted" on the railroad platform, and the entire troupe of singers and players is deposited in the New York station between two and three in the morning, after which there is a rush for home, lest to-morrow's rehearsal activities suffer from want of sleep.

The post-season tours are considerably more elaborate. Throughout the season, the Management is in communication with distant cities that apply for a visit from the Metropolitan Opera, arranging details of time, repertory, and casts. These tours are planned in a single circuit of "trouping," with no trips home until the engagement ends. The tour begins the week following the close of the New York winter season. Scenery, properties, and costumes are sent ahead; the orchestra, the stage crews, and the other working departments stay with the "show," while the principal singers and choristers join it as they are needed.  The visits to each city vary in length from two to ten performances of selected repertory.

In 1936, the Management inaugurated its first supplementary Spring Season of opera, offering four weeks of standard works, at a reduced scale of prices.  The Spring Season gets under way early in May, immediately after the company's return from its tour.  The project was launched to extend the duration of an operatic year, to provide wider opportunities for gifted young artists, and to offer the facilities of the Metropolitan Opera to the public within a generally accessible price range.  At the close of the first Spring Season, several of the performers and one of the operas had given such excellent accounting of themselves that they were carried over into the roster and repertory lists of the regular winter season.  The Spring Season is being continued, the direction of its second year of life coming under the charge of Mr. Lee Pattison.

CHAPTER XII

## OPERA BROADCASTING

### 1.

ON CHRISTMAS DAY of 1931, there took place an event which served to lift Metropolitan Opera permanently out of the ranks of a local, metropolitan institution. On that day, the National Broadcasting Company assumed the rôle of Santa Claus on a large scale, and presented the country as a whole with its first broadcast of a complete opera from the Metropolitan stage. The work was *Haensel und Gretel,* with a cast including Queena Mario, Editha Fleischer, Dorothee Manski, and Gustav Schuetzendorf. From that time forward, Metropolitan opera has become national (and, for one season thus far, international as well) ; America as a whole has begun a personal acquaintanceship not only with opera, but with the finest productions of opera available.

The broadcasting of Metropolitan Opera was beset with difficulties. In most cases, it is the performer who seeks "time on the air." In the case of the Metropolitan, the process was reversed. For some years prior to 1931, NBC officials had been desirous of sending out Metropolitan performances, and Mr. Gatti had steadily refused his consent, on the grounds that radio reproduction was not yet capable of transmitting a faithful reflection of the work that represented his own best efforts, and that anything short of such a faithful reflection would create a false picture of Metropolitan standards in the public mind. There had been opera broadcasts before, chiefly from the stage of the Chicago Civic Opera. Mr. Gatti had listened to them, and by them had been inspired to cling even more tenaciously to his decision of barring the microphones from the Metropolitan.

NBC had sent Mr. Charles Grey to Chicago, as the engineer in charge of the opera work, and Mr. Grey had learned much by way of discovering and solving the problems that had caused difficulty. On his return to New York, Mr. Grey was asked by NBC to undertake studies which would make practical use of the fruits of his experience, and would tend toward the perfection of operatic broadcasting. The direct result of Mr. Grey's research is the unique apparatus now in use in the opera broadcasts, some of which he designed himself. When his experiments had reached the practical stage, further negotiations were opened with Mr. Gatti. Gatti's response was entirely characteristic and entirely fair.

"I must continue to withhold my consent to broadcasting the Metropolitan performances until it is proven to me that my objections are groundless."

NBC's answer was to ask Gatti to set a time when he and his staff of conductors would be free to listen to proof. Gatti replied that a performance of *Madama Butterfly* would be given three days hence, in the regular repertory; if the NBC engineers cared to try sending it out, they were welcome to do so. The trial broadcast was private. Gatti and his musical staff joined the broadcasting officials in the Board Room at NBC headquarters, and the intricate apparatus was installed in the House solely to "pipe" that single performance in there.

All obstacles seemed ended when NBC finally secured permission to enter the House at all. But that early smell of triumph was blown away by the difficulties surrounding the test case. There was less than three days in which to get things ready. Mr. Grey had never witnessed a performance of *Madama Butterfly;* there had been no full rehearsal for him to watch; he had had no time, what with installing his equipment within the brief time limit, to study the score or to make a detailed acquaintanceship with the acoustic properties of the Opera House; and he was completely at sea as to when to arrange for tonal adjustments on his new controlboard. Thus equipped, he placed his microphones by his general knowledge of acoustics and his memories of Chicago, installed his sending apparatus in Box Forty-four of the Grand Tier by grace of Mr. Gatti, and set to work.

A telephone connection had been installed between Box Forty-four and the NBC board room, and presently the light flashed.

"They say they want a little more orchestra and a little less singing," whispered Grey's assistant.

Whereupon Mr. Grey did things with the faders. Ten minutes later, the light flashed again and the request was repeated. Ten minutes after that, a third flash heralded a request for a little less orchestra and a little more singing. Each flash drew icy beads to the brow of Mr. Grey, who interpreted these requests only as the gentle breaking of a lost cause. Still, the experimental broadcast went on. When it was done, at last, Grey turned his back resolutely on the telephone and

tried to concentrate upon the winding up of cables.
Then the light flashed a fourth time.

"You've done it!" came the official voice of NBC.
"We're putting the 'Met' on the air for good!"

The perfection with which the operatic performances
reach the public to-day must stand as the most fitting
tribute to that category of "radio stars" which does not
often find its way to the attention of the "fans." Radio
itself was no longer an experiment, of course, by the time
the Metropolitan reached the air. But the normal radio
routine centered chiefly about the regular studio program, for the sending out of which the program itself is
fitted to the measure of broadcasting requirements.
That is to say, the engineers regulate the position of the
microphones, these microphones are fixed there as the
focus of the "show," and the performers are grouped
about them in locations best adapted to the picking up
of sound. Further, the programs are carefully rehearsed, with frequent interruptions from production
directors and engineers, who offer suggestions as to
timing, tonal volume, emphasis, and the like. Finally,
the entire program normally originates in a studio already equipped with the best facilities for further amplification and reproduction. Political or "special
dinner" programs which originate outside the studios,
have, at least, the advantage of fixed microphones.
There had been some experimenting with mobile units,
or portable microphones, such as are used in interview-
ing unsuspecting individuals along Broadway on Elec-
tion Day night; but these microphones could be kept
entirely visible and could be moved within the desired
range of distance of the persons speaking into them. In
carrying the microphones into the Metropolitan Opera

House, the NBC engineers found conditions which could scarcely have differed more drastically from the accustomed radio routine, if they had been especially designed to do so.

No microphones in any fixed position could pick up a balanced blending of tone proceeding at the same time from an orchestra that sat still and a company of singers moving freely about a hundred-foot stage. All microphones had to be kept invisible, so as not to disturb the appearance of the House, and therefore could not be carried near to the singers. Radio rehearsals of the performance were impossible. And the sum-total of the operatic pick-up had to be "piped" back to NBC headquarters for further amplification and resending. The solution of all these problems involved the most expert engineering ingenuity.

There was an opera in progress upon the Metropolitan stage, and there were microphones waiting to pick it up. The two could be welded into a successful union only by supplying, from the outside, that acoustic perspective which the opera patron supplies for himself, by watching the stage as well as by listening. In their Chicago days, the NBC experts had learned that a microphone rigged up in an orchestra chair in the opera house does *not* transmit the same tonal effects heard by the auditor sitting in that same chair. Not only does the auditor see the stage action, but, through seeing it, he makes unconscious adjustments in his reception of tone. If, for example, the soprano leaves her place at the footlights to rush to the rear of the stage in search of the baritone, the auditor watches her move, and adjusts himself to expect her next tones to sound forth from a greater distance. A microphone, unassisted, makes no

such adjustments.  It simply mirrors a faithful reflection of a "near" tone and then of a "far" tone.  And the
listener in Fargo, North Dakota, who is completely unfamiliar with the soprano's deportment, wonders what
can be wrong with his radio set, to account for the sudden unevenness of tone.  Further, if he has recently
paid to have his radio repaired, his wonder will increase
to resentment.  He will arrive at the inescapable conclusion that opera is not all it is said to be.  Thus,
the NBC engineers assumed the task of supplying, for
the listener in Fargo, North Dakota, a complete acoustic perspective.  By virtue of which, the radio audience
hears a performance which is equal in *effect* to the performance heard in the House, and even more perfect in
tonal *balance*.

### 2.

The broadcasting of Metropolitan Opera is settled
between the microphones on the stage, and the engineer's controls, set up specially for each performance,
in Box Forty-four.  Five nights a week, this box is
adorned by society.  On Saturday afternoons, its adornment proceeds from Mr. Grey, Mr. Milton J. Cross,
NBC's veteran announcer, and Mr. Herbert Liversidge, NBC's operatic production director.  Mr. Cross
sits in the rear of the box, behind a glass door through
which he can observe the stage.  The door is sound-
proofed.  Mr. Grey and Mr. Liversidge sit in the front,
in open contact with the body of the House, and amid a
mass of the most sensitive engineering equipment.
House people often refer to the intricate set-up of amplifiers, volume indicators, telephone cables, and con-
trol-panels as "the stuff you stumble over."  Whereupon

the NBC representatives give voice to their own opinions on the stumbling qualities of back-drops and set-pieces on the stage. Again, it all depends on the point of view.

There are four microphones permanently installed in the footlights. Others—varying in number from two to four, according to the tonal properties of the operas to be broadcast—are placed above the orchestra pit. In the Chicago days, the orchestra's microphones were set on the floor, exactly as though they were additional musical instruments; but experiments proved that the sound came over better when caught from above. Although as many as eight microphones may be used in a given performance, no more than four are ever in action at the same time. Often a broadcast may run for half an hour on only two microphones. A microphone installed at great cost, may be used for no more than five minutes of the broadcast performance.

The microphones were formerly set straight upright, to catch the voices of the singers, until Mr. Grey applied certain findings in the matter of reflected sound, which impelled him to invert them. Seventy-five per cent of all tone heard in the House is reflected tone. A singer whose voice can easily fill the auditorium during a performance, could not be heard at all if the stage were padded with thick carpets and hung with heavy draperies. Working on these principles, Mr. Grey found he could send out more sharply defined tone by inverting the microphones. All microphones are now angled downward, so that they pick up the voices and the orchestra, not as they issue forth from throats and fiddles, but as they are reflected, in greater intensity, by the

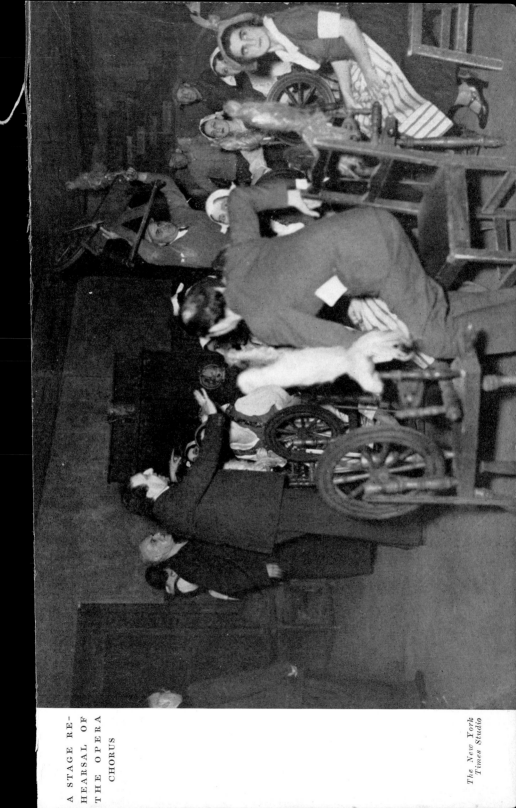

A STAGE RE-
HEARSAL OF
THE OPERA
CHORUS

The New York
Times Studio

THE OPERA BROADCAST.   RIGHT, CHARLES GREY AT THE CONTROLS

wooden floor of the stage. All microphones are connected with the engineer's control-board by cables, installed especially for broadcasting, and which run from the back of the stage, through the body of the House, into Box Forty-four.

Each microphone is responsible for the sounds within its own angle of pick-up. The engineer's control-board, or mixing-panel, is equipped with as many faders as there are microphones, each fader regulating the volume of sound picked up by its own "mike." As the performance progresses, Mr. Grey constantly tunes in those microphones which must pick up that particular moment of sound, and tunes the others out. The microphones in actual use are determined by the point on the stage where the action is taking place.

Further, to assure complete tonal balance, the engineer's equipment makes it possible for him to bring up the volume of any tones which sound weak and to take down the volume of those which are over loud. If the orchestra, for example, is in danger of drowning out a singer, Mr. Grey restores immediate balance on his mixing-panel; if a singer asserts himself too vociferously over the orchestra or the other vocal groups, another twist of the fader-knob maintains the equilibrium in the opposite direction. (In certain Wagnerian scores, however, the orchestra overshadows the singers in such a way that it would present an inaccurate musical picture to interfere with it.) While the volume-indicator registers the sum-total of outgoing sound at any given moment, the balance between the various units of the performance is maintained by the unusually acute ear of Mr. Grey.

Because of the delicate problems arising from the broadcast of a moving performance of opera, which is quite unrehearsed as far as the microphones are concerned, Messrs Grey and Liversidge spend much time familiarizing themselves with the operas—their scores, their action, their sound by phonograph records; the orchestral routine, the solo and choral routines, the combinations of voices and instruments, and the voice qualities and idiosyncrasies of the individual singers. They translate both sound and action into terms of radio adaptability, and prepare for the mechanical set-up of the broadcast.

From notes made during the regular operatic rehearsals, the footlight microphones are adjusted as to the angle at which they must face the floor. The angle is determined by the voice quality of the singers and the nature and location of the stage-sets. The measured position of the sets and properties makes it possible to adjust the microphones with accuracy, but the spontaneous movements of the "stars" can always inject a note of interesting speculation into the process. If the lady who turned left at Thursday's rehearsal becomes suddenly inspired to turn right on Saturday afternoon, Mr. Grey may have a moment of acute activity at the control-board in Box Forty-four.

Acoustic problems may arise which cannot be "cured" in advance, and which, for the radio audience, must be righted at the controls. When Strauss' *Elektra* was broadcast, some seasons back, the rehearsals indicated no undue difficulties; yet, during the performance, the voice of one of the singers suddenly sounded "dead." Mr. Grey quickly slipped off his ear-phones, to check the broadcast version of the opera to which he had been listening, with the flesh-and-blood version in the House. The singer had moved a step or two forward by that time, and his voice rang out vibrantly through the auditorium.  Slipping his ear-phones on again, Grey found that the trouble had stopped.  As the singer crossed the stage, then, the "dead" sound came back.  It dawned upon Mr. Grey at last that these tonal variations were being caused by the draperies in the stage-set, which interfered with the reflection of sound.  The stage was set with three entrances, each covered with rich hangings.  When the singers stood in front of one of these doorways, their voices, in radio parlance, "went sour"; directly they stepped aside, their voices came back to normal.  Throughout that performance, Mr. Grey had to work hard at his mixing-panel to compensate for the decorations!

In the broadcasting of *Emperor Jones,* the unusually heavy use of drums in the score necessitated the installation of a complete double set of microphones.  Microphones are "afraid" of drums.  Because of the shape of the sound-wave set up by these instruments, a single drum can occupy a microphone to the exclusion of all other instruments or voices sounding at the same time. The normal number of microphones, operating normally, would have brought the radio public the impression of a solo recital of the tom-tom going on in the Opera House.  There was no way, of course, of getting rid of the drums or of altering their effect.  So Grey hazarded a means of counteracting their influence.  For that broadcast, he set up the microphones in pairs, depoled each pair, and put them out of phase with each other.  Throughout the afternoon, he worked those double microphones in pairs, so that one could cancel the other, thereby eliminating the siege of the drums and allowing the other sounds to pass through.

There are other problems, not of an exclusively acoustic origin, that can make Saturday afternoon a busy time in Box Forty-four. Chief of these is the business of conveying the sheerly dramatic value of an opera by means of sound alone. There are moments when the continuity of the performance may depend chiefly on the stage action, the music, important though it be, serving as an accompaniment. That is why broadcast opera never can, and never should, sound quite like a reproduced concert. The Card Scene in *Carmen* offered notable difficulties along the lines of dramatic presentation. There is music throughout this scene, but its chief value, to the audience, lies in following *Carmen's* turning of the cards. House patrons have only to observe the stage to understand the progress of events. But how to convey a fortune-telling-by-cards via the radio? Ultimately, Mr. Grey hit upon the plan of angling the microphones in such a way as to pick up the sound of the cards themselves, as *Carmen* flicked them from the pack and slapped them down upon the stage. At a slight sacrifice of orchestral values, the radio audience was allowed to follow the play of the cards.

One of the queerest of radio problems involves the singers' pronunciation. "Good diction," which is among the goals of every artist, means the clearest possible enunciation of the words of the text. For technical reasons, however, operatic enunciation is brought over the air as better than it actually is. Thus, when a singer's pronunciation is normally excellent upon the stage, a problem arises: speech excellencies are intensified, causing the singers who enunciate most clearly to give

the impression of over-emphasizing their articulation.
One of Mr. Grey's chief tasks is to tone down, on the
mixing-panel, the results of that "excellent diction"
which the singer has probably labored long and hard to
acquire. He does this by closing the microphone near
the singer, and using one at a greater distance.

Sitting, as he does, in the open House, Mr. Grey
works entirely in the dark. He has designed his control-board with notched fader-knobs, and manipulates
them by their feel. Generally, he works two with each
hand, controlling four microphones at one time. He is
equipped with ear-phones, which bring him the sound of
the opera as he sends it out. By slipping these off, he
can check the tonal proportions of his broadcast with
those heard in the House. He does this frequently, lest
too great a concentration upon the broadcast alone lead
him into over-emphasizing any one unit of the performance.

Beside him sits the production director, who follows
the score, by a hooded light on his music stand, and
provides Mr. Grey with a pre-view of what is about to
happen on the stage. Although Grey watches the stage,
he must be prepared for the various tonal effects *before*
they take place. All expected entrances, concerted passages, high notes, low notes, *crescendi,* and *decrescendi,*
are announced to Mr. Grey a moment or two in advance
of their advent. They are announced to him by hand
positions and finger signals, since strict quiet must be
observed in the House during a performance. Through
a study of the score and the action, Grey knows when
the "mixing" of tonal balance is due, and the pre-view
cues indicate to him the exact split-second of time when
it must be prepared. Loud tone and soft tone, for ex-

ample, cannot be picked up simultaneously by the same microphone. Thus, if a *piano* passage blends immediately into a sharp *crescendo,* the advance-announcement of the conductor's down-beat enables Grey to reach for the proper fader and tune in the second microphone at the precise moment it is needed. All changes in tone quality or volume, as well as the shiftings of position in the stage action, are announced and prepared by these signals. In the normal radio program, the production director is responsible for the casting, timing, rehearsing, and general effectiveness of the "show." In the Metropolitan Opera broadcasts, however, where these duties are in the charge of opera officials, NBC's production director is limited to translating the opera's progress into signals for the engineer. The importance of these signals make it imperative that the operatic production director be a musician as well. Mr. Liversidge is a professional organist. Constantly on the alert for the least variation in tonal quality and intensity, Grey "mixes" the sounds at the same moment they come from the stage, affording the radio listener that correct balance of tone which the score demands.

The mechanical equipment of the opera broadcasts is so arranged that it is virtually impossible for accidents to occur. Lest potential defects in the electrical equipment of the Opera House cause interference, the broadcasting apparatus is not connected with the Opera building in any way. It is grounded to a water-main in West Thirty-ninth Street, and fed by batteries of its own, under the stage. If, by any emergency, the lights in the House should be blown out, the broadcast could continue undisturbed. Further, every piece in the pick-up and sending apparatus is duplicated. Beside the mechanism actually in use, there are double amplifiers, with the tubes kept heated up throughout the performance; a second mixer (more accurately, perhaps, a twin-mixer, the only one of its kind, built into the same case as the one at work); and extra microphones. Should the least defect show itself in any of the apparatus in use, a few seconds of adjustment would transfer the broadcast from one set of equipment to the other, while the performance was in progress. Only twice has there been "trouble" in the sending out of Metropolitan Opera, and neither time was the broadcasting equipment at fault. Once there was an electric leakage in the subway, which runs under the West side of the Opera's ground, and once, a similar leakage in the system of the New York Edison Company.

During the week, the broadcasting equipment is stored in an unused elevator in the Fortieth Street lobby. On Saturday morning it is set up in Box Forty-four, under the supervision of Mr. Grey, and taken down again immediately after the matinée. The business of broadcasting is accomplished by Mr. Grey, Mr. Liversidge, Mr. Cross, two assistant engineers, kept busy at the telephone circuits and other equipment, and a sixth representative, whom NBC stations in the left wings, to telephone to Box Forty-four, by specially installed wire, any emergency delays on the stage, and to advise the engineer of the moment when the conductor leaves for the orchestra pit. Mr. Cross announces the conductor's movements through his own microphone, behind the glass panel, and the "show" is on. Cross signals his readiness to speak by flashing a special light, built into the control-board. Should any talking run over into the beginning of the performance, Grey can switch it out.

From the broadcasting point of view, the operas present vastly different problems, each of which must be settled by microphone adjustments, or "mixing." The French operas are the most difficult to send out, because of the prevailing lightness of their orchestration and other tonal combinations; while the solidity of the German works makes them less subject to distortion.

Once the opera leaves the apparatus in Box Forty-four (to be amplified, taken by telephone wires to the master apparatus at NBC headquarters in Radio City, re-amplified, re-routed, and re-telephoned to individual broadcasting stations of that NBC network all over the country), its progress is that of all radio programs. Believing as they do that the sending out of Metropolitan Opera is the most important institutional program on the air to-day, NBC officials devote to it the most elaborate engineering equipment yet devised. It is never a grateful task to set forth the costs involved in the carrying out of other people's business, but it may safely be said that the expense of bringing Metropolitan Opera before the country would go far towards setting up a rival operatic organization.

### 3.

And so the Metropolitan Opera was put "on the air." Which offered no indication of what would happen to it once it got there. How would it be received by the vast and heterogeneous public which makes up America? Up to the time of that first broadcast in 1931, grand opera was neither a natural nor a native form of American entertainment. Maurice Grau once said that he regarded his New York opera venture as a strict bit of business, involving the selection of famous voices for fashionable ears to hear, and bearing little on art "as art." (Grau said this, it is interesting to note, around 1903, when the times and the tastes had not yet been tinged with modernism, War reactions, or the manifestations of the jazz age.) Grau's successors modified this outlook to a great extent, but, even under the best circumstances of the best boom years, grand opera remained a strictly "exclusive" commodity.

There were reasons for this, to be sure, rooting partly in operatic costs and partly in native tastes. One could argue that America didn't "like" opera because it didn't get it; one could argue just as well that America took no steps to get opera because it didn't want it. But whichever factor was the more potent, the result remained that only a limited section of the public enjoyed opera. The rank-and-file citizens were believed to look upon it as something alien and "highbrow" (when they troubled to look upon it at all). They took their personal amusement at the movies. The movies were cheap and accessible.

Then came the Metropolitan broadcasts, which carried opera into the living-room, where it was even cheaper and more accessible than the movies. The American public found itself very literally presented with a form of entertainment which was so strange that its entertainment-value was best symbolized by a question-mark. On the one hand, it was "highbrow," which was damning at the onset. On the other hand, it was "fashionable," which might make it worth a trial at least. What further attractions it might possess were an unknown quantity.  In the average Austrian city, the boy who pushes the butcher's delivery-cart may be heard to lighten his labors by whistling the *Preislied* from *Die Meistersinger,* with which he has been perfectly familiar since his cradle days.  It remained to discover how the average American, reared in complete innocence of operatic tradition, would receive the operatic form.  He might take pleasure, this average American, in reading accounts of a Metropolitan opening; of the thrilling discovery of a new "star"; or the details, as set forth in the tabloid press, of operatic peccadillos. But this was something different.  This was a personal, intimate, head-on encounter with the substance of opera itself, denuded of all such glittering caparisons.

It is a difficult thing to determine the success with which any radio program is received.  There is no applause, no statement of circulation, no box-office count. Mechanical vote-devices are being developed, but have not yet come into general use.  To date, there are but two ways of estimating a program's popularity.  Some experts rely on commercial rating charts for their "popularity count"; some cling to the fan-mail reactions; and all admit that neither system is perfect.  The chart rating system is based upon personal questionnaires which cannot possibly reach every listener, while the fan-mail system reflects the views of only those listeners who trouble to write in.

In the case of the Metropolitan Opera, however, there came a response by what might be termed spontaneous generation, which is unique even in radio annals, and which leaves no doubt as to the genuine enthusiasm with which the nation has received a form of entertainment which, to the largest proportion of that nation, was a completely alien thing.

After the first months of broadcasting, letters began to find their way into the House and to NBC. They differed from the regulation "fan" documents in that they supplemented their praise (and occasionally censure) with requests for information. Would the Opera's management announce its repertory longer than a week in advance, so that people might have time to "read up" on coming productions? Where could librettos be purchased, and what would they cost? Which was the best book on opera plots? Which were the best musical biographies? Or histories? Where could one read facts about the singers?

The next year or two marked an important change in the character of these letters. Where the earlier crop had come from interested individuals, there now poured in requests from organized groups—clubs, schools, choral and musical organizations, and also from a new type of group which had never existed before. These were the Opera Clubs. The Clubs were formed by a nucleus of men and women who met regularly at one another's homes on Saturday afternoons, took tea together, and listened to the Metropolitan broadcasts in exactly the same spirit in which they played bridge at other times. These groups asked for more than isolated facts about librettos and books. They wanted good, solid material on which to base discussions of opera, so that they might be better equipped to enjoy the Saturday broadcasts.

In time, all this mail came to take on the proportions of a first-class problem. Both the Metropolitan and NBC were accustomed to straight statements of praise or blame, but neither was prepared to send out the working materials of a class in grand opera. At the same time, the officials of both organizations realized that something very like a miracle was asserting itself in the realm of public taste. In the case of even the most popular forms of entertainment, the normal procedure is for press-agents and publicity departments to bestir themselves to devise ways and means of arousing public interest. Here, the process was reversed. The entertainment in question was perhaps the last in the world which astute showmen would have styled "popular," yet the public, of its own accord, was deluging two managements with requests for information about it. There had been no undue publicity; no "contests" were announced; no "prizes" were offered; no "drive" had been organized to solicit response. The people who wrote in for information about the opera did so because they were personally interested in knowing more about it. And all the while that the Opera and the broadcasting officials were discussing what should be done about all this accumulating mail, the requests and the interest and the Opera Clubs went on growing.

# CHAPTER XIII

# THE METROPOLITAN OPERA GUILD

## 1.

THE solution of the radio-information problem finally came through the co-operation of an organization which already stood pledged to a policy of furthering just such an interest in opera. This was the Metropolitan Opera Guild, organized in 1935, under the vigorous leadership of Mrs. August Belmont, for the purpose of bringing together two musical needs, to the point where they might complement each other. On the one hand, there was a growing curiosity on the part of the public as to the "inside" and the "glamour" of opera. On the other hand, the Metropolitan stood in need of wider public support. Mrs. Belmont proposed to offer the public the more intimate insight it wanted, in a way that would bring the Metropolitan the support it needed. Hence Mrs. Belmont refers to her work as "a two-headed Janus, but of an entirely amiable temper, which looks in the direction of the public as well as in that of the Opera."

Guild members were to be given something in return for their dues; something that should bring them into closer personal contact with the object for which those contributions were asked. Accordingly, the Guild offered its members "treats" which have come to be integral parts of its annual program. The first was a great party, designated as an "At Home," held on the stage and in the auditorium of the House, and calculated to bring an opera-minded public into personal contact with the artists and managerial staff of the Metropolitan. Secondly, the Guild invited its members to attend a regular dress rehearsal, from which the public is normally excluded. Within the brief period of its existence, the Guild has enrolled something upwards of three thousand members, most of whom report that encountering the singers and "watching the wheels go 'round" have brought them a keener personal pleasure in the opera than did years of mere attendance on performances.

Further, the Guild began a ticket-purchasing service for its members; and organized an Artists' Memory Fund, supported by voluntary contributions, for the purpose of honoring outstanding members of the Metropolitan Opera in a way that should increase general opera interest. In the first year of the Fund's existence, the artists thus honored were Emma Calvé and Jean de Reszke, and in the second, Ernestine Schumann-Heink and Antonio Scotti. The Fund is spent entirely at the Box-office, on special-rate ticket-coupons, which are sold at fifty cents and one dollar each, to students in music and general academic schools. In exchange for the privilege of hearing opera at reduced prices, the Guild requires that the students chosen by their schools be genuinely musical and honestly studious, and that they write the Guild a letter setting forth their personal reactions to a performance which they might not otherwise have been able to witness. During the first season of the student-coupon plan, more than six hundred tickets were distributed, for seats in all parts of the House, at a saving of from one to six dollars to their purchasers.

During the season of 1936-37, the Guild enlarged its program. It began the publication of its weekly *Opera News* (a bulletin of operatic events, anecdotes, and the like); and it launched the experiment of a special Students' Matinée. The Guild bought out the entire House, sold the boxes at advanced rates to help meet expenses, pledged any deficit from its own treasury, and offered the seats at prices ranging from twenty-five cents to a dollar "top," to an audience made up entirely of school-children. To select a suitable opera for such a group, the Guild invited to its Students' Matinée Committee the heads of the Music Departments of public, parochial, and private schools in New York City and within a fifty-mile distance. There was balloting, and *Aida* was finally chosen, for its spectacular interest as well as its musical worth. Some weeks in advance of the matinée, the participating schools set aside periods for the study of the plot and themes of *Aida,* of Egyptian history, the characteristics of Egyptian dress and gestures, the background of the artists who assumed the rôles, and like subjects. On the day of the performance, buses were chartered to bring the youthful spectators from Westchester, New Jersey, Connecticut, Park Avenue, and the New York Public Schools. And the result of the experiment was tersely summed up by one boy of fourteen, who was heard to exclaim:

"Well, if this is op'ra, I'm done with the movies!"

Except that it has no unfriendly designs upon the welfare of the motion picture industry, the Guild is endeavoring to foster exactly this approach—to convince strangers-to-opera that a personal participation in it, bulwarked by no more irksome preparation than is required by any good game, results in first-class fun.

The Missourian principle of "being shown" is entirely
American, and its adoption has already brought heartening results.  From being "scared" of opera, the
American public has progressed to the point of listening
to it; thence, to being curious about it; and next, to
putting out voluntary feelers towards satisfying that
curiosity.

2.

Such was the nature of the organization which ultimately took over the requests for information that
came from the opera's radio audience.  The Guild undertook to answer all letters, and, in addition, to act as
liaison officer in organizing new Listening Groups.

Among its means of disseminating information on
operatic subjects (and in addition to personal replies
to all mail), the Guild has prepared a bibliography of
works bearing on opera plots, themes, structure, musical
biography, history, and the like, which is sent to Opera
Clubs throughout the country.  Further, the Guild
launched its Thursday afternoon broadcasts, conducted
by Mrs. Herbert Witherspoon, and sent out over
stations on the same NBC network which broadcasts
the Saturday afternoon performances.  These broadcasts are presented as informal discussions rather than
"educational lectures."  They present the plot and the
musical characteristics of the coming performance; make
known "human interest" anecdotes about the composers
and participating artists; include talks on allied subjects
by authorities in those fields; invite guest speakers
from the Opera's roster and from the ranks of prominent opera-lovers; and offer their material in a way
that will stimulate further voluntary acquaintanceship

with it.  The Guild's Thursday programs are at present reaching something over seven thousand Listening Groups, of men and women of all ages, backgrounds, occupations, and interests.

The nature of the letters received by the Guild's Radio Committee points to an ever-deepening opera-interest on the part of the American public which, up to a few years ago, was believed to have no taste for opera at all.  A woman who never witnessed a performance of opera inquires about an inexpensive piano edition of the best-known themes.  Great curiosity is shown in the cuts in the Wagnerian works: how are they decided?  are they uniform in all opera houses?  People inquire about the names and methods of the teachers of the various artists; about the way in which operas are mounted and rehearsed; about details of costuming and make-up.  College students ask for suggestions as to how they can "get the most out of an opera."

Not all of the Guild's mail is of the question variety, however.  Many letters come from people who have left New York, have heard no "personal" opera since their departure, and take pleasure in animating the broadcast version with the faces and figures they knew thirty years ago.  Listeners report the enjoyment they derive from the imaginative adventure of supplying the music with sets and scenes and people of their own creation.  Frequently letters outline the snow-ball growth of opera-interest in this or that distant community.  A woman in Indiana wrote at some length of a particularly interesting development of this kind.

An opera-enthusiast herself, she set about using the Saturday broadcasts as a practical means of demonstrating the worth of her hobby. She invited a group of her bridge-mates to an early Saturday luncheon, spent half an hour telling them the plot of the coming opera, another half-hour playing its chief themes on the piano, and climaxed these preparations by turning on the radio when the broadcast began. The following week, she was invited to repeat her "performance" at the home of a neighbor, who had invited a group of her own. Within a short time, an Opera Club was organized, and the next winter a second such club had to be formed, to take care of the overflow enthusiasts who could not be got to fit into the rooms of the original group. When both clubs had been some time in a state of flourishing existence, the woman gave a large musical party. During the week, she was approached by one of the Senior Class officers of the local High School. The Seniors had planned to hold their annual dance on the night of her party, but had unanimously voted to postpone it if they could secure invitations to the musical affair. These were readily issued, the High School group came in a body, and admitted a desire for an Opera Club of their own. One girl brought with her a notebook into which she had copied down those themes of *Die Walkuere* which she had "liked best" during the broadcast and had later looked up. The High School group elected a program of deeper study in music appreciation, and finally formed a Choral Club for the pleasure of participating in the rousing operatic choruses as well as listening to them. Yet less than a decade ago, opera was completely unknown in this particular Indiana community.

Metropolitan Opera lunches, it is reported, are popular in Colorado, where the broadcast comes in just before the lunch hour, and the listeners sustain themselves with sandwiches from trays during the intermissions. Hockey and basket-ball matches are being transferred from Saturday to week-day afternoons, so that school and high school students may join their own opera groups for the broadcasts. Garage mechanics in small towns and farm-folk in isolated regions write in of their interest. And the Cody Museum, in Wyoming (normally devoted to the mementos of Buffalo Bill), throws open its doors each week for the opera broadcast and discussion.

For one performance in the week, at least, the world occupies front seats at the Metropolitan. Opera breakfasts are among the social events of Honolulu. In South America, interest in the Metropolitan broadcasts is such that NBC has put on a special commentator, who is not heard by the American audience, but broadcasts intermission talks in Spanish for the benefit of listeners in the Latin republics. When the Australian soprano, Marjorie Lawrence, made her Metropolitan début, radiograms were delivered to her between the acts, from her brother who was listening to her in Sydney, and from her teacher, who sat before her radio in Paris. And Mme. Flagstad's mother listens regularly from her home in Oslo.

The most encouraging aspect of these various reports is, not that the Metropolitan Opera is being sent out on the air, but that people are receiving it with spontaneous personal pleasure. They try it, like it, and come back for more. The aura of strangeness is wearing away from "grand opera"; it is coming to be a natural, livable

part of American existence, quite as it is abroad.  The
European is given his first taste of opera by the traditions of his family and his community.  The American,
thus far, gets his from a little black microphone.  The
important thing, however, is that, regardless of its
source, he *does* get it, and getting it, finds that it re-
sponds to some need of his own, which must have existed all along, but which there was no previous means
of satisfying.

Given such a closer approach to opera, the coming
generation of Americans will have a firmer grasp on
the key that unlocks the world of art than the past
hundred and fifty years brought to their parents.
High School youngsters who to-day take active steps to
secure operatic entertainment, and make their first attempts at copying out Wagnerian themes, will demand
opera as a matter of course in the communities they
come to direct, twenty years hence.  It is not inconceivable that the long-awaited local opera houses may
come, and sooner than one has been taught to expect,
as the direct result of the opera-interest which is asserting itself to-day.  Largely through the means of
radio (one of those "mechanical devices" thought to
"kill" art), the artistic outlook of a nation has become
more thoroughly revolutionized within the brief space
of a decade than in all the previous years of its existence.  The opera is at last sloughing off its "strangeness" and its "highbrowism," to take its place among
the familiar and pleasurable aspects of American life.
The Metropolitan may look forward to a second
Golden Age of opera, when it may choose its "stars"
from among native Americans who have been getting
their experience in local houses anywhere between Port-

land, Maine, and Portland, Oregon; when it may send its artists as guests to permanent local companies, staffed by American orchestras, American choruses, and American beginners; when it will no longer be forced into the position of the only permanent proving-ground for gifted young singers, but will advance to still greater heights as the foremost musical tradition in American life.

# INDEX

# INDEX

Abbey, Henry E., 7, 9
*Africaine, L'*, 8
*Aida*, 8, 113, 171, 200, 206, 221, 222, 223, 228, 229, 256, 267, 268, 269, 275, 309
Albers, Henri, 14, 15
Althouse, Paul, 253
Alvary, Max, 8
Amato, Pasquale, 76, 183
American Ballet, The, 273
*Amore dei Tre Re, L'*, 78
Angelis de, Jefferson, 9
*Apollo, or The Oracle of Delphi*, 9
Astor, Mrs. Caroline Schermerhorn, 109

Bada, Angelo, 72
*Barber of Seville, The*, 72, 228
Barnay, Ludwig, 26
Barrett, Lawrence, 26
*Bartered Bride, The*, 232
Bates, Blanche, 75
Beethoven van, Ludwig, 53
Bégué, Bernard, 49, 153
Belasco, David, 26, 75, 76
Bellini, Vincenzo, 257
Belmont, Mrs. August, 307
Bernhardt, Sarah, 9
Bispham, David, 14, 113
Blass, Robert, 43, 49, 53
Bodanzky, Artur, 79, 80, 204-206
*Bohême, La*, 77, 138, 172, 229, 232, 270, 273
Boito, Arrigo, 57, 147

Bonci, Alessandro, 22, 29, 51
Bonelli, Richard, 61
Bonn, Ferdinand, 26
Booth, Edwin, 26
Borgia, Lucrezia, 203
Bori, Lucrezia, 78, 90, 121, 203 204, 232
Brandt, Marianne, 8
Breil, Joseph C., 61
Bressler-Gianoli, Clotilde, 51
Brown, Hugh R., 165, 247, 248
Bruning, Dr. Henry F., 285
Buchter, Jacob, 239, 240
Burgstaller, Alois, 28, 43, 157, 158, 163, 164
Burrian, Carl, 47

Cadman, Charles Wakefield, 61
Calvé, Emma, 12, 14, 20-22; 28, 51, 113, 117, 118, 138, 167, 308
Campanari, Giuseppe, 14, 28, 113
Campanini, Cleofonte, 51
Campanini, Italo, 7
*Canterbury Pilgrims, The*, 61, 80
*Carmen*, 113, 117, 118, 138, 197, 198, 204, 223, 298
Carpenter, John Alden, 61
Caruso, Enrico, 171-189; *also* 22, 29, 30, 37, 40, 41, 49, 50, 52, 60, 76, 82, 83, 116, 124-126; 140, 149, 151, 152, 169, 170, 190-192; 202, 204, 212-214; 252, 260, 261, 262, 273, 285
Case, Anna, 61

319